W9-ACL-937

SPIRITUALLY ORIENTED SOCIAL WORK PRACTICE

DAVID S. DEREZOTES

College of Social Work
University of Utah

PEARSON

Boston   New York   San Francisco
Mexico City   Montreal   Toronto   London   Madrid   Munich   Paris
Hong Kong   Singapore   Tokyo   Cape Town   Sydney

Series Editor: *Patricia Quinlin*
Editorial Assistant: *Sara Holliday*
Marketing Manager: *Laura Lee Manley*
Manufacturing Buyer: *JoAnne Sweeney*
Cover Coordinator: *Kristina Mose-Libon*
Production Coordinator: *Pat Torelli Publishing Services*
Editorial-Production Service: *Lynda Griffiths*
Electronic Composition: *Publishers' Design and Production Services, Inc.*

For related titles and support materials, visit our online catalog at www.ablongman.com.

Between the time Website information is gathered and then published, it is not unusual for some sites to have closed. Also, the transcription of URLs can result in typographical errors. The publisher would appreciate notification where these errors occur so that they may be corrected in subsequent editions.

Cataloging-in-Publication data not available at press time.

0-205-42040-0

Printed in the United States of America

10 9 8 7 6 5 4 3 2 1   09 08 07 06 05

To Tami, Nate, and Taylor, Jaiya and Liani,
Nick and Ruth, Jim and Au-Deane, Roger, Don, and Jake,
Zena, turtle, and Buddy—all my spiritual teachers.

CONTENTS

PREFACE

Spirituality Oriented Social Work Practice will help inform and support social workers who want to add spiritual content to their practice. I feel more hopeful about our human tribe, which I believe will continue to co-create a society that values as sacred all people, living things, and ecosystems, and that supports the Highest Good of our decedents as well as those of us fortunate to be alive today. Also, I hope to increasingly walk my own talk, which writing this book has especially challenged me to do.

ACKNOWLEDGMENTS

There really is nothing new under the stars, at least on Earth. This book is an attempt to categorize, summarize, and simply describe, as much as appropriate, the methods of spiritual practice that I have studied, taught, and incorporated into my own work. I acknowledge the many generations of people who have lived before us, who have not only built our great cities, towns, and farms but who have also created the many wisdom traditions that still inform us today. I also acknowledge the growing number of people today who are currently working to foster the spiritual development of the world.

My appreciation goes to the following reviewers for their helpful comments on the manuscript: Ann Conrad, Catholic University School of Social Service; Dennis T. Haynes, University of Texas, San Antonio; Hugo Kamya, Boston College; and Robin Russel, Binghamton University, State University of New York.

CHAPTER 1

INTRODUCTION

PURPOSE AND CONTENTS

Purpose

The purpose of the book is to provide social workers with practical theory and research-based methods for spiritually oriented practice with individuals, couples, families, groups, institutions, and local and global communities and ecosystems.

A Second Phase of Literature

The literature on spirituality, which expanded rapidly over the past two decades in such fields as social work, psychology, nursing, and medicine, has helped create a beginning theoretical and research foundation for the use of spirituality in practice. This research and theory development constituted what could be called a first phase of the literature in spirituality and practice. In this phase, scientists and artists have shown that spirituality can contribute to the healing and highest well-being of people. Science has learned that there are spiritual factors associated with the etiology of every biopsychosocial–environmental problem and challenge, and that spiritual approaches may significantly contribute to the effectiveness of our attempts to deal with our current problems and challenges.

Growing global interest in spirituality in the past decade has been accompanied by a parallel global growth in church affiliation. A divide has developed between these two great trends, in spirituality and religiosity, intensified by mutual fear and mistrust. On one hand, critics of the new spirituality have questioned whether this movement may be promoting excessive self-centeredness, as people focus more on their own experiences and pleasure than on the doctrines, rituals, and beliefs of community and religion. On the other hand, critics of the new religions worry about the theocratic and patriarchal nature of some churches that threaten the rights and well-being of children, women, sexual minorities, and other disempowered people.

Although the concerns of both sides are not unfounded, spirituality and religiosity are not mutually exclusive. The divide between spirituality and religiosity can be healed, both on the individual and collective levels. Social workers need practical methods that can be used with clients across the diversity of spiritual and religious belief and practice. Such methods should promote both the free expression and the exploration of individual spiritual development.

What is now necessary in the field of spirituality in professional helping is what might be called a second phase of literature, which builds on the foundations of the first phase to construct theory and research-based *methods* that can be used in the spiritual dimension of practice. Social workers now want to know how to incorporate spirituality into their practice with specific populations and problems.

This second phase of spirituality is concerned not only with personal spiritual growth but also with personal transformations that lead not only to changes in individual consciousness but also toward individuals taking increased responsibility for the welfare of their families, communities, and ecosystems. Thus, there is a growing awareness that spiritual development brings with it an increased responsibility to serve, and that personal spirituality and service are themselves interconnected and interrelated.

An Inclusive–Integrative Approach to Theory and Practice

An inclusive view of spirituality is taken in this text. Much of the first phase of spiritual literature did not integrate theories of spirituality with other theories of practice that are informed by the many different disciplines of science and the humanities. Social workers were given some theory and methods in spirituality, but were not shown how to use spiritual methods in concert with traditional methods of assessment, intervention, and evaluation.

In this book, spirituality is conceptualized as a dimension of human experience, development, and environment that is interconnected with and inseparable from all other human experiences, developmental dimensions, and environments. Since the most advanced theory is the most inclusive and integrative, theories of spiritual practice do not replace existing theories but are included together with them.

Thus, since spirit impacts everything in the human world, spiritual work is best practiced from a biopsychosocial–spiritual–environmental (BPSSE) perspective. The book shows how to include the physical, emotional, cognitive, social, and environmental levels in making spiritual assessments and interventions. Issues of individual spiritual development (such as personal transformations during or following traumatic experiences or other kinds of suffering) are also linked to issues of global human development (such as collective transformation in response to threats to global well-being and survival and threats to our natural ecosystems).

All levels of spiritual practice are seen as interconnected and inseparable across the range of practice. Thus, direct work with individuals, couples, families, and groups (microlevel practice), as well as leadership, administration, supervision, and activism with institutions, local communities, ecosystems, and global communities (macrolevel practice) all have common spiritual elements that can inform work on each level. In addition, microlevel practice is conceptualized as always having a macrolevel impact and macrolevel practice is conceptualized as always having a microlevel impact.

The path of *self-work* on one's own individual consciousness and the path of *service* devoted to the welfare of the greater community are also linked together. Thus, as professionals and their clients raise their consciousness, they become more response-able to the welfare of their families, institutions, communities, and natural environments.

Both the differences and the connections between spirituality and religiosity are examined. Methods of assessment and intervention with religiosity are described. The book also provides methods of working with religion to foster biopsychosocial–spiritual–environmental well-being.

MULTIPLE INTERRELATED VIEWS OF SPIRITUALITY

The spiritually oriented social worker views spirituality from multiple and interrelated perspectives. A common theme in all of these perspectives is the idea that spirituality is a connecting force that can help the social worker bridge across apparent dualities. Thus, for example, spirituality can help heal the divide found between people and their environment, between science and religion, between different religions, or between different cultures.

Spirituality as a Loving Connection

Human spirituality can be most simply understood as a person's desire for and expression of loving connection with everything. The most basic expression of spirituality, then, is loving kindness toward one's self, other people, other living things, and the ecosystems that support all life.

Spirituality and Religion

In practice, the social worker distinguishes spirituality from religion because she or he realizes that spirituality can offer a set of beliefs, rituals, and language that can help bridge differences between different religions and between religion and science. The social worker also realizes that clients can react negatively to religious beliefs, rituals, and language that are different from those of their own religion.

Spirituality can be seen as the *individual's* sense of connectedness, meaning, peace, consciousness, purpose, and service that develops across the life span. In contrast, religiosity can be seen as *socially* shared rituals, doctrines, and beliefs that may or may not support and enhance the individual's spiritual development.

Creative Spirit: What Makes Everything

Most people share the belief that there is a purpose, force, or power behind the on-going creation of everything; this could be called *Creative Spirit*. From this perspective, Creative Spirit is not just what happened long ago, perhaps at what astronomers call the Big Bang. Many physicists believe that our universe may in fact be just one of many universes that are continually being created and perhaps destroyed in a vast Multiuniverse. Similarly, our reality is constantly being recreated and humans are partners in that creative process. Creative Spirit is by definition vast, complex, and mysterious. Creative Spirit cannot be completely known by any single person; a community of people can collectively know more about Creative Spirit than any single individual in that community.

God and Spirituality

Although most people in the United States indicate that they believe in God, there is a variation across religion and individual people about what *God* means. For example, some people view God as having a masculine energy, some prefer to use the word *Goddess* to denote feminine energy, and many others see God as being both masculine and feminine. There are also religions that do not believe in a God. In sensitivity to the diversity of beliefs both within religions as well as in the populations that do not believe in God, in this book, the term *Creative Spirit* will sometimes be used to describe the experience of the ultimate that most people share. In some cases, the word *God* or *Goddess* will also be used.

Spiritual Perspective: The Biggest Perspective

The spiritual perspective is the biggest perspective, taken across both space and time. The size of the human body is somewhere midway between the infinitesimal size of the smallest known particles and the immense size of the Multiuniverse. People also stand in a present moment between the apparent eternities of past and future time. Spiritual healing can occur when human experience and behavior is viewed from such perspectives.

Spirituality as an Archetypal, Meaning-Making Process

Human beings are *meaning-making mammals* and our spirituality is in part a meaning-making process usually done through symbolic language. Like poetry, spiritual experiences are often not understood as literal truths but instead can be worked with as metaphors or *archetypes* that can be given different meanings. Instead of "shrinking" people down into diagnoses or labels, spiritual archetypes *expand* people into archetypes that are rich, unending sources of multiple meanings.

Thus, spirituality is a living story; like the tales handed down by our ancestors from tribal elders to their children and grandchildren, spirit is reinterpreted and given new meaning by each individual and by each family, culture, and generation. In our era of written language, books, journals, and now information technology, spiritual traditions can become doctrines that are no longer reinterpreted as environmental conditions change.

Spirituality as a Mystical Experience

Spiritual experience is *mystical* experience, which simply means that spirituality can be experienced in the here and now. Although consciousness can become deeper and expanded over one's lifetime, the loving and connective experience of spirituality is available to every human being in every ordinary here-and-now moment.

The Soul as a Synapse between Creative and Individual Spirit

Many of the world's wisdom traditions describe an essence inside of every person, sometimes called the *soul*, that is indestructible and even immortal. The spiritually oriented social worker can also view the soul as the connection or synapse between the person and Creative Spirit (or God). In this book, the word *soul* will be used to describe that essence of the person.

Spirituality as a Transformational Experience

Spirituality is ultimately transformational, which means that a person makes deep and lasting developmental changes in consciousness. From a life span perspective, every person gradually develops an identity (or "mask") during life and ultimately experiences perhaps the ultimate transformation beyond that mask at death. Spiritual experiences can support transformations before death.

Communities of Spiritual and Universal Diversity

From the spiritual perspective, all forms of human diversity are equally sacred and beautiful individual expressions of Creative Spirit. Similarly, spirituality also reconnects humans with other nonhuman life and with everything else in the Multiuniverse, since everything is viewed as sacred expressions of Creative Spirit.

The word *religion* means literally "to bring together." Religions often bring people together, but also often exclude others (usually nonbelievers) from their community. A religion is a *Community of Spiritual Diversity* when it brings together all people as equally valued and sacred members, not just some people with certain characteristics, beliefs, or behaviors and not just members of one particular tribe of people.

Universal community includes everything in the entire Cosmos, including all animals, plants, rocks, other matter, and energy. A religion is a *Community of Universal Diversity* when it brings together and values as sacred, not only the diversity of humanity but also the diversity of the Multiuniverse with all of its elements—animals, plants, matter, and energy.

SPIRITUAL PRACTICE

Spiritual Practice as a Personal Healing Practice

From a spiritual perspective, most people today live their lives deeply disconnected from "parts" of who they are. A person might, for example, lose intimacy with her own body, mind, heart, or soul. In such a situation, the person no longer can have a relationship with all of her "parts" in which an internal dialogue between body, mind, and spirit is possible. Instead, one "part" of the self may dominate, perhaps the outer cortex, silencing the rest of the body, mind, and spirit through worry or other excessive mental activity. Spiritual practices are healing practices because they help us become *whole* beings again, reconnected to our bodies, minds, hearts, and souls. Such work ultimately leads to increased awareness of love for and care of the self.

Spiritual Practice as a Bridge across Social Divides

People today also often feel deeply disconnected from other people, even from those people living in their own homes and communities. They may dismiss relationships with other people, for example, because of conflicts regarding various religious, political, moral, or economic positions. It is not that such conflicts are in themselves unhealthy; people are inevitably going to disagree on some issues. It is the *way* that such conflicts are managed that can move people out of relationships and dialogues into the monologue of violence. Disconnection often intensifies when one side tries to dominate the other, and winning the conflict becomes more important than staying in the relationship. Spiritual methods of practice can help people go back into relationships and dialogues with other people. Such work ultimately also leads to an enhanced sense of well-being and a life full of loving service to other people.

Spiritual Practice as a Service to Other Living Things and the Ecosystems That Support Life

Most people are not only disconnected from themselves and from other people but also from other living things and ecosystems. Spiritual practice helps people reconnect with everything in the Multiuniverse. The sense of specialness and the pain of alienation can both soften. Ultimately, such deep-felt connection leads to a sense of responsibility for and life of stewardship toward other living things, and to the ecosystems that support all life.

CONSCIOUS USE OF HIGHER SELF

Decades of outcome research has helped social workers understand the primary importance of the helping relationship in practice. The ability of the social worker to form relationships is much more significant than either a practice technique or client characteristics in predicting case outcomes. The traditional tool of relationship building has been *Conscious Use of Self*, which involves the intentional engagement of the social worker in co-creating a helping relationship with the client. Typically, Conscious Use of Self involves the use of talk therapy, in which the worker shares ideas and sometimes feelings with the client.

In spiritual practice, the social worker expands on this idea, and uses and addresses all the elements of self in the helping relationship. Thus, Conscious Use of Higher Self involves the intentional use of the physical, emotional, cognitive, social, and spiritual dimensions in the co-creation of the helping relationship. In each session, the social worker attempts to relate to the client on a physical, emotional, cognitive, social, and spiritual level. Similarly, the social worker relates to the client as if they are both body–mind–spirit–environmental beings, connected not only to their own bodies, brains, and souls but also to other people, living things, and ecosystems. Gradually, the client hopefully will also learn to value and use all of his or her "parts."

When using Conscious Use of Higher Self, the social worker uses and integrates both the scientific and intuitive ways of knowing in her or his assessments and evaluations. Whereas scientific ways of knowing primarily utilize the outer cortex of the brain, intuitive ways of knowing utilize the entire body–mind–spirit–environment. The intuitive social worker might, for example, sense the client at times through "gut" feelings the worker feels in his intestines, or perhaps at other times through sensations in the worker's stomach. The experienced social worker both checks out his intuitions with his science and his science with his intuitions.

Conscious Use of Higher Self involves the fluid and intentional use of all the levels of consciousness. These levels are described by the major religious and spiritual traditions of the world and increasingly confirmed by scientific research (see Table 1.1). Prepersonal consciousness is characterized by a childlike view of the Cosmos that emphasizes impulses over reason or intellect, but that also allows for the experience of pleasure. Personal consciousness is characterized by a greater focus on the needs of other people, communities, and ecosystems; more responsibility in using reason; and the ability to postpone pleasure to examine one's own shadow and to accomplish goals. Transpersonal consciousness is disidentified from the hedonism of the child and the duty of the parent, and thus is free to experience the soul directly.

TABLE 1.1   Levels of Consciousness in Transpersonal Theory

LEVEL OF CONSCIOUSNESS	RELATIVE STRENGTH OF THREE EGO STATES	RELATIVE EMPHASIS ON PERSONALITY CHARACTERISTICS
Prepersonal	Parent: relatively weak Observing self: relatively weak **Child: relatively strong**	Responsibility & reason: relatively weak Disidentification: relatively weak **Spontaneous impulse: relatively strong**
Personal	**Parent: relatively strong** Observing self: relatively weak Child: relatively weak	**Responsibility & reason: relatively strong** Disidentification: relatively weak Spontaneous impulse: relatively weak
Transpersonal	Parent: relatively weak **Observing self: relatively strong** Child: relatively weak	Responsibility & reason: relatively weak **Disidentification: relatively strong** Spontaneous impulse: relatively weak

Note: Levels of consciousness from Wilber (2000).

As the social worker uses all levels of his consciousness to help the client, he also models such fluidity for the client. Thus, the spiritually oriented social worker practices what he preaches, and fluidity between levels of consciousness is part of both his own Conscious Use of Higher Self and his ultimate goal for the client.

Spiritually oriented social workers believe that health and healing is about integrity of being, which means wholeness. Healthy people have all of their parts of self and divine self and use them wisely for the highest good of their self and divine self. Healing is not the elimination of suffering, but the loving care and inclusion of the body–mind–spirit–environmental whole.

The Highest Good Rather than Just Symptom Reduction

The spiritually oriented social worker holds the intent that her work will lead to the Highest Good for the client. The *Highest Good* is always about both individual and collective well-being, because the well-being of any person is interconnected with and inseparable from the well-being of other people, living things, and ecosystems.

Social workers also realize that, although they hold an intent for the Highest Good, the precise outcomes of any interventions are always unknown. Professional helpers strive to do the very best assessments and evaluations in their practice, but they also appreciate the role of *Sacred Mystery* in practice, which is the unknowable, transrational aspects of every experience, usually accompanied by such human responses as awe, respect, curiosity, reverence, and wonder.

Being Human Rather than Being Perfect

Many social workers are concerned that they are not perfect enough to do spiritual work, as if only the most evolved workers on the planet are qualified to use the spiritual dimension in practice. However, clients do not need their social workers to be perfect so much as they need their workers to be aware and accepting of their own imperfections. This is in part because most clients are very aware of their own imperfections. Often they have come to the social worker involuntarily, perhaps sent by the court because of some behavior about which they are embarrassed. Usually they carry significant shame about themselves.

The client can best identify with a social worker who is human. A social worker who is human is a social worker who has all of his "parts" and is capable of expressing or controlling all of those parts as they emerge in his life. To be human means that the social worker does not feel that he has to know all the answers, fix the client, always be calm, say wise things, or do anything else that he happens to think represents "perfection." Instead, the social worker is aware and accepting of his own strengths and imperfections. He sees himself as an ever-evolving being who is a "good enough" social worker (rather than necessarily "the best"). He has pure intent, which means that he is more interested in his inner development and his service to other beings and ecosystems rather than in his outer appearance and the recognitions and rewards he receives.

The social worker is willing to be transparent about himself when he thinks that such openness will benefit the client. Typically, for example, when working with a client who is going though a "dark night of the soul," the worker might share that he went through a similar experience successfully years ago.

The Social Worker Works in Partnership with Creative Spirit or God

In spiritually oriented social work, the practitioner sees herself as a healer, but understands that the deepest healing happens on a spiritual level, and that she is most effective when she partners with Creative Spirit in the helping process. In contrast to today's typical professional helper who views himself as the doctor who provides such curative medicines as psychotropic drugs and therapy, the spiritually oriented social worker views herself as a partner in the healing process who works with the client and Creative Spirit.

The professional helper today often has a vertical relationship with the client, in which the helper may be unable to disidentify with his persona of "helper" and also sees himself as superior and even indispensable to the client. The spiritually oriented social worker develops a *horizontal* relationship with his clients in which both the healer and the client are equal partners, working together with Creative Spirit for healing and change. For example, such a social worker recognizes that the "natural external" world of sky, air, earth, and water, or the "natural internal" world of body, mind, and spirit, may often ultimately be the most powerful medicines for the client.

Process Focus Rather than Just Goal Focus

The social worker values the client's own "spiritual process" as ultimately the best "medicine." The client's process is her own mystical, here-and-now experience of what is happening in her body–mind–spirit–environment. The spiritually oriented social worker views people as meaning-making mammals who want to find personal and sacred significance in their experiences.

Since the outcome of spiritual work is always uncertain, the social worker resists building all of his interventions around established goals. Although the spiritually oriented social worker can write behaviorally anchored goals as well as any other helping professional, he believes that the client's process is just as important as the goals in driving assessments, interventions, and evaluations.

Presence Rather than Just Technique

The spiritually oriented social worker emphasizes presence rather than just technique. Although she strives to continually "practice" her practice by honing her techniques that can foster change, she also equally values and practices her ability to be fully conscious in the here-and-now moment with her client without any expectations of change. Such modeling of presence can assist the client in also learning how to be in the here-and-now moment.

Fluidity of Spiritual Language

Spiritual practitioners need to be fluent in many tongues, in the sense that each client, family, and community uses a unique language to describe spirituality. People can attach great significance to their words, often with strong emotional or cognitive "charge," so the wise practitioner works within the client's language when possible. Each generation, the revision of traditional words and phrases can give the language of spirituality new and sharper meanings. Such revision can also help the New Century practitioner develop his or her own language, relatively free from emotional and cognitive charge, to use when working with spiritual issues. The following definitions are introduced here so that the reader can understand the terms used in this text.

Spiritual Work as Radical and Transformational Service

Spiritual work is viewed as a *radical* approach to practice because the roots of human consciousness, suffering, and transformation are dealt with directly. Spiritual work is a *transformational* practice method, focused on creating fundamental changes in the way individuals and communities view and live in their world.

Spiritual work is both an individual practice and a social activism. *Spiritual Practice* happens as a person takes response-ability for the development of her own consciousness, in a way that is balanced between over- and under-responsibility to self and others. Spiritual Practice leads to Spiritual Activism as the individual becomes increasingly aware of her interconnection with everything else, and understands that practice and activism are essentially two sides of the same coin. Spiritual work is *Spiritual Activism,* as people take increasing response-ability in working to foster the highest good of their families, communities, and ecosystems. Spiritual Activism fosters Spiritual Practice as the individual becomes increasingly aware that she must continue to work on herself to effectively serve others.

In this text, the terms *social worker* and *practitioner* refer to the professional helpers who serve the client. The term *client* refers to the individual, couple, family, or group that the practitioner is serving. There is a recognition that, although the practitioner is usually receiving some kind of payment and/or recognition as the helper, both people are partners in the helping relationship. In other words, the client also has a responsibility for his own transformation and service.

STUDY QUESTIONS

1. What was the first phase of the spiritual literature about? What would a second phase contain?

2. What is an inclusive or integrative approach to spiritually oriented practice?

3. What is the relationship between spirituality and religion? How are they the same and different? In your own life, how are they related?

4. What is Creative Spirit? What word do you prefer using for this concept?

5. What is meant by the word *soul?* Do you identify with having a soul? What is its function?

6. Describe a Community of Spiritual Diversity. Why is this concept important to social work? Have you ever been part of such a community? What was it like?

7. Describe a Community of Universal Diversity. Why is this concept important to social work? Have you ever been part of such a community? What was it like?

8. What is meant by the term the *Highest Good?* How can one know what the Highest Good is?

9. Have you ever felt that Creative Spirit or God was your partner when you were helping a client? Describe the situation.

10. What are the three levels of consciousness? What does it mean to be fluid in these levels?

11. Why is fluidity in spiritual language important? What kinds of spiritual language are you most and least fluid in?

RESOURCE

Wilber, K. (2000). *Sex, ecology, spirituality: The spirit of evolution.* Boston: Shambhala.
  This book includes
  1. Descriptions of prepersonal, personal, and transpersonal consciousness
  2. Descriptions of quadrants of ways of knowing
  3. Wonderful reference list

CHAPTER 2

ASSESSING IN SPIRITUALITY

THEORETICAL ASSUMPTIONS
GUIDING ASSESSMENT

In this chapter, methods of assessment and evaluation of spiritually oriented practice are described. These methods do not replace existing assessment strategies in current use, but are meant to be *added* to those strategies. The theoretical assumptions underlying these methods are summarized below.

Vast and Complex Causes

The practitioner in spirituality assumes that the ultimate "cause" of any human experience and behavior is everything. In other words, all human experience and behavior is linked with the totality of the Multiuniverse and the complex interactions between all of its many parts.

Multiple Ways of Knowing

Since no twenty-first-century practitioner is capable of assessing the entire Multiuniverse, the best assessments must utilize the ways of knowing currently available. Social workers can draw from both transrational and rational techniques as they make assessments at varying complexity levels. *Rational* ways of knowing include scientific and "evidence-based" practice methods. *Transrational* ways of knowing include the use of intuitive and other artistic practice methods. As suggested in Table 2.1, these techniques each have advantages and disadvantages.

The best assessments utilize *combinations* of ways of knowing, in which the practitioner skillfully confirms or denies hypotheses based on one way of knowing with other ways of knowing. For example, an intuition about the emotional state of a child might be confirmed (or invalidated) by the results of a formal psychological testing instrument and by the independent reports of the child's school teacher.

Transrational Ways of Knowing

Transrational ways of knowing utilize intuition. Intuition is transrational in that it involves not only the brain and its cognitive processes but also the whole

TABLE 2.1   Two Ways of Knowing across Two Levels of Complexity

	COMPLEXITY LEVEL ONE: INTRAPSYCHIC ASSESSMENTS OF INDIVIDUALS	COMPLEXITY LEVEL TWO: INTERPERSONAL AND ENVIRONMENTAL ASSESSMENTS
Transrational Ways of Knowing	*Example:* intuition about client's emotional state	*Example:* intuitition about fractal patterns in client's environment
	Advantage: more inclusive assessment, includes all intrapsychic factors	*Advantage:* more inclusive assessment, includes all environmental factors
	Disadvantage: countertransference issues and other biases may reduce accuracy	*Disadvantage:* countertransference, life history, and other biases may reduce accuracy
Rational Ways of Knowing	*Examples:* formal psychological testing, single-subject design	*Examples:* program evaluation, community needs assessment
	Advantage: provides mathematical and/or standardized data on client's perceptions and observable behaviors	*Advantage:* provides mathematical and/or standardized data on agency and community
	Disadvantage: reduces complex intrapsychic etiology to oversimplified factors	*Disadvantage:* reduces complex environmental etiology to oversimplified factors

body–mind–spirit. Intuitions are therefore often nonverbal and are often experienced as spontaneous and immediate. Each individual seems to sense intuition differently. For example, a father might have a "gut" feeling about his children; he senses with his intestines. A woman, the CEO of a large organization, might intuit her business decisions with her heart, because that is her most sensitive organ-system.

Some scientists suspect that intuition may have developed in animals (and probably plants) as a way of quickly assessing the complex environments in which they live. Intuition may have especially evolved to sense *fractals,* which are the patterns that exist in all complex natural systems. The term *fractal* is used by scientists to describe the order found throughout nature. For example, just like the structure of a small branch suggests the larger structural patterns of the entire parent tree, the structure of a person's behaviors and experiences suggest what might be called the "ecofractal" patterns of her or his familial history, current cultural environment, and lifelong developmental path.

Obviously, all living organisms had to evolve some way of avoiding danger, navigating ecosystems, predicting daily and seasonal changes, mating, and finding food and other resources. In our current world, many humans may not have the same intense and "natural" need to utilize intuition for survival. However, we do use intuition daily as we navigate though such challenges as selecting groceries at the store, dealing with social relationships, and making decisions while driving.

Currently, intuition is probably our best tool in sensing the ecofractals that can help reveal the main themes in the complex etiology of human life. Although it may seem surprising or even contradictory that intuition often works better than scientific ways of knowing in sensing aspects of reality, Einstein himself stated that he used intuition to develop his most famous formula, $e = mc^2$. Many other scientific discoveries and theories have been developed through intuition as well. Effective practitioners trust their intuition, strive to further develop their intuition across their life spans, and recognize that their intuition can sometimes become less accurate when their own feelings and beliefs interfere. Students often learn how to use intuition by noticing how their whole body responds to various situations.

Rational Ways of Knowing

The practitioner who works with spirituality does not, however, discard scientific ways of knowing. Although intuitive processes usually act quicker than rational processes and may also seem more "natural," our higher cognitive processes also evolved for a purpose. Some scientists believe that our more rational cognitive processes developed at least in part to help us "check out" our instinctive and intuitive processes. Although rational thought processes usually are relatively deliberate and slower than unconscious or transrational mental processes, they do give humans another way of knowing that probably gave humans an "edge" over competing animals in the ongoing battle for survival. Students often learn how to use rational thought by explaining their assessments through written or spoken language.

Today, many people believe that science is not a particularly helpful process, since it has brought us the ability to destroy ourselves through environmental destruction, terrorism, and war. Practitioners, however, realize that scientific ways of knowing sometimes can help us refine or correct our intuition, particularly when intuition is invalidated by other human processes such as countertransference reactions and cultural biases.

What kinds of scientific ways of knowing help in spiritual assessments? A variety of assessment tools have been developed to help practitioners measure elements of spirituality and religiosity. Such tools can help guide and inform practice. In addition, scientific methods can be used to measure the efficacy of spiritual interventions.

Use of Transdisciplinary Lenses in Assessing Spirituality

Since the ultimate "cause" of any human experience and behavior is everything, and since all scientific disciplines explore only some aspects of the Multiuniverse from a limited perspective, no one scientific school or discipline can adequately describe the etiology of human behavior and experience. Today's multidisciplinary

TABLE 2.2   Levels of Scientific Assessment

LEVEL OF SCIENTIFIC ASSESSMENT	VIEW OF LEVEL AND EXAMPLE OF LEVEL	ADVANTAGES AND DISADVANTAGES
Single School within Single Discipline	Emphasis on a common doctrine and/or method	Has the most narrow and exclusive focus
	Example: cognitive psychology (beliefs are primary causes of emotion and behavior)	Creates unnecessary dualities and conflicts *within* disciplines
Single Disciplinary	Emphasis on the theoretical position of a particular discipline	Has a narrow and exclusive focus
	Example: psychology (the science of mind and behavior)	Creates unnecessary dualities and conflicts *between* disciplines
Multidisciplinary	Includes more than one theoretical position	Has a broader and more inclusive perspective
	Example: evolutionary-psychology (links biology with evolutionary science)	Insufficient emphasis on the *interactions* of the different elements in the assessment
Transdisciplinary	Is a synthesis of all theoretical positions	Has the broadest and most inclusive perspective
		Emphasizes the complex *interactions* of all elements in the assessment

perspective can also be inadequate in assessing spirituality because only some disciplines are typically included and because no synthesis of these disciplinary views is made. *Synthesis* here refers to an ongoing process where the different disciplinary views are either combined into a whole perspective or as ecofractals of the whole. As illustrated in Table 2.2, the transdisciplinary lense goes beyond the single-school, single-disciplinary, and multidisciplinary perspectives.

Valuing Mystery in Assessment

Regardless of the skill of the practitioner, there is always an element of mystery and the unknown in every assessment. Rather than viewing mystery as only a limitation, the practitioner is aware of the advantages of accepting and working with the inevitable unknown parts of the assessment. Not only is any illusion that the practitioner is all-knowing shattered but also the client is given permission to learn how to live in the mysteries of life.

Assessing Level of Consciousness

Although spirituality, like emotionality or cognition, exists in people from birth to death, spirituality can also develop across the life span. As described in Table 1.1, spiritual development can be viewed as a process in which the individual gradually develops the ability to move intentionally into any of the levels of consciousness available to humans. Any individual can become "stuck" at one of the levels of consciousness, and may begin to develop observable imbalances in the way he or she thinks and acts in the world. As summarized in Table 2.3, the practitioner can assess at what levels of consciousness the client can function (and at what levels the client may be stuck) through observing behaviors and thought patterns.

Of particular importance in assessing the level of consciousness is what Wilber (2000) has called the "pre-trans fallacy." In our culture, and perhaps throughout history in most cultures, many people have confused the nature of prepersonal and transpersonal consciousness. The simple reason for this confusion is that the two levels of consciousness both involve a shift away from consensus re-

TABLE 2.3   Distinguishing between Levels of Consciousness That Are Healthy (Fluid) and Stuck

LEVEL OF CONSCIOUSNESS	OBSERVABLE HEALTHY FUNCTIONING WHEN LEVEL IS INTENTIONALLY CHOSEN	OBSERVABLE UNHEALTHY (IMBALANCED) FUNCTIONING WHEN "STUCK" ON LEVEL
Prepersonal	1. Is able to enjoy such "animal" behaviors as eating dinner, having sex, watching a sunset, walking	1. Deals with shame by focusing blame on other people's faults and denies personal limitations
	2. Is able to spontaneously express the self through such activities as dance, art, poetry, song	2. Emphasizes the immediate needs of self over the needs of other people, other living things, and ecosystems
Personal	1. Is able to postpone immediate gratification for Highest Good, such as saving money to pay bills	1. Deals with shame by blaming the limits of self and minimizing the limitations of other people
	2. Can give empathy and presence to other people, other living things, and ecosystems	2. Emphasizes dutiful consideration of the needs of other people, other living things, and ecosystems over self-needs
Transpersonal	1. Lives fully in every moment, as if it could be the last moment, because death has been faced	1. Minimizes the "animal nature" of self by neglect of diet, exercise, sleep, sexuality, relationship
	2. Is capable of spiritual love for self, other people, other living things, and ecosystems, which is a conscious choice/intent to serve	2. Although identification from self is reduced this is replaced with a subtle identification with success in spiritual development

ality. In our culture, consensus reality is really an emphasis on such goals as intellectual control, task- and solution-focused activity, productivity, material consumption, speed, wealth, narcissism, power, and beauty. The differences between the two levels of consciousness are perhaps more subtle.

Prepersonal functioning shifts away from consensus reality by minimizing responsibility and emphasizing immediate gratification, personal experience, and free expression. Such consciousness is typical in young children, who seldom reflect on all the consequences of their actions or on all the root causes of their experiences and behaviors. A child may not feel a need to develop a rational and responsible understanding of self and the Multiuniverse. Therefore, prepersonal functioning is also prerational functioning. When in prepersonal consciousness, a person escapes some aspects of reality though play. Although play is neither good nor bad, right nor wrong, an imbalanced emphasis on play can lead to addictive behaviors that could mimic transpersonal states.

In contrast, transpersonal functioning, defined as the passage "beyond the mask of personality," can occur only after a person has developed a self that can be transcended. Transpersonal functioning shifts away from consensus reality through an intentional, rational choice to disidentify from the goals of consensus reality. Thus, transpersonal functioning can lead to ecstasy, which literally means to "stand beside oneself." When in transpersonal consciousness, a person does not escape reality, but "watches" or experiences reality from the Observing Self, thus standing besides oneself, with Creative Spirit, in both joy and suffering.

Personal consciousness is therefore a prerequisite of Transpersonal Consciousness. Personal Consciousness occurs when a person constructs a self. Although from a transpersonalist perspective, the self is an illusion, each person constructs a personality, or mask, that is the perfect container for his or her soul in his or her lifetime. The personality is therefore the body–mind container that Individual Spirit climbs into at birth and leaves at death. Personal Consciousness is the consciousness of the responsible adult who becomes immersed in the imperatives of the family, institutions, and communities in which the person lives. Responsible adults are able to look at their own shadows, which means that they can examine their own limitations without being overwhelmed by shame and worthlessness.

None of the levels of consciousness is better or worse than the others. A healthy person is a flexible person, able to intentionally shift from one level to another, often many times in a day.

Inclusion of All Dimensions of Development

Spirituality is viewed as a dimension of human development related to and inseparable from all other levels of development. Thus, individual spirituality is best evaluated as part of a biopsychosocial–spiritual–environmental (BPSSE) assessment. Not only is spirituality added to the assessment but also the *interrelationship* between the spirituality of the client and all other BPSSE factors are included. The BPSSE assessment includes individual factors, environmental factors, and fractal analysis.

Individual Factors

The individual is assessed as a being with lifelong development along interrelated spiritual, physical, emotional, cognitive, and social dimensions.

Spiritual maturation (SPM) includes the increasing ability to move fluidly between all the levels of consciousness in order to foster the Highest Good in self and divine self. As described earlier, these levels of consciousness include the prepersonal (child centered), personal (parent centered), and transpersonal (centered in observing self). Spiritual maturation also involves the acceptance of spiritual diversity in self and in other people.

Physical maturation (PHM) includes the increasing ability to accept, listen to, and care for the body in ways that foster the Highest Good in self and divine self.

Emotional maturation (EMM) involves the increasing ability to understand, accept, and consciously express or control emotions.

Cognitive maturation (COM) involves the increasing ability to see the complexities of the Multiuniverse that are hidden from dualistic thinkers. Cognitive maturation also includes the ability to value and fluidly use all ways of knowing when observing the Multiuniverse.

Social maturation (SOM) includes the ability to be intimate with other people, nonhuman life, and the nonliving parts of the Multiuniverse *(horizontal intimacy)*. Social maturation also involves development of *vertical intimacy,* which is the ability to be both alone (out of contact with humans) and at the same time intimate with self and divine self. Finally, SOM involves the increasing ability to conduct spiritual activism with people.

Environmental Factors

An individual's environment has many complex, evolving, and interrelated levels, including family, friends, and other informal social systems; institutions and other formal social systems; local and global communities; local and global ecosystems; the Multiuniverse; and the human mysteries.

Family, friends, and other informal social systems include the most intimate people in the individual's life. Informal social systems also include the casual relationships that an individual has created to meet her or his social needs.

Institutions and other formal social systems include schools, churches, agencies, health centers, and other programs and centers that the individual utilizes to meet his or her personal needs.

Local and global communities include all the political and cultural organizations the individual lives in, such as neighborhoods, towns, cities, counties, states, countries, and global regions.

Local and global ecosystems include all the natural environments that the individual lives in, which usually cross over the cultural, political, and economic boundaries of local and global communities. These include the land, water, and atmospheric systems and the plants and animals those systems support.

The Multiuniverse includes our home universe and everything else consisting of matter and energy, including the smaller and larger worlds.

Human mysteries are everything in the Multiuniverse that humans individually or collectively still do not completely sense or understand.

■ ■ ■ ■ ■

BOX 2.1

INDIVIDUAL ECOFRACTALS

Spiritual Fractal	Pattern of individual consciousness, such as a prepersonal, personal, or transpersonal focus, or a sense of peace, meaning, or connectedness
Physical Fractal	Pattern in the relationship an individual has with her or his body, such as exercise, rest, diet, body symptoms, acceptance, and self-care
Emotional Fractal	Individual feeling-pattern such as resentment, gratitude, and fear, or psuedo-feeling-patterns such as anxiety, shame, and depression
Cognitive Fractal	Pattern of perception that the individual has about his or her life, including self-concepts, value hierarchies, and attitudes about the world
Social Fractal	Pattern of interpersonal interaction the individual has with other people or with animals, plants, and ecosystems

Note: Each individual ecofractal may reflect patterns in the history and current nature of this person at the individual, couple, family, institutional, community, and/or Multiuniverse levels.

Fractal Analysis: Recognizing Patterns of Interaction between Individual and Environment

Although the client's world is obviously vast and extremely complicated, observable ecofractals, or patterns of interaction between the individual and the environment, can usually be identified. Each of these ecofractals identified in Boxes 2.1 and 2.2 may offer the practitioner data about the the connections between an individual's BPPSE history, inner and outer worlds, and possible future directions. When several ecofractals either correlate or conflict with each other, the practitioner has *fractal patterns* that provide additional collaborating evidence.

Fractal analysis is the systematic review of patterns in the client's history and current life and environment. These patterns will be of different levels of complexity, ranging from the client's own patterns of thinking and behaving, for example, to global patterns of human thought and behavior that may "mirror" the client's individual patterns.

For example, an elderly woman lived all of her life in an isolated rural area and now lives alone, complaining of depression and anxiety. Her husband died five years ago. She was raised in the xyz religion, and still believes in a male God who is very judgmental and punitive. This spiritual fractal suggests that the woman might have been exposed not only to doctrines of patriarchal religion but also to patriarchal men in authority positions. Such possibilities and others could be further explored. The woman also complains constantly of physical problems, such as fatigue, stomach pains, and arthritis, and feels that her doctors do not care or are incompetent. This physical fractal may also be related to many factors, of

---

BOX 2.2

EXAMPLES OF INDIVIDUAL ECOFRACTAL PATTERNS FOR ELDERLY CLIENT

Spiritual Fractal	Fear of, no trust in judgmental and punitive God
Physical Fractal	Physical suffering and little trust of medicine
Emotional Fractal	Depression and anxiety, no trust of others
Cognitive Fractal	No trust she or he has worth when not working
Social Fractal	Little trust she or he is lovable or that love exists
Cross-Fractal Patterns	Little trust in her or his own self-worth, little trust in that the Multiuniverse is friendly

---

course, such as her aging process, her feelings about her own body, disappointments with the medical model, and the ways her family of origin may have responded to her childhood illnesses.

The elderly woman also talks about feeling depressed and worried. She thinks that her life has been a failure, despite having mothered several healthy children who are all now themselves married and successful. This emotional fractal may perhaps be linked to society's devaluing of women and domestic work or to the woman's use of anxiety in her childhood to deal with sexual trauma, or to biogenetic factors that predispose her to what we now call depression. The woman tells her therapist that no one in her family really cares about her anymore and that they only pretend to want to spend time with her. She also seems to believe that she has no value and is unlovable now that she is unable to do any physical work. These cognitive fractals could be related to many factors, such as the emphasis on obligation in her extended family, the emphasis on being productive in the larger society, and her own childhood experiences of emotional neglect.

The woman also has few friends and complains about being alone but resists her family's attempts to get her to go to adult day health care for socialization. She says that she feels most happy when she is able to get out in nature. Like all ecofractals, these social fractals suggest many possible issues and experiences in her life. Perhaps, for example, she has always felt more alone than she wanted to be, and dealt with her suffering by increased social withdrawal. Perhaps her connections with nature began when she lived on a farm as a child. All of these possibilities and others could be further explored. Finally, these ecofractal examples seem mirrored in *cross-fractal patterns*, which are general themes in this woman's life. As illustrated in Box 2.2, the ecofractals suggest several common cross-fractal patterns in her life; she is a woman who has lost trust in her own worth and in the friendliness of her God.

Observable ecofractals can also be found in the interactions within groups of people. As illustrated in Table 2.4, these collective ecofractals may offer the practitioner data about the BPPSE history held by all the members of any group of people. Column 3 in Table 2.4 provides illustrations of the ecofractal types. Each ecofractal may reflect patterns in the history and current nature of a couple at the individual, couple, family, institutional, community, and/or Multiuniverse levels.

In the first row, for example, a couple reports communication and intimacy problems. The practitioner can see how this fractal may reflect patterns at many levels. On the individual level, neither people may have learned communication and intimacy skills as children. On the couple level, they may have both reacted to suffering by withdrawing further from each other each time they were hurt. On a family level, none of their parents may have modeled good communication and intimacy. On an institutional level, their schools and religions may have neglected including educational content on effective communication and intimacy skills and values. On the local community level, most other couples they know are actually

TABLE 2.4   Collective Ecofractals

ECOFRACTAL NAMES	ECOFRACTAL CONTENT	EXAMPLES OF ECOFRACTALS*
Couple Fractal	Interaction pattern in the couple relationship, including spiritual, physical, emotional, cognitive, and social interactions	A couple reports that they have poor communication and little intimacy
Family Fractal	Interaction pattern in familial relationships, including spiritual, physical, emotional, cognitive, and social interactions	Across generations, the men in the family usually have alcohol addictions and the women are codependent
Institution Fractal	Interaction pattern in institutional relationships, including spiritual, physical, emotional, cognitive, and social interactions	The college seems to always have political infighting, which reduces collegiality and productivity
Local Community Fractal	Interaction pattern either between people or between people and local ecosystems, including spiritual, physical, emotional, cognitive, and social interactions	The medium-sized city segregated along religious and racial lines in both subtle and overt ways
Global Community Fractal	Interaction pattern either between people or between people and local ecosystems, including spiritual, physical, emotional, cognitive, and social interactions	The poor nations continue to grow poorer and more oppressed, and the rich nations grow richer and more oppressive

*Each collective ecofractal may reflect patterns in the history and current nature of this group at the individual, couple, family, institutional, community, and/or Multiuniverse levels.

less intimate than they publically act like they are. On the global community level, the goal of marriage has changed so quickly from economic advantage to intimacy that most people in the current generations have not yet learned how to reach those goals in one lifetime.

A similar analysis can be done at, for example, the global level. The fractal of growing inequality between have and have-not nations can be linked at the local level to the growing inequality between have and have-not families in most communities in the United States. Similarly, the fear and insecurity that many couples and families currently have about the economy is a fractal of the fear and insecurity that many nations seem to have about the global economy.

The Client's Greatest Suffering Is Often in Shadow

The client often has intense shame and guilt about the circumstances of his most intense suffering, and therefore may try to hide his pain from other people. Psychologists might say that he hides his symptoms in shadow. This *shadow* includes all the parts of a person that he cannot yet fully own or accept.

For example, a 40-year-old father with symptoms of dysthymia and anxiety complains to his therapist that his wife has had an affair and wants to leave him. As they talk, the therapist starts to realize how difficult it is for this man to identify his needs and ask other people for anything. In this case, this man's shadow is, in part, his heart's desire for love and his pain around his aloneness.

In another example, a teenager presents with depression and suicidal ideation. She has a 4.0 grade-point average in high school and is popular with her peers. However, she tells her therapist that her mother has been drinking alcohol heavily since her father lost his job and that lately her father and mother have had frequent angry outbursts. The therapist determines that the girl's sadness, hurt, and anger about her parents' relationship is in shadow.

The social worker can often assess the sources of a client's suffering by also studying where the client's shame most seems to be. Thus, shame is an indicator of where some of the most important work needs to be done. For example, many adolescent and adult sex offenders have tremendous shame about their sexuality, and these clients usually have a history of sexual trauma and related sexual issues that greatly trouble them. In another example, many clients who have symptoms of Obsessive Compulsive Disorder also have shame about their repetitive thoughts and behaviors, and these symptoms are often identified by such clients as the most significant cause of their unhappiness.

ASSESSING SPIRITUAL–RELIGIOUS IDENTITY

The spiritually oriented social worker assesses the Spiritual–Religious Identity (SRI) of each client and client population. As illustrated in Table 2.5, one way to assess SRI is to use spirituality and religiosity to create four categories. Studies of baby boomers in the United States indicate that Category I (*strong spiritual identity* and *strong religious identity*), which includes the two subcategories of *Born Again*

TABLE 2.5   Categories of Spiritual–Religious Identity

	STRONG SPIRITUAL IDENTITY	WEAK SPIRITUAL IDENTITY
Strong Religious Identity	**Category I: Strong religious and strong spiritual identity** Born Again Christian (33%) Mainstream believer (26%)	**Category II: Strong religious and weak spiritual identity** Religious dogmatist (15%)
Weak Religious Identity	**Category III: Weak religious and strong spiritual identity** Metaphysical believer (14%)	**Category IV: Weak religious and weak spiritual identity** Secularist (12%)

Note: Categories and percentages from Roof (1999).

Christian and *Mainstream believer,* is the largest, making up 59 percent or close to two-thirds of the population. The other three categories are much smaller; each contains roughly only one-seventh of the population.

The social worker puts a client or population into a category, knowing that each individual and population has unique characteristics and is more than a label. However, the social worker uses the SRI assessment to help her be more sensitive to the unique beliefs, rituals, and metaphors that each client and population may use. Examples of these unique characteristics are illustrated in Table 2.6.

Therefore the spiritually oriented social worker assesses the SRI of her client as quickly as possible so that she can begin using language and methods of transformation with which the client is likely to be most comfortable. For example, if the social worker assesses that the client has a Category II SRI, then she might look for beliefs, rituals, and metaphors that the client uses in his life that are similar to the examples given in Table 2.6.

TABLE 2.6   Examples of Beliefs, Rituals, and Metaphors That May Be Found in Each SRI Category

	STRONG SPIRITUAL IDENTITY	WEAK SPIRITUAL IDENTITY
Strong Religious Identity	**Category I: Strong religious and strong spiritual identity** *Belief:* I have found the real God *Ritual:* Praying to God from the heart *Metaphor:* My sins are forgiven	**Category II: Strong religious and weak spiritual identity** *Belief:* This is God's only true religion *Ritual:* God talks through clergy and bible *Metaphor:* God the father
Weak Religious Identity	**Category III: Weak religious and strong spiritual identity** *Belief:* I see sacredness in nature *Ritual:* Drumming and dancing *Metaphor:* Mother earth, Father sky	**Category IV: Weak religious and weak spiritual identity** *Belief:* There is no God *Ritual:* Knowing reality through science *Metaphor:* Heaven and Hell are on Earth

STUDY QUESTIONS

1. What does it mean to say that human behavior has vast and complex causes? Do you experience your own behavior as having such causes?

2. What are the different ways of knowing available to practitioners? What way of knowing are you most comfortable with? Which is least comfortable? Explain why.

3. What are the challenges and advantages of single-disciplinary, multidisciplinary, and transdisciplinary approaches to assessment? Which of these approaches do you have experience in? Which do you prefer? Explain why.

4. How much of assessment do you think is usually in mystery? How do you deal with the unknowns you encounter when you do assessments?

5. What are the three major levels of consciousness in transpersonal theory? Which of the three levels do you spend most of your time living in? Why do you think this is your primary level?

6. What are the dimensions of human development? In what dimensions are you personally most developed or mature? In which dimensions are you least developed? To what extent do you think these differences in your development is caused by nature, environment, or spirit?

7. What are fractals? Do you notice fractals in your own life? Do you notice factals in your intergenerational family? Explain.

RESOURCES

Bird, R. J. (2003). *Chaos and life: Complexity and order in evolution and thought*. New York: Columbia University Press.
   This book discusses
   1. How the Multiuniverse is a complex and chaotic system
   2. How chaotic systems are actually well ordered and somewhat predictable
   3. How living things have "chaostability," which means that they preserve the degree of information (entropy) that they have
   4. How order in chaotic systems is the result of interactions between the observer and what is being observed
   5. How the most complex mathematical objects are fractals, which result from many iterations of the same functions
   6. How the best way to study human beings (the most complex systems known) is by observing a few principles, which are actually patterns or fractals

Brockman, J. (2003). *The new humanists: Science at the edge*. New York: Barnes & Noble Books.
   This book covers
   1. How fifteenth-century humanism was about the idea of one intellectual whole
   2. How the First (Literary) Culture and the Second (Scientific) Culture is now being followed by a Third Culture of "New Humanists" who join together the arts and the sciences
   3. How the New Humanist science-based humanities scholars are intellectually eclectic, use many sources of information, and implement ideas that work

Derezotes, D. S. (2000). *Advanced generalist social work practice*. Thousand Oaks, CA: Sage.
   This book discusses
   1. How to include all the dimensions of human development as well as all the dimensions of the human environment in assessment
   2. Using both the art and science of practice
   3. Biopsychosocial, local community, and global community interventions

Greene, B. (1999). *The elegant universe: Superstrings, hidden dimensions, and the quest for the ultimate theory.* New York: W. W. Norton.
This book includes
1. An interesting description of emerging theories in current physics
2. A frank discussion of what is known and what remains in mystery to physicists

Mandelbrot, B. (1991). "Fractals: The geometry of nature," in N. Hall (Ed.), *Exploring chaos: A guide to the new science of disorder* (pp. 122–135). New York: W. W. Norton.
This chapter provides
1. A useful introduction to fractal theory
2. A linkage between chaos theory and fractal theory

Roof, W. C. (1999). *The spiritual marketplace: Baby boomers and the remaking of American religion.* Princeton, NJ: Princeton University Press.
This book provides the concepts and percentages described in Table 2.6.

Siegfried, T. (2000). *The bit and the pendulum: From quantum computing to M Theory—The new physics of information.* New York: John Wiley & Sons.
This book covers
1. Information theory
2. How all of natural activity is information processing
3. How information is a physical entity

Walker, E. H. (2000). *The physics of consciousness: Quantum theory and the meaning of life.* Cambridge, MA: Perseus Books.
This book includes
1. Descriptions of emerging theories in physics that may support transpersonal theory
2. A fascinating scientific theory of how consciousness, life, and matter are linked

Wilber, K. (2000). *Sex, ecology, spirituality: The spirit of evolution.* Boston: Shambhala.
This book includes
1. Descriptions of prepersonal, personal, and transpersonal consciousness
2. Descriptions of quadrants of ways of knowing
3. Wonderful reference list

Wilson, E. O. (1998). *Consilience: The unity of knowledge.* New York: Random House.
This book discusses
1. How consilience is the establishment of interlocking causal connections across scientific disciplines
2. How real-world problems have multifaceted etiologies that go beyond the scope of any one discipline and require the expertice of all disciplines
3. How few theoretical maps exist that describe these multifaceted real-world problems

CHAPTER 3

METHODS IN SPIRITUAL TRANSFORMATION

METHODS OF TRANSFORMATION

This chapter is an overview of the seven paradigms of spiritually oriented practice. In Chapters 4 through 10, each of these seven paradigms of spiritually oriented social work are further described. In the first part of this chapter, *methods* of spiritual transformation are introduced. The characteristics of transformation are described here.

Radical Change

Transformations are radical because they involve root-level change. Observable changes in behavior, which by themselves may not be maintained or generalized over time, are rooted in changes in mind, heart, and soul.

Integral Change

Transformations bring about more integrity, or wholeness. The person rediscovers parts of herself that have been lost. She finds that her heart, mind, body, and spirit have become aligned, so that each part of herself cooperates in forming a balanced, common view of how she fits in the Cosmos.

Enhanced Equanimity

Transformations also bring a calm, centered approach to life. Rather than going into unconscious or destructive reaction to life events, equanimity allows the person to make proactive and creative decisions about how to think and act.

Temperance

Transformations also tend to foster harmony and moderation. The person learns how to mix emotions, thoughts, and behaviors and other aspects of self in order to establish a balanced pattern of being.

Greater Ecstasy

Ecstasy occurs when the person sits in his witness or supervisory self, from where he can watch his personality, the Cosmos, and Creative Spirit with equanimity. He does not sit there alone, but in fact sits in increased intimacy with Creative Spirit, made possible by his movement from "immersion in" to "observation of" the material world.

Increased Capacity

Transformations create more capacity for consciousness, love, compassion, and wisdom. Capacity is also increased for spiritual power, transrational knowing, imagination, and aliveness. The person has greater capacity to not only develop the highest levels of well-being but also to examine the shadow aspects of self.

Here-and-Now Change Potential

The potential for transformational change always exists in the here and now. Although each person is a unique embodiment of Creative Spirit, every person can initiate her own unique next step in her transformational process at any time in her life.

New Value Hierarchies

If there are no changes in values, then there has been no transformation. Transformations bring new value hierarchies. The person in transformational change helps co-create communities of spiritual diversity and communities of universal diversity, in which the Highest Good of all individual parts and the Highest Good of the collective whole are highly valued.

Service-Activism

If there are no changes in behaviors, then there has also been no transformation. Transformations bring new patterns of behavior, rooted in evolving value hierarchies. Transformations lead to greater response-ability for service and spiritual activism in support of the Highest Good of other people, living things, and ecosystems.

THEORETICAL ASSUMPTIONS

Methods of transformation do not necessarily replace any interventions that professional helpers currently use, but they do *add* the spiritual dimension to all practice situations. This relationship can be described by the expression:

Intervention + Spirituality = Transformation

TABLE 3.1   Some Theoretical Assumptions Underlying Interventions and Transformations

METHOD	ELEMENTS IN INTERVENTION*	ELEMENTS ADDED IN TRANSFORMATION
Microlevel Change	*Emphasis:* Personality *Disease model:* Dysfunction *Goal:* Function, symptom reduction *Technique:* Cognitive-behavioral *Change agent:* Practitioner and drugs	*Emphasis:* Transpersonality *Disease model:* Spiritual disconnection *Goal:* Reconnection with Spirit *Technique:* Invite and allow Spirit *Change agent:* Spirituality
Macrolevel Change	*Emphasis:* Productivity, competition *Problem:* Success of enemy *Goal:* Wealth, power, status *Technique:* Economic-military force *Change agent:* External coercion	*Emphasis:* Global healing, Highest Good *Problem:* Suffering of others *Goal:* Deep peace *Technique:* Universal community making *Change agent:* Spirituality

*Characteristics of interventions often observed in current practice

Thus, a spiritual perspective can be taken with any of the existing intervention methods, to create more inclusive methods of transformation. Inventions help people create a functional personality; transformations help people welcome Spiritual Power into their lives. Such power helps people stop identifying solely with their personality, with consensus reality, and with the material values of the culture they are in.

A brief summary of some of the differences between the theory that guides typical methods of intervention and the theory that guides methods of transformation is given in Table 3.1. In general, interventions focus on helping people reduce their symptoms, function in society, and create a self. In contrast, transformations help clients move beyond their self-focus to a more spiritual focus informed by Spiritual Values.

Spiritually Inclusive Practitioner

The most effective practitioner is spiritually inclusive, which means that she is open to including spirituality in her practice assessments, methods, and evaluations. She is open to continue using any existing intervention strategy she has learned, and she is also open to discovering what might happen when she invites the spiritual dimension into her work with her current practice strategies.

Spiritual Values

Like all methods of practice, spiritual methods are rooted in a set of values. Since spiritual work is potentially the most powerful of all practice methods, the spiritually inclusive practitioner especially needs to have a set of values that serve to help guide him or her toward fostering the Highest Good and reducing the possibility of causing unnecessary suffering.

■ ■ ■ ■ ■

BOX 3.1

A POSSIBLE SPIRITUAL-VALUES PRACTICE HIERARCHY

SPIRITUAL VALUE	IMPLICATIONS FOR WHAT PRACTITIONER EMPHASIZES WITH CLIENT
Service	Taking responsibility to foster the Highest Good of people, life, and ecosystems
Consciousness	Developing each person's prepersonal, personal, and transpersonal development
Love	Holding intent for the Highest Good in self, others, and ecosystems
Imagination	Imaging the Highest Good for one's self and divine self
Integrity	Approaching every moment with all parts of one's self and divine self
Connectedness	Living in interrelationship with self, divine self, and Cosmos
Ecstatic Aliveness	Developing capacity to experience joy and suffering from observing self
Meaning Making	Developing capacity to find spiritual significance in all of life experiences
Sacred Mystery	Approaching life and its mysteries with awe, gratitude, and respect

Spiritual Values are radical because they deal with the fundamental roots of such experiences as suffering, happiness, and ecstasy. Values by definition exist in a hierarchy of levels of importance. Box 3.1 shows a possible hierarchy of Spiritual Values that might guide the practitioner in working with a client. As can be seen, service and responsibility to other people, living things, and ecosystems is held as the highest value in this hierarchy.

Apparent Dualities of Transformational Work

Spiritual transformations may superficially seem to be full of conflicting realities, but a study of spiritual processes indicates how these apparent dualities are not mutually exclusive. For example, although spiritual transformation may involve subtle body–mind–spirit processes, they can also lead to the most dramatic changes in self and the world. In addition, although spiritual work can look self-absorbed and self-serving, it can lead to radically selfless spiritual activism. Finally, although spiritual work deals with the most serious life challenges and can require facing the most painful experiences, spiritual interventions can also be fun and can bring the highest ecstasy possible in life.

PARADIGMS OF TRANSFORMATION

The methods in this book are organized into seven interrelated paradigms of transformation (see Table 3.2). These new paradigms are built on traditional practice paradigms, symbolized by the simple expression:

TABLE 3.2   Seven Paradigms of Spiritual Transformation

NEW PARADIGM OF SPIRITUAL TRANSFORMATION	THEORETICAL BASE NEW PARADIGM IS BUILT ON	WORK WITH INDIVIDUALS, COUPLES, FAMILIES, AND GROUPS	WORK WITH LOCAL AND GLOBAL COMMUNITIES AND ECOSYSTEMS
1. Spiritual momentum	1st Force: Psychodynamic	Transforming individual spiritual momentum	Transforming collective spiritual momentum
2. Mindful daily living	2nd Force: Cognitive behavioral	Developing a pattern of mindful living	Teaching mindfulness and Right Actions to others
3. Spirit with heart	3rd Force: Experiential-humanistic	Developing consciousness by experiencing and sharing the full range of emotions	Teaching love, forgiveness, and compassion in service to other beings
4. Religious self	4th Force: Transpersonal	Developing consciousness by using rituals from world's wisdom traditions	Teaching the rituals of any of wisdom traditions
5. Bio-consciousness	Biopsychosocial	Developing consciousness through body work and the embodiment of experience	Teaching the embodiment of consciousness
6. Community consciousness	Community organizing Global work	Developing consciousness though local and global community work	Co-creating and practicing in communities of spiritual diversity
7. Eco-consciousness	Deep ecology Ecotherapy Shamanism	Developing consciousness though ecowork	Co-creating and practicing in communities of universal diversity

Traditional paradigm + Spirituality = More inclusive paradigm
of transformation

The first four paradigms of transformation correspond to the four forces of psychology: psychodynamic, cognitive behavioral, experiential humanistic, and transpersonal. Since transpersonal psychology is essentially a study of human consciousness, it is the paradigm that changes the least when spirituality is added. The other three paradigms build on several other theoretical areas that are not included in the four forces. These are biopsychosocial theory, various community-level models, and ecological theories.

The paradigms represent seven levels of transformation. The levels represent increasingly complex, large-scale, and subtle transformational work. The first five levels are about developing a spiritual self (through work on the past and future, the mind, right actions, the heart, wisdom traditions, and the body). The last two levels move "beyond" sole focus on self to focus on the more inclusive divine self (communities of people, other living things, and the ecosystems that support all life).

Each of the seven levels has two interrelated service methods: Spiritual Practice and Spiritual Activism. *Spiritual Practice* transforms individual consciousness, individual heart, and individual mind, whereas *Spiritual Activism* transforms collective consciousness, collective heart, and collective mind. In the fourth column of Table 3.2, the term *teaching* is used in an inclusive manner, referring not only to instruction but also to mentoring and modeling. Since individual consciousness is inseparable from collective consciousness, each type of service leads to the other, as shown by the expression:

Spiritual Practice <—> Spiritual Activism

The most effective practitioners utilize methods of both Spiritual Practice and Spiritual Activism drawn from all seven paradigms because the paradigms, when added together, address the major aspects of self and divine self that interact with our spirituality.

Spiritual Momentum (Chapter 4)

These methods build on the traditional first force or psychodynamic paradigm of practice. The goal of traditional first force practice is to help people gain insight into the historic origins of their internal conflicts so that their current needs are better understood and met. The goal of *spiritual momentum* is to free people to foster transformations of momentum so people can be fully present in the here and now. Spiritual momentum is the overall direction that a person's soul is heading, and could be thought of as similar to the concept of karma, without the requirement that soul direction necessarily continues across lifetimes. The primary methods of transformation are the use of altered states of consciousness to take healing journeys across time and space and the use of these journeys to gain insight into how issues in the past and future still obstruct the individual's ability to be present in the here and now.

Mindful Daily Living (Chapter 5)

These methods build on traditional second force or cognitive-behavioral therapy (CBT) methods. The goal of the traditional CBT methods is to help people develop more "functional" ways of thinking and acting. The goal of *mindful daily living* is to foster a pattern of right actions that is rooted in a discipline of mindfulness. Mindfulness is the development of a spiritual perspective through intellect. Right actions are behaviors that are consistent with the individual's own spiritual perspective, and are consistent with the value of service for the Highest Good. The principal methods involve the use of intellect to transform the mind and the use of intent to transform behavior.

Spirit with Heart (Chapter 6)

These methods build on traditional third force or humanistic-experiential methods of practice. Those third force methods traditionally focused on helping people become aware of, accept, and express their emotions. The goal of *spirit with heart* is to foster transformations of the heart in the here and now, which ultimately fosters greater love, forgiveness, and compassion. The methods utilize awareness, acceptance, and expression of the emotional self to explore and express spirituality.

Spirit through Religious Self (Chapter 7)

Religious self methods foster development of the religious self, which is the manifestation of spirituality in the social dimension. The religious self is capable of relating with loving intent on any or all of the prepersonal, personal, and transpersonal levels of consciousness. These methods adapt, sometimes modify, and apply techniques drawn from the wisdom traditions of the world. These methods support the individual's lifelong free choice and wise use of a menu of spiritual disciplines that best support his or her spiritual development and ultimately the spiritual development of other people as well. Key tasks in this lifelong quest for spiritual maturity are the development of temperance and equanimity. The development of the religious self leads to increased responsibility that the individual takes in helping her or his religion become a community of spiritual and universal diversity.

Bioconsciousness (Chapter 8)

Most interventions utilize talk therapy, which can be primarily an above-the-neck activity. These methods build on biopsychosocial theory, which describes a body–mind connection in all human beings. The goal of *bioconsciousness* is to foster that connection, which leads to healthy functioning. Whole-body (above, below, and including the neck) methods are used, such as aerobic exercise, expressive dance, slow stretching, breath work, and martial arts. Body-consciousness transformations expand the definition of health (or wholeness) to a biopsychoso-cial–*spiritual* connection. Practitioners help clients learn to listen to Creative Spirit with their bodies and learn to embody spirituality in their daily lives.

Community Consciousness (Chapter 9)

These methods build on family and group counseling theory and community-level practice strategies, which help people by changing family and group dynamics and institutional and social policies and other local and global community structures. The goal of *community–consciousness* transformations is to co-create and practice communities of spiritual diversity that support the development of individual consciousness and the individual and collective Highest Good. Methods include conscious intimacy, conscious dialogue, conscious service, and conscious activism designed to support the development of communities of spiritual diversity.

Eco-consciousness (Chapter 10)

Eco-spiritual techniques build on the theories of ecotherapy and shamanism (the earliest-known religions of people). The goals of deep ecology and ecotherapy are to foster better caretaking of the Earth's life and supporting environments, which in turn fosters the well-being of people who live on the Earth. The goals of shamanism are complex, but usually involve the use of ecstatic journeys in which healers use visualizations that incorporate drumming; journeys onto different levels of consciousness; and the intent to heal. *Eco-consciousness* methods build on these ancient and recent traditions for the purpose of fostering spiritual transformations and developing communities of universal diversity. These methods might include visualizations involving animals, plants, and landscapes; experiences that combine therapy with interactions with nature, and activism in the service of other living things and ecosystems.

Spiritual work could be viewed as the fostering of individual and collective spiritual development. Since humans are biopsychosocial–spiritual–environmental beings, the dimensions of human development are all interrelated. Each of the seven paradigms has a focus on one dimension of human development (see Box 3.2).

GENERAL PRINCIPLES OF SPIRITUALLY ORIENTED SOCIAL WORK PRACTICE

Spiritual and Religious Transference and Countertransferences

Often, the first clue that the practitioner has about where the client is at in his or her life spiritual journey comes from spiritual and religious transferences and countertransferences (see Table 3.3). All of these reactions are normal aspects of human

---

■ ■ ■ ■ ■ ▬▬▬▬▬▬▬▬▬▬▬▬▬▬▬▬▬▬▬▬▬▬▬▬▬▬▬▬▬▬▬

BOX 3.2

DIMENSIONS OF HUMAN DEVELOPMENT IN THE SEVEN PARADIGMS

Level One: *Spiritual momentum*	Development of orientation in time and space
Level Two: *Mindful daily living*	Cognitive development
Level Three: *Spirit with heart*	Emotional development
Level Four: *Religious self*	Social (religious) development
Level Five: *Bioconsciousness*	Physical development
Level Six: *Community consciousness*	Community development
Level Seven: *Eco-consciousness*	Ecosystem development

TABLE 3.3   **Definitions of Spiritual and Religious Transferences and Countertransferences**

	TRANSFERENCE	COUNTERTRANSFERENCE
Spiritual	Feelings and beliefs (with roots in both the client's past and present experience) that client has about the practitioner's spiritual nature and path	Feelings and beliefs (with roots in both the practitioner's past and present experience) that practitioner has about the client's spiritual nature and path
Religious	Feelings and beliefs (with roots in both the client's past and present experience) that client has about the practitioner's religious affiliations, beliefs, doctrines, rituals, and practices	Feelings and beliefs (with roots in both the practitioner's past and present experience) that practitioner has about the client's religious affiliations, beliefs, doctrines, rituals, and practices

interaction, and are *always present in every helping relationship,* although they can vary in intensity. These transference and countertransferences usually have roots in both the past and present. Past roots occur when their interactions on the spiritual and religious levels activate previous experiences and associated emotions and beliefs that the client and practitioner have had with other people. Present roots occur because the client and practitioner also can have here-and-now reactions to each other's spirituality and religiosity. The work of the therapeutic relationship is to sort out what reactions are rooted in the past and what reactions are rooted in the here and now.

The practitioner can respond to spiritual and religious countertransferences in a variety of ways, utilizing any of the seven paradigms for spiritual transformation. In Table 3.4, examples of methods of practice drawn from the first three paradigms are summarized.

Conscious Use of Higher Self in the Spiritual Partnership

The quality of the *relationship* that the practitioner can build with the client is the most important factor in successful therapeutic outcomes. It is through that relationship that the client learns to love herself and develop her consciousness. Conscious use of Higher Self in the spiritual partnership is the intentional engagement of the practitioner with the client, with the aim to foster the spiritual development and Highest Good of the client.

The characteristics of the practitioner are typically associated with the quality of the helping relationship. Decades of research show that practitioner characteristics are more important than techniques and client characteristics in predicting such outcomes. Perhaps most important of all of these characteristics is *genuineness,* which is the ability of the practitioner to be fully present with the

TABLE 3.4 Selected Methods of Practice in Response to Spiritual and Religious Transferences and Countertransferences

	TRANSFERENCE (T)	COUNTERTRANSFERENCE (CT)
Spiritual	*Level One: Spiritual momentum* Identify any past spiritual wounds that may contribute to the client's T *Level Three: Spirit with heart* Establish spiritual intimacy in helping relationship in which issues related with client's T can be safely discussed *Level Two: Mindful daily living* Replace client's old T reactions associated with spiritual woundedness with new ways of thinking and acting	*Level One: Spiritual momentum* 1. Identify past spiritual wounds that may contribute to the CT reaction 2. Then find what client characteristic(s) may also contribute to the CT reaction *Level Three: Spirit with heart* Practitioner is "transparent" with client about her own CT and spiritual wounds *Level Two: Mindful daily living* Practitioner responds proactively with the intent to foster the client's Highest Good
Religious	*Level One: Spiritual momentum* Identify past religious wounds that still echo in here-and-now transferences *Level Three: Spirit with heart* Explore emotional and spiritual intimacy with practitioner in which T can be safely discussed and thus healed *Level Two: Mindful daily living* Replace destructive reactions coming from religious woundedness with more creative, loving, and service-oriented ways of thinking and acting	*Level One: Spiritual momentum* 1. Identify past religious wounds that may contribute to the CT reaction 2. Then find what client characteristic(s) may also contribute to the CT reaction *Level Three: Spirit with heart* Practitioner is "transparent" with client about his own CT and religious wounds *Level Two: Mindful daily living* Practitioner responds proactively with the . intent to foster the client's Highest Good. Spiritual and religious diversity is respected and supported

client in integrity in each moment. Although genuineness may be conceptualized as the part of the normal state of human consciousness, most people learn to give up parts of their integrity or wholeness as they navigate through the often painful experiences of childhood, adolescence, and adulthood.

Another important characteristic is *love*, because if the practitioner does not care about the client and somehow show the client that love, the client may not benefit from the work. The effective practitioner also accepts the client as she or he is in the here-and-now moment.

Clients also *want to be seen*, although their initial reaction to being seen by the practitioner may be characterized by guilt, shame, and defensiveness. Therefore, the effective practitioner strives to eliminate obstacles to his ability to see his clients accurately, such as biases, fears, and other reactions.

Clients also develop most quickly when they experience *radical acceptance* from the practitioner. Radical acceptance means that the client is viewed by the practitioner as being perfect, lovable, and on her spiritual path in every moment. Such acceptance does not mean that the client is therefore free to do whatever she wishes to do. Rather, the practitioner knows that as people learn to truly love themselves, they become more responsible for fostering the Highest Good of themselves, other people, and ecosystems. The practitioner is compassionate and forgiving toward the client, but she also challenges the client to move toward transformations in his life. There really is no duality between the goals of creating an atmosphere of safety and acceptance and challenging the client to grow because the most radical changes occur when the person loves himself. Said differently, the best way to *not* have a spiritual transformation is to hold on to guilt and shame about one's self.

Since love and narcissism are so often confused in our culture today, the practitioner needs to make sure he or she can distinguish between the two opposite characteristics. Love of self combines self-awareness with self-acceptance; narcissism is characterized by a sense of self distorted by self-hatred and compensatory self-inflation.

Spiritual Self-Work

The effective practitioner engages in spiritual self-work throughout her career. The goal of such work is to continue to foster the practitioner's own spiritual development through service to herself, other people, and ecosystems.

In preparation for practice, the practitioner engages in her own personal exploration of every method that she wants to use with her client. The client is more likely to respond favorably to a practitioner who has done the same work that she is asking the client to do.

In response to practice, the practitioner also views each client as a spiritual teacher, in the sense that the client has come into her practice for a reason and that there is always something to learn. Thus, the practitioner always considers what lessons are to be learned during the course of any case.

Ritual

The word *spiritual* includes the word *ritual* within it, suggesting that rituals help us embody spirituality in our lives. Rituals are sacred ceremonies during which aspects of spirituality can be played out. Rituals can be done individually or collectively, and can be spontaneous or planned and repeated acts.

The practitioner strives to co-create rituals with her or his clients that are enjoyable and relatively safe to do. The practitioner also works with the client to co-create meaning for every part of the ritual. All the methods in this text can be seen as rituals of spiritual growth and healing.

Ethical-Value Issues

Some general principles of ethics and values can be described here.

1. The practitioner needs to be aware of the current literature that describes the methodologies he is using. The practitioner makes himself aware of the various theories, debates, outcome research, and state of the art practices in the methodologies used.

2. The practitioner is aware of the general potential risks and benefits of the methodologies. She is also able to assess potential risks and benefits specific to each of her clients, and can describe these specific risks and benefits to each client.

3. The practitioner is able to relate his spiritual practice to more conventional theories and interventions and ethics in his profession. He can see similarities and differences, and can describe ways to integrate both views into his practice.

4. The practitioner can form an effective helping relationship with the client, in which she employs conscious use of self in that relationship (see Chapter 6).

5. The practitioner continues to develop himself, in the physical, emotional, cognitive, social, and spiritual dimensions, across his lifetime. He also is responsible to the Highest Good of other people, other living things, and the ecosystems that support all life.

6. The practitioner can evaluate her practice and make appropriate modifications in her practice, based on these ongoing evaluations.

STUDY QUESTIONS

1. What are transformations? How are they different from interventions?

2. What kinds of spiritual transformations have you experienced in your own life? What seemed to facilitate those transformations?

3. Which of the eight aspects of transformation are most important to you today? Which of these are most developed in yourself? Which are least developed?

4. What are the seven paradigms of transformation developed in this text? Which of these paradigms seem to be the most interesting to you? Why do you think they appeal to you?

RESOURCES

Derezotes, D. S. (2000). *Advanced generalist social work practice.* Thousand Oaks, CA: Sage.
   This book explains
   1. How to include all the dimensions of human development as well as all the dimensions of the human environment in assessment
   2. How to use both the art and science of practice
   3. Biopsychosocial, local community, and global community interventions.

Derezotes, D. S. (2005). *Re-valuing social work: Implication of emerging science and technology.* Denver: Love.
   This book discusses
   1. How hierarchal values systems can help inform social work practice
   2. How new knowledge and theory from other disciplines can help inform social work practice

CHAPTER 4

SPIRITUAL MOMENTUM

SPIRITUAL MOMENTUM

The overall purpose of the spiritual momentum paradigm is to foster individual transformation of spiritual momentum, which is the general direction that the soul of the person is moving in. Momentum is more positive, for example, when the person is moving toward her own multidimensional healing and maturity, is learning to love herself and the world more deeply, and is participating in the creation of communities of spiritual and universal community. Momentum is more negative, for example, when the person is losing a loving connection with parts of himself and his world, is becoming increasingly regressed and stuck in some stage of his development, and is losing reverence for the diversity of human beings, other living things, and the ecosystems that support all life.

Work in the spiritual momentum paradigm fosters higher consciousness across the past, across the future, and across spatial distance so that the person can be more fully present and conscious in the here and now. When in such higher consciousness, people have a sense of *sacred continuity*, which is the experience that one's everyday human life is connected with and inseparable from the experiences of their ancestors and descendants across time. There is also a sacred continuity people have with other living things and the ecosystems that support all life. For example, a person gazing into the Grand Canyon may have an enhanced sense of connection with the Earth as she or he realizes how much time it has taken to create all the layers of rock now revealed by erosion. From a spiritual perspective, a sense of reverence for sacred continuity is an essential ingredient in a person's well-being.

From this perspective, people could be viewed as having one of two kinds of difficulties. First, they may be "stuck" in the past or the future, which inhibits their ability to be fully present in the here and now. People may be stuck, for example, by worrying excessively about the future. They may also have persistent feelings of guilt or anger or unhelpful beliefs about past events, which intrude into their present consciousness.

A second kind of difficulty is disconnection from sacred continuity. This happens when people live their lives as if they have no connection with their ancestors or descendants. Our ancestors and descendants include not only our human relatives (grandparents and grandchildren) but also the other living things and natural ecosystems that came before us and that will follow us.

In spiritual momentum, the client and practitioner essentially become co-travelers across time and space, exploring individual, collective, and divine time-space. Such spiritual momentum is ultimately a journey toward higher consciousness, which involves exploration into all three kinds of timespace:

1. *Individual time-space* is the person's own unique life story, over the course of one lifetime. Psychodynamic methods have traditionally addressed only individual time (not necessarily also across space), for the purpose of helping people resolve past issues and related inner conflicts so that current needs can be met. Typically, a client is asked to tell parts of his or her story to the practitioner, and then the practitioner responds, perhaps with an interpretation of the meaning of the story. Individual time includes the experiences a person has both in waking time and in dream time (when the person is asleep).

2. *Shared time-space* is the shared story of a family, community, or other human grouping, which may extend over many individual lifetimes. Stories about shared time are often best told in a circle or other interactive group setting. These stories are not completed until the voices of all the people involved are heard. Each new generation may reinterpret the stories and their meanings as time goes on.

3. *Sacred time-space* is the collective experience of all the stories of people, other living things, and ecosystems across all time. Stories about shared time continue to evolve forever because they are infinite in scope and because they continue to be created by the voices of all people and other living things, and the rest of Cosmos. Sacred time includes not only the experiences a person has had in his or her lifetime, but also the experiences all people have had, are having, or will have in their lifetimes in the past, present, and future. Sacred time also includes the stories of the other animals and the plants that have lived or will live on the Earth, as well as the stories of the Earth itself, with its evolving continents, oceans, atmospheres, and landscapes.

All Times and All Locations Are Right Here and Now

From a spiritual momentum perspective, human consciousness can access all experiences across all time and space. Science has never found the limits of the human imagination. Although science has never proven that such things as collective unconsciousness, past lives, and simultaneous universes actually exist, many people across the world, including prominent scientists, *believe* they exist. The practitioner is not as concerned with the ultimate truth of any particular client's experiences as she is concerned with the potential meaning, practical usefulness, and healing potential of the experience for the client.

Symptoms and Life Trauma from a Spiritual Perspective

The spiritually oriented social worker does not want to replace other theories, but is willing to look at the relationship between symptoms and life trauma in different ways than the traditional psychologist or psychiatrist might view the relationship. Instead of considering just nature and nurture in the etiology of human characteristics, the social worker is also willing to consider the spiritual dimension as a third source of human characteristics.

Modern psychology and psychiatry teaches that people have symptoms (such as depression, anxiety, etc.) because they were traumatized, perhaps by a caregiver, a family, an institution, or even by the entire culture. The client may also have a genetic predisposition that adds to the symptom. In addition, when the symptom is eliminated, the client is "cured." From a spiritual perspective, however, what is called a symptom could also be viewed as part of a person's spiritual momentum that his soul brought into his lifetime. Thus, the symptom could be viewed as a characteristic that was necessary for the soul's journey during at least part of the lifetime.

For example, an adult client may be viewed from a traditional perspective as being hypervigilant about intimacy because he is unable to commit to a marriage-type relationship. The social worker might determine that the man was traumatized by an overintrusive mother when he was a boy. In traditional psychodynamic work, the social worker would help the man "work through" the past trauma so that he can gain insight into his past and get his needs met in the present. Medications might also be given to help the man "balance his brain chemistry." From this perspective, if the worker can help the client stop being so vigilant, then he is "cured."

From a spiritual perspective, however, the man may have been "given" the spiritual "gift" of vigilance so that he could survive his childhood intact. The goal then is to help foster a transformation in which the man creates a new spiritual momentum in which he can open up his heart and soul to a lover if he so desires. The "old" momentum is not viewed as a pathology to be cured, but is instead viewed as a spiritual gift that is no longer needed. The shift in perspective can help some clients let go of the old momentum more easily than if they view it only from the narrow psychological perspective. This is because, for many clients, what they resist truly does tend to persist.

Thus, the social worker's task is in part to help the client view his or her trauma from three interrelated perspectives: past trauma, biogenetic predisposition, and spiritual momentum.

Imaginative Journeys

One of the principal methods used in spiritual momentum transformations is the *imaginative journey.* The imaginative journey is used to travel intentionally from the present moment to other moments across time-space. In general, there are seven steps to the method: intent, focused relaxation, departure, the story, reentry, process, and practice.

Intent

The imaginative journey begins with a shared intent between the practitioner and the client(s). The general intent is the desire for transformation, so that the client can become more present in the here and now and live with an appreciation for sacred continuity. The specific intent will vary according to what part of the past or future is to be explored and what issues need to be addressed. There is an agreement that the outcome is a mystery.

Clients may wish to work on traumatic experiences in their own lifetimes that involved what many Shamanic traditions called "soul loss." Shamanic theory suggests that children are born into the world still well connected with Creative Spirit. Soul loss occurs as children are inevitably traumatized in the imperfect world they live in, and as a result become more disconnected from spirit. Part of the healing process (becoming reconnected again) often involves the reexperience of the traumatic event.

Clients may also want to experience "past lives" for a variety of reasons. Many people believe that they have experienced lives in the past that still influence them in this life. Some think that there are collective past lives that we all share; others believe that each person has a soul that has experienced unique past lives over time. The therapist's job is not to prove or disprove any of these beliefs, but to help people use their past life experiences as catalysts for transformation. Some clients are curious and also believe that such work will lead to their spiritual growth; others believe that certain specific past life trauma still limits their health and well-being today.

Visits to the future may also be motivated by curiosity and an interest in spiritual growth. Another motivation has to do with taking more responsibility for the impact of our lives on our descendants. Some tribal cultures believed that a person should always consider the impact of her behaviors on future generations before she makes any significant decision. With our culture's current focus on immediate economic gain, we often seem to devalue and minimize the long-term effects of our behaviors on the quality of life for our children, grandchildren, and great-grandchildren. The therapist's job is not to predict the future, but to help people appreciate the connection they have with the future of other living beings and ecosystems.

Focused Relaxation

The client then begins his work by relaxing, using one of the many different kinds of relaxation techniques. The client also remains focused on his intent for transformation during the relaxation. One favorite relaxation method involves the creation of a secure situation. The client is given permission, if he needs it, to give himself some time to work on his own issues. He is invited to imagine a secure situation to be in—a situation that may or may not yet exist in his own reality. The location could be indoors or outdoors. This situation should be a place where the client can be safe enough to do the work he needs to do without any unwanted interference. He then imagines being in that situation, and lets himself actually smell, feel, see, hear, and even taste elements of that safe environment. The client can be encouraged to imagine that he is spiritually safe and protected as he does his work. As a human being, no client is ever safe from emotional or physical suffering, but the client can experience himself as a spiritual being who cannot be harmed.

Departure
The client leaves for another time-space by going through an departure ritual, usually involving some kind of visualization. In each case, the practitioner's task is not to discover or judge whether or not the client's experiences are literally "true." Instead, the task is to support the client in finding the right experience that will help move her in the direction of her intention. The practitioner can choose to trust that the visualization that the client will have will be the perfect experience that the client needs.

If the intent is to revisit a scene from a past time in the client's present lifetime, the departure ritual might have the following components, for example. The client visualizes a CD player, a television, and a library of CDs in her secure situation, each with a particular segment of her life (such as year one, year two, etc.). She selects the appropriate CD, puts it into her disk player video, and watches the scene.

Studies suggest that the majority of adults in the United States believe that they may have had past lives. If the intent is to explore past life experiences, the departure ritual might look different. For example, the client visualizes standing next to a spacecraft, perhaps a rocket ship. He enters the ship and gradually goes into orbit around the earth. The client circles the earth, watching the continents and oceans go by, until he sees a particular spot that he is drawn to, that he wants to visit. Then he lands there and steps out of the rocket ship.

If the intent is to visit the future, the client's departure may be guided through another mechanism. For example, if he wants to visit his human descendants, he might try a DNA visualization. Essentially, the client imagines his DNA in his body start to divide and evolve over one, two, three, or even more generations. When he has "arrived" at the iteration he wants to be at, he lets the DNA manifest in his visualization into a particular human descendant.

The Story
In this part of the journey, the client lets his imagination take him through a story. If the story is one that "actually happened" in his own life, then he revisits that story, perhaps looking at it with fresh eyes like a person who is watching a good movie for the second time. The practitioner guides the client back to the appropriate time and place. One way to do this is to have the client sit in a secure situation, put a CD in the machine, and watch the past scene on a television screen.

If the story is taking place in a past life, then the client might be directed to briefly set the stage. After he steps out of the rocket ship, to continue the visualization, he looks at the clothes he is wearing (if any) and then at his surroundings for clues as to where he has landed in time-space. Perhaps, for example, he is wearing sandals and a robe and is an Arab female in a desert kingdom maybe 500 years ago. Then he looks around again. Is he alone? If not, who and what does he see? He lets his imagination take him through a little story.

The start of the future story might be similar. After arriving at the generation he wants to visit, he becomes the descendant and watches the story begin.

Reentry
Wherever the client's imagination goes, he will eventually need to return to the here-and-now moment. The practitioner calls the client back, and the client returns via his television, spacecraft, or DNA strands. The client is asked to open his eyes and fully come back to the present moment, taking with him any useful insights, feelings, or memories that will contribute to the realization of his original intent.

Process
Most clients need to talk about their story with their practitioner. After the story is told, the practitioner often helps the client find insight and meaning in the experience. The client reviews his original intent in this process. The practitioner encourages the client to look at the outcomes of his work (the story experience) as being exactly the outcomes that he needs in his transformative work.

Practice
Insight and meaning are not the final steps in transformation. A transformation also includes the emergence of new beliefs and behaviors. The practitioner encourages the client to build on his new insights and experiences and practice living more in the moment with increased responsibility to the ancestors and descendants who are part of his sacred continuity.

CASE STUDY 4.1
PAST LIFE JOURNEY

A 40-year-old financially successful, single man asks his therapist for help in exploring his past lives. The therapist talks with the man about his intent for the work. They agree that they will both hold the same intent in the work, which is that the client will become more present in the here and now and that he will live with more reverence toward sacred continuity.

The client chooses to sit in a comfortable chair with his eyes closed while the therapist leads him through the imaginative journey. The client finds a secure situation to do the work, which happens to be on an ocean beach. The therapist leads the client through the entry visualization of the orbiting spaceship. The client is drawn to a jungle area in Africa. When he lands and walks out, he realizes he is an African woman. The story he sees in his mind's eye involves his interactions with the other people in the tribe. The African woman prepares food for her family. Then she walks to the fire with her husband and children and participates in a dance with the men and women.

When the client finally "returns" to the room with the therapist, he bursts into tears. In their processing of the visualization, the client says that he realized how much he longs for a family and community to belong to in his own life. The man makes a commitment to work less hours every week and to put more energy into creating family and community in his life.

CASE STUDY 4.2
NEAR-FUTURE LIFE JOURNEY

A 49-year-old man named Ralph is conflicted about his marriage of 11 years. He currently has two children with his wife, and they are 8 and 6 years old. He tells his therapist that the main reason he is staying in his marriage is "for the children." Ralph decides to take a journey to discuss this with his children when they are adults and he is no longer living. He goes on an imaginative journey and asks each of them how they feel. They tell him that they feel guilty and are very sad and angry that their parents stayed together mainly because they were afraid to hurt them, and that it is difficult for them to feel permission to have happy marriages in their own lives. Ralph later tells his therapist that this visualization helped him feel free to make a decision about his marriage based on his own sense of the Highest Good.

CASE STUDY 4.3
DISTANT-FUTURE LIFE JOURNEY

A 22-year-old college student named Mary goes to the Student Counseling center. She is unsure what she wants to major in, and is unsure in general about what her life goals should be. She is currently dating a young man named Fred who is pressuring her to marry him. In discussing different methods that the client could use to help her clarify her situation and goals, the young woman decides to do a journey into the future.

The counselor leads the woman through a visualization in which the woman goes to visit a descendant 200 years in the future. The client watches her DNA evolve through five generational iterations. Then she "becomes" a young teen of age 13 in the year 2204. The teen lives in a lovely glass city on the Moon. She is looking at a holographic photo album of her ancestor who was born near the end of the twentieth century. She has a homework assignment to write a story for her teacher about her favorite ancestor and she has decided on "Great-great-great-grandmother Mary." In her essay she writes about how proud she is that Mary became the first woman in her family to become an astronaut and how she was famous for having the first baby born on the Moon.

At the end of the journey, Mary tells her counselor that she wants to be both a mother and some kind of scientist. "Maybe I won't go to the moon, but I know I am here for a reason," she says. The woman decides to put off Fred for now because "I should not make that kind of decision until I am sure I want it. And I know I am not sure about marriage yet."

Making Meaning from Individual Time

Most people struggle with traumatic stories from their past, present, and future. From a spiritual perspective, every event across a person's life span has a spiritual meaning and purpose. Spiritual momentum practice in individual time helps clients make such meaning and purpose in all their life experience. Several methods that can be used are discussed next.

The Before-Birth Game

This game, like any other, involves rituals that require participation in the rituals and symbolism of the game. The practitioner first asks the client to retell the story of her trauma. Then the practitioner asks the client to play the before-birth game. In the game, the client imagines that she met with Creative Spirit (or God, Goddess, etc.) before she was born and that she co-designed with Creative Spirt all the events of her life. Then the client re-examines the trauma story from this pre-birth perspective and asks the question, "Why did I agree to have this experience and how does it fit into my life journey and purpose?" A process of significance-making follows. Then the practitioner has the client build upon the new meanings by creating new rituals, thoughts, and behaviors that bring the meanings to life.

CASE STUDY 4.4
IMAGINATIVE JOURNEY

A 25-year-old man with moderate anxiety and depression complains to his therapist that "nice guys finish last." He has had a series of male lovers, all of whom have, in his words, "dumped me for other guys." In the course of the work, the therapist asks the young man to play the before-birth game and the client agrees. After determining that the young man believes in a God, the therapist leads the client into an imaginative journey.

In his journey, the client has a discussion with his God during which they talk about what will happen during the client's early twenties. Then he talks with his God about why he has to have a series of painful relationships with men. The answer he gets is that he needs to learn about what he does not want in a relationship before he can learn about what he does want.

After the imaginative journey is complete, the therapist asks the client to explore what has not worked for him in his recent relationships. The man realizes that he has given much more than he has taken in all of his relationships. His homework assignment is to begin a journal in which he records his behaviors, thoughts, and feelings as he interacts with other people. Gradually over time, the man is able to identify unhealthy relationships and end them more quickly.

Storytelling Rituals

Clients can gain a spiritual perspective from the telling and retelling of their life stories. There are many ways to facilitate such spiritual storytelling. All of them are essentially methods of time travel that use human imagination. These imaginative journeys can include any part(s) of a person's life, including the past, present, and anticipated future.

Group Stories

In group settings, participants can take turns telling their life stories over a set period of time (for example, an hour). During the telling of a story, the other participants listen but cannot interrupt with questions or comments until the story is over. The group facilitator can also ask that the stories be told in a special way. For example, each participant can tell his or her story in the third-person tense, so it might begin, "Once upon a time, a baby was born to an unwed mother in a large city . . ." The discussion following each story can be directed toward finding a spiritual perspective that can help the storyteller.

CASE STUDY 4.5
A PURPOSE TO EVERYTHING

A facilitator is running a closed group for court-ordered female alcoholics. She decides to ask each participant to tell the story of her life. They will do one story each week, so with nine women in the group the storytelling will last nine weeks. The facilitator asks each woman to explain what she learned spiritually from each life event in her story. The other women are asked to remain silent until the story is completed and then they go around the circle and offer any additional insights they may have into how the storyteller's alcoholism and eventual recovery could be part of her spiritual journey.

The woman who volunteers to go first tells a story full of experiences of child abuse and domestic violence. She tearfully tells the group that she believes that her inability to deal with her trauma as a child led to her drinking and that her drinking led her to start looking at her trauma when she was ready and had people to help her. When she is done with her story, one of the other participants, the elder of the group, says, "I wonder if all the things that happen in our life, both good or bad, are actually perfectly designed to teach us what we need to learn here on Earth." The storyteller agrees.

Reentering the Story

Another way to facilitate storytelling is to ask a client to reenter a traumatic story through an imaginative journey and then invite some kind of spiritual transformation to occur. The practitioner and client can co-create the target story and the intended change in the story before the journey begins. One way to invite a change is to have the client go back into the story as the person he is today and then have a conversation with the child or younger adult that was once him. Another way to facilitate change is for the client to invite a wise elder (such as a medicine woman or minister) or an animal sacred to the client (see Chapter 8) into the story to deliver a spiritual insight or message.

CASE STUDY 4.6
A HEALING JOURNEY BACK IN TIME

An elderly woman is struggling with her feelings about her marriage with her now-de-ceased husband, who was repeatedly unfaithful to her during their long 52-year mar-riage. She tells the therapist, "When I was young I should have just left him the first time he had an affair; I was such a fool! Instead, I stayed with him and became de-pressed. I am still depressed. It's all I think about these days." In the course of their work together, the therapist asks the woman to prepare for an imaginative journey. The therapist tells the woman to consider who she would like to have visit her when she was a young married woman. She chooses herself. During the journey, the elderly woman sits down next to the young woman and holds her hand and says, "Dear, there are some things I want to tell you. First, God loves you. You are so beautiful and lov-able, despite how you are treated. Second, it is not your fault that you married him and have stayed with him, because you have not had any support in your life to do anything different. Finally, God wants you to be happy." A week later, at the beginning of the next session, the woman says, "You know, I didn't think about him as much this week."

End-of-Life-Story

Most terminally ill people report that the biggest regret in their lives is not that they took too many chances, but that they did not take enough risks. A client at any age could be asked to look at her current issues from this end-of-life perspective. This can be done through an imaginative journey, in which the client sees her life through the lenses of imminent death. After such a journey, the practitioner can help the client take the new insights she developed and actively apply them to her life. The practitioner hopes that the client will start living her life as if she will even-tually die, because then she is more likely to live in a state of Aliveness, which was defined in Chapter 1 as the state of being fully present in the here and now, with all parts of the self and divine self fully available.

We all actually live in a place of imminent death, of course, since life could end at any moment. However, few people live in that state of consciousness. Al-though this process of developing what could be called "death consciousness" can be initially disturbing and may not be helpful to every client, such work can ulti-mately be freeing. Most of the major religious and spiritual traditions of the world offer people ways to make life more meaningful by dealing with their deaths. The alternative to facing death is to live as if one will never die, which paradoxically tends to decrease aliveness.

CASE STUDY 4.7
A HEALING JOURNEY FORWARD IN TIME

Billy's parents bring him to a therapist because the 15-year-old has failing grades in most of his classes and has been withdrawn and belligerent at home. The therapist cannot get the boy to talk at all to her. Fortunately, she had just read this book and decides to try a creative and spiritual transformation with her new uncooperative client.

She takes the boy out on a field trip (with all the appropriate permissions) to get a sandwich, but on the way there stops at a nursing home. They walk in and the boy quietly looks at the very frail elderly people in the center. They meet a 90-year-old man in a wheelchair who, despite being thin and bent over, says hello to the boy and shakes his hand. The therapist says nothing but takes Billy over to the local health food store for lunch. There, she brings up the subject of aging and death and asks the boy if he would like to do an imaginative journey with her. He nods unenthusiastically (which is 100 percent more aliveness than she has seen before) and she leads him though an exploration of what he might think about his life if he was old and terminally ill. The boy at first has difficulty with the journey, but then is able to imagine being the 90-year-old man he met at the nursing home. He imagines that he may never like school but that he does not want to end up "like a bum." Instead, he wants to be successful at something. Maybe he *can* get through school. It was the beginning of a turning point in his life.

Imagining the Next Chapter

Another method of time travel enters the immediate future. Sometimes people can benefit from having a sense of what the next life tasks are that will confront them. Such a journey, which can be taken at any age, can help people identify what they need to focus on and do *today*. The method is to ask the client to take an imaginative journey a week or month or maybe a year ahead. Then they watch to see what they will be doing.

CASE STUDY 4.8
AN EXPLORATION OF FUTURE DREAMS

In January, Sally goes to her therapist because she will be graduating from college in a few months and she is uncertain what she wants to do. They discuss her choices, which include going to graduate school, traveling in Europe, joining the Peace Corps, and staying in town and working full time at a local business. Sally takes an imaginative journey to see her life in July. She finds herself in an old city on a warm sea, and realizes it is Venice, Italy. She is studying Italian and working at a coffee house in a museum. She is also in love, in a romantic city. She tells the therapist about the visualization and makes a decision to use her savings to travel.

Spiritual Interpretations

Much of the work in spiritual momentum involves making sense out of various experiences. Clients usually seek meaning in their experiences and they may even ask the practitioner directly for help in interpreting the significance of an experience they have had. An interpretation made by the practitioner about spiritual issues can be very helpful and can also be harmful to a client. Interpretations become more valuable when they more accurately reflect the client's process, rather than the practitioner's own process. The most effective practitioner consistently strives to know herself well enough to understand when her own biases may be inhibiting her ability to see her client accurately.

Because of the danger that the practitioner may project his process on the client, some educators believe that practitioners should avoid making any interpretations. Such a strategy is probably too extreme because some practitioners have the ability to see a client more accurately than the client can see herself. The other extreme should probably also be avoided, which is making frequent interpretations. In addition to the danger of projection, there is also the issue of dependency and growth. The practitioner wants to help the client stay at her *edge* of growth, which means that the client works with issues that are neither too easy (no growth occurs) or too hard (no success occurs) to process. If the practitioner makes all the interpretations, then the client will never learn to trust her own ability to make significance out of her life.

Enhancing Sacred Continuity

The practitioner often asks clients to reflect on the extent to which they experience sacred continuity in their daily lives (see Case Study 4.1). Sacred continuity has to do with a sense of connection with the client's past and future.

Reconnecting with Past

Work with the past means enhancing connection with both human ancestors and other ancestral life forms. Many people in the United States no longer feel a connection with their familial and cultural roots. A greater connection with human ancestors may enhance the client's sense of identity, self-esteem, and responsibility to others (both inside and outside of the client's family and tribe).

Work with the past can focus on a family hero, even a hero from the distant past who is little known. For example, the practitioner can ask the client to focus on a particular relative during an imaginative journey. The client is asked to choose the relative, still living or perhaps even long deceased, to whom he is most drawn. Then the practitioner asks the client to explore such questions as:

1. What qualities about this person do I most admire and why?

2. In what ways do I also have these same qualities, even if they are not yet fully developed or expressed?

3. If this ancestor could talk to me, what encouraging words would he or she give me?

4. What new beliefs and behaviors would my ancestor encourage me to develop?

Reconnecting with Future

Work with the future means enhancing connection with both human descendants and other life forms that follow us. Many people live as if their lives have no impact at all on the lives of those who will live after us. Such denial tends to be destructive not only to our descendants but also to ourselves. We hurt our descendants, for example, as we allow destructive intergenerational patterns of abuse or substance abuse to continue, hungrily consume nonrenewable resources; destroy the last wilderness ecosystems; pollute our lands, waters, and air; and overpopulate the planet. We harm ourselves in part because we cannot engage in such destructive behaviors without living in a state of disconnection from ourselves and from the planet that is our home.

The work with the future can focus on an individual or on many people or even on an ecosystem. For example, the practitioner can ask the client to take an imaginative journey into the future to see what impact her actions may eventually have on her descendants. Then the client can be encouraged to consider what new behaviors she might want to develop.

ETHICAL-VALUE ISSUES

Implications of Outcome Studies

Spiritual momentum, like any methodology, is not effective with every client in every situation. The literature suggests that First Force, psychodynamic interventions may not work as well with clients who have limited intellectual ability or limited motivation to do the insight work required. There is also evidence that clients do best when the practitioner helps them understand why the interventions are being used. Similarly, spiritual momentum transformations may require intellectual ability, motivation, and an understanding of the rationale for the methods used.

How can practitioners reduce the chance that spiritual momentum methodologies might cause possible harm? As with any other method, practitioners must consider client, community, and practitioner issues when choosing, using, and evaluating spiritual momentum transformations.

Issues of Client Diversity

The social worker is careful to make certain that the client has agreed to do work in the past and future. The social worker also does not insist on any interpretation of the experiences the client may have, but encourages the client to find her or his own meanings.

Some clients may object to work in the past or future on religious grounds. For example, a client may not believe in evolution, or may feel uncomfortable with the idea of a "past life." The social worker is always respectful of such feelings and beliefs and never tries to change the client's religious beliefs.

The practitioner is aware of the formal and/or informal contract he or she has with the client. The practitioner asks questions about the fit of the method to the client. What goals does the client now have? Is the client comfortable with spiritual momentum methodologies? Are these methodologies likely to help the client move toward personal goals?

Also, the practitioner needs to respect the metaphors each client may currently use to describe his or her spirituality. The practioner uses the client's language as much as possible.

The practitioner is sensitive to the client's development, on the physical, emotional, spiritual, cognitive, and social levels, because the client will not succeed if he is asked to take steps that he is not developmentally prepared to take. Is the client ready and able to do the insight work necessary to understand the historical roots of his suffering?

Issues of Family and Community Diversity

The practitioner is sensitive to the collective values, doctrines, and rituals held in the practice setting and culture in which she works. Are spiritual momentum methodologies consistent with these values, doctrines, and rituals? If not, can and should the practitioner advocate for the client doing this work?

The practitioner recognizes that she has a responsibility to support the Highest Good of the families and communities with whom the client associates. Therefore, the practitioner consistently encourages the client to provide service to his family and community.

Issues of Practitioner Diversity

The practitioner evaluates his competence to do spiritual momentum. He also constantly monitors his own needs, so that he knows that his choice of these methods are in response to the client's needs, rather than just his own.

In addition, the practitioner seeks appropriate professional training and personal experience in First Force or psychodynamic theory and interventions, and in spiritual momentum transformations.

The social worker also reads the current literature to understand the key theories, outcome studies, criticisms, and other relevant information about the methods he is using.

Issues of Ecosystem Diversity

The social worker also recognizes that he has a responsibility to support the Highest Good of the ecosystems with which the client associates. Therefore, the social worker consistently encourages the client to provide service to her family and community. As the client reaches out with her awareness to consider the suffering of other beings, she tends to become less focused on her own suffering.

STUDY QUESTIONS

1. What is the goal of the spiritual momentum paradigm?

2. What is sacred continuity? To what extent do you feel a sense of sacred continuity with the past and future? How might you enhance your current sense of sacred continuity?

3. What does it mean to be "stuck" in the past or future? Where do you notice you are currently most stuck in the past and future?

4. From a spiritual perspective, why do you think it is important to be present in the here and now? To what extent do you live your everyday life in the here and now?

5. What is an imaginative journey? What are the main steps in the process?

6. Do an imaginative journey on your own. Describe what happened.

7. Lead your class in an imaginative journey. Describe what happened.

8. What are some issues of diversity that the social worker can address when planning and implementing a spiritual momentum transformation? If you were a client, what issues of diversity would you hope a social worker would address when working with spiritual momentum issues with you?

RESOURCE

Washburn, M. (1994). *Transpersonal psychology in psychoanalytic perspective.* Albany: State University of New York Press.
   This book includes
   1. Summary of key theories in psychodynamic paradigm
   2. Summary of transpersonal theory

CHAPTER 5

MINDFUL DAILY LIVING

MINDFUL DAILY LIVING

The overall purpose of Mindful Daily Living is to foster a pattern of Right Actions based on disciplined mindfulness. The mind is freed from destructive illusions and is used instead to serve the soul and Creative Spirit.

Mindfulness is the practice of living life in a state of increasing reverent awareness and presence in every moment. As this awareness and presence deepens, fundamental and lasting change occurs in the person and then she becomes increasingly responsible in living a life of service through Right Actions. These *Right Actions* are the methods of Spiritual Activism, in which the individual works to foster the Highest Good of self, families, communities, and ecosystems.

Mindful Daily Living builds on Second Force, cognitive-behavioral therapy (CBT) interventions that help people change their thoughts and behaviors. Mindful Daily Living utilizes intentional cognitive and behavioral strategies to foster transformations. Two interrelated goals, greater consciousness (or reverent awareness) and more evolved attitudes, are a part of Mindful Daily Living.

The client develops *greater awareness* of both Inner and Outer Worlds. The *inner world* is the multidimensional and interconnected aspects of the developing self, including the physical, emotional, cognitive, social, and spiritual. The *outer world* is that part of the Cosmos that exists outside of the individual's human body. As the client becomes more conscious, he identifies the mental obstacles that still get in the way of his ability to manifest transformation.

The divine self includes all the "parts" of the person as a body–mind–spirit–environment system. Part of the client's self and divine self will be in *light* and part will be in *shadow.* The part that is in light is the part that the client already is aware of and accepts. The part in shadow is that which the client is unaware or cannot yet accept. The work of consciousness building in Mindful Daily Living usually increases awareness of shadow material.

For example, a client may not be aware of how lovable he is, or even of how little he still loves himself. Or, a client may not be aware of how angry she is, or who she is angry at. A client may also not be aware of how afraid he is of the future, or how little he trusts his ability to create what he wants in the world. Shadow aspects may also be about soul and Creative Spirit. For example, a person may not be aware of how angry she is at God, or how disconnected he is with his soul.

The client also develops *new attitudes* about her inner and outer worlds. A client may, for example, begin to increasingly value consciousness, connectedness, sacred mystery, meaning making, imagination, aliveness, integrity, love, or service. New attitudes might also contribute to increased *spiritual maturity*, which is associated with an awareness and acceptance of one's gifts and limitations, as well as the acceptance of spiritual diversity in other people.

Mindful Daily Living also can help a person live in increased personal integrity and to promote the Highest Good. Integrity means that the individual acts with all her parts in wholeness and harmony; consequently, her body, mind, and spirit all "agree" on how to behave.

Right Actions

Right Actions are based on disciplined mindfulness and thus are done with integrity and pure intent for the Highest Good. At the same time, the person engaged in Right Actions also lets go of expectations for any specific outcome. The practitioner helps the client engage in Right Actions because of the benefits to the client and the client's larger family, community, and ecosystem. The client benefits indirectly because service to others tends to result in the enhancement of the client's own well-being. Family, community, and ecosystem benefit directly from the service provided by the client.

The Directing-Self

Mindful Daily Living involves the development of a directing-self, a "part" of the self from which the individual not only watches the Cosmos but, through disciplined mindfulness, also supervises and modifies the attitudes that she has toward everything in the Cosmos. Like the director of a movie, who watches and supervises all artistic aspects of the project, the directing-self watches and supervises all aspects of the self. Like a muscle that gradually gets stronger when exercised, the directing-self also develops as the individual increasingly uses it. The directing-self is a natural part of every person, but is not equally developed in every person. There are, however, methods that can be used to help enhance the client's ability to sit in his directing-self.

CASE STUDY 5.1
THE DIRECTOR'S CHAIR

Eight recently widowed women are attending a closed hospice program bereavement group. All are over 60 years old. The women talk openly in the first session about all the losses they have had in the last year. Their husbands died, their children moved away, their health deteriorated. The hospice social worker, who is facilitating the group, asks the group members if he could teach them a technique to use in dealing with loss.

The next session, the worker has the women sit in movie director chairs and imagine that they are movie directors, watching their lives like a director would watch a film. They first talk about their bodies and how they have aged. The social worker asks them to imagine what they would be without their bodies. All the women agree that they can imagine that they are not just their bodies, and that the loss of their youth has not resulted in the loss of what some of them call "soul" or "spirit." Over two sessions they learn how to look at their bodies, and then their minds, from the directing-self position. Later, they practice looking at their children and their husbands from the same perspective. All report that these kinds of meditations help them see their losses from a new perspective that is very helpful.

Dis-Identification

Since there is no part of the self that the directing-self cannot observe, the individual is able to see that he is "more" than any part of himself. In this process of *dis-identification* (discussed in Chapter 7) an individual does not give up who he is, but becomes less identified with the many "parts" of self that he has constructed in his life. Thus, as illustrated by the examples in Table 5.1, a person may begin to realize that he is not just his mind, or his feelings, or even his body.

The developing person can also discover that her mindfulness can help her dis-identify from parts of her divine self with which she may have previously identified. As the examples in Table 5.2 illustrate, an individual can use mindfulness to dis-identify from things outside of one's self. Again, dis-identification does not mean that a person necessarily gives up something, but does mean that a shift in attitude has occurred.

TABLE 5.1   Dis-Identification from Parts of Self: Examples of Identification Shifts

PART OF SELF	STILL IDENTIFIED (EXAMPLES OF IDENTIFICATIONS)	LESS IDENTIFIED (EXAMPLES OF DIS-IDENTIFICATIONS)
Physical	I am my headache. I am my physical beauty.	I observe my headache, I am more than it. I observe my beauty, I am more than it.
Emotional	I am my sadness. I am my gladness.	I observe my sadness, I am more than it. I observe my gladness, I am more than it.
Cognitive	I am my belief. I am my anxiety.	I observe my belief, I am more than it. I observe my anxiety, I am more than it.
Spiritual	I am my rituals. I am my level of consciousness.	I observe my belief, I am more than it. I observe my consciousness, I am more than it.
Social	I am my political party. I am my family.	I observe my politics, I am more than it. I observe my family, I am more than it.

TABLE 5.2   **Dis-Identification from Parts of Divine Self: Examples of Identification Shifts**

DIVINE SELF PART	STILL IDENTIFIED (EXAMPLES OF IDENTIFICATIONS)	LESS IDENTIFIED (EXAMPLES OF TRANS-IDENTIFICATIONS)
Possessions	I am my house. I am my car.	I observe my house, I am more than it. I observe my car, I am more than it.
Power	I am my authority over others. I am my job.	I observe my authority, I am more than it. I observe my job, I am more than it.
Status	I am my hierarchical position. I am my neighborhood.	I observe my position, I am more than it. I observe my neighborhood, I am more than it.
Fame	I am my publicity. I am my publications.	I observe my publicity, I am more than it. I observe my publications, I am more than it.
Money	I am my stocks. I am my savings account.	I observe my stocks, I am more than it. I observe my savings, I am more than it.

DEVELOPING MINDFULNESS

Mindfulness can be understood as a method of becoming more fully present and alive in the here and now. All mindfulness methods begin with an intention to develop such presence and aliveness.

Meditation

One method of developing mindfulness is through meditation. The many forms of meditation can be organized into two types: focused-attention methods (sometimes called *sitting* meditations) and opened-attention methods (sometimes called *walking* meditations). In focused-attention methods, the individual directs and narrows her concentration, whereas in opened-attention methods, the individual opens his awareness to everything around and inside of him. Some clients will benefit more from focused-attention methods; others will benefit from opened-attention methods or from a combination of methods.

Focused-Attention Methods

Creating Space   The first step in doing meditative mindfulness work is to create a space in which to do the work. The individual begins by concentrating on the intent for the work. The intent may be simply to relax, to clear the mind, to study a challenge or problem, or any number of other objectives. The practitioner may simply respond to the client's intent, or may work with the client to help him identify his intent.

Next, the practitioner helps the client find a quiet, safe, and comfortable location to do the work. Such a location may help the client withdraw his senses from normal operation, and thus may contribute to the quieting of his mind. The safe place may at first be the practitioner's office. Later on, the client may want to do his work at home or even outdoors.

Body posture is often helpful to mindfulness work. Some clients prefer sitting in an upright position; others lie down. Most clients close their eyes, unless the focus target is an object outside of themselves that they want to watch.

Focusing The client can learn to focus on any number of things. Many meditation traditions focus on breath. The word *spirituality* literally means "the breath of life," perhaps as a way of recognizing the miraculous way we breathe in air and then use the air as fuel for life. The practitioner can ask the client simply to notice his breathing, perhaps in the four stages of breathing in, holding lungs full, breathing out, and relaxing lungs while empty. There are many possible variations of watching breath. Some clients like to change the rate of their breath—for example, slowing it down. Others breathe in with one nostril and out with the other. Some clients imagine breathing in love from their God and breathing out blessings for other people or the world.

Many people who do focusing work have certain expectations that can become obstacles to their healing. For example, often people believe that they should be able to sit still without difficulty, or that they should be able to keep their minds completely empty of thoughts.

CASE STUDY 5.2
SIMPLE FOCUSING FOR TEENS

One of the programs in a community-based agency is designed for adolescent sex offenders. The new program director decides to incorporate breath work and yoga into the group session with the teens. In the first group session, he has the boys sit in their chairs or lie on their backs on the rug and then says: "I want to first close my eyes and notice what comes into my mind. Whatever thoughts I may have about the past or future or anything else may kind of float past me like clouds eventually blow across the sky. . . . Good. . . . Now I am going to start watching my breath. I am watching my inhale, and then how I pause and hold my lungs full of air, then my exhale, and then how I pause with my lungs empty. . . . Now as I breathe in, I am going to imagine I am breathing in good, positive energy from the mountains above us. I will hold that energy in for a moment, feeling compassion, love, and forgiveness for my self. Now as I breathe out, I give love and compassion to the people in my life I have hurt, and forgiveness to those who have hurt me."

Over time, most of the boys report that they feel better about themselves and begin to feel moments of inner peace. They report better ability to control unwanted sexual impulses. None has reoffended. Some of them ask to continue in the trainings after their court-ordered program is completed.

Other focusing targets might include mental images, drawings, pictures, natural scenery, and the person's own organs and muscles. Research seems to indicate that the body–mind–spirit has a natural response to all relaxation and focusing methods. The outcome is thus not dependent on the specific focus target.

Opened-Attention Methods

Instead of sitting or lying down in a quiet place, opened-attention methods apply mindfulness to normal everyday activities. The practitioner teaches the client to observe her self and her surroundings from her directing-self. Then the client is encouraged to practice mindfulness while engaged in various actions, such as eating, bathing, dressing, walking, exercising, working, playing, and so on. Since these are the activities that people routinely engage in, and because few can devote much time on focused-attention, opened-attention methods can be very important in spiritual development.

Identifying Spiritual Lenses

In traditional cognitive-behavioral therapy, the practitioner works with the client to help him identify and replace thinking errors that get in the way of his healthy functioning. In Mindful Daily Living, the practitioner helps the client question every spiritual belief and value he currently holds and identify and replace destructive spiritual lenses. *Spiritual lenses* are perspectives that the client has about his self and the Cosmos. Spiritual lenses can be held individually and collectively, by people in families, institutions, cultures, and local and global communities. They are destructive to the extent that they work against the Highest Good, and they are creative when they support the Highest Good.

Spiritual lenses are identified and replaced by the director-self. The client may choose to modify some of his lenses as he examines whether they stand up to emerging truth. As some mystics say, one must be willing to shatter one's most cherished beliefs on the rock of truth. Examples of spiritual lenses are illustrated in Table 5.3.

TABLE 5.3   Examples of Destructive and Creative Spiritual Lenses

LEVEL OF SPIRITUAL LENSE	DESTRUCTIVE LENSE	CREATIVE LENSE
Human identity	I am a being with a mind separate from the Cosmos.	Every person and mind is interconnected.
Protection	I need to focus on self-protection.	There is no self to protect.
Interpersonal conflict	I need to defend and retaliate when I am attacked.	I will forgive the other because his or her attack is a request for help.
Growing up	I am a victim of the world and so I can and must take whatever I want.	The peace and healing I give the world gives me peace and healing.
War	We need war to have peace.	War brings fear, only love makes peace.

Replacing Spiritual Lenses

Many of the complaints that practitioners hear about have to do with the suffering their clients experience in their interactions with other people. Common are such complaints as the insensitivity of a work supervisor, the competitiveness of a colleague, the rigidity of a parent, the moodiness of a current spouse, and the selfishness of a former spouse. All of these kinds of difficulties can be dealt with through the replacement of spiritual lenses.

The method is simple, but each case may have its own unique characteristics. The practitioner first helps the client study her self, so that she can uncover what spiritual lenses are causing her suffering. Then the practitioner helps the client replace the destructive lenses with more creative lenses.

CASE STUDY 5.3
SPIRITUAL LENSES

A couple come to a spiritually oriented practitioner for marriage counseling. Referred by their pastor, they say they want to save their marriage but do not know how. Their last child just moved out a year ago and for the past months they have been in almost constant conflict. The man says that his wife is cold and withholding and the woman says her husband is a loser.

Part of what the practitioner does is to help each partner examine the spiritual lenses that are intensifying the suffering in the marriage. With help, the man realizes that his wife's "coolness" is actually a cry for help, and he starts to have compassion for her again. The woman starts to see her husband's struggles with his career differently as well, and she sees his withdrawing behavior as his way of showing pain. She says in one session that her husband is "God's gift to me, to teach me how to really love . . . and how to accept love too; it's not that easy to do. I am glad he still wants me. I thought I hated him, but it was myself that I hated." The man says, "I am finally learning how to say what I want and don't want around her now. It took me 23 years of marriage to learn it." The therapist replies, "I am proud of you both that you can make transformations. It is as hard as it feels to learn compassion and forgiveness in a marriage."

Activism

As the client develops her mindfulness (and any other aspects of her spirituality), she has increasing response-ability to serve other people, communities, and ecosystems. How does mindfulness help create the ability to serve? Mindfulness is a key tool in developing the ability to understand and foster the Highest Good of families, communities, and ecosystems. Activism without mindfulness is out of balance, and can lead to blind actions that may bring harm to self and divine self. Mindfulness without activism is also out of balance and can lead to a spiritual withdrawal from the world that can bring harm to self and divine self.

The practitioner does not know what kind of service the client needs to be engaged in, but the practitioner can help the client determine what she needs to do and then become actively engaged in a discipline of service. The wise practitioner also helps the client discover for herself how her mindfulness leads to service and how her service leads to increased mindfulness. The word *education* literally means to "draw out," and the practitioner helps the client explore her own service interests. The practitioner also helps the client stay mindful of how she does her service activities, using opened-attention meditation techniques.

CASE STUDY 5.4
VOLUNTEER SERVICE

A 16-year-old boy came to the practitioner with complaints of dysthymia and anxiety, with occasional suicidal ideation. The practitioner does a suicide contract with the boy, which the boy agrees to sign (indicating that he agrees to call one of several people before he makes an attempt to harm himself).

During several months of therapy, the client begins to learn how to do focused and opened-attention meditation. The practitioner encourages the boy to become engaged in some kind of service in his community, and the boy decides to volunteer to help elderly people at the local senior center. With the practitioner's help, the boy learns to become more aware of the feelings of the elderly people with whom he is working. His awareness of his own emotions also starts to improve over time. As he becomes more aware of everyone's feelings, he notices the suffering of not only people but also animals around him. The boy becomes less focused on his own suffering and gradually becomes less concerned about his depression and anxiety, which no longer seem so intense. He learns to use the occasional depression and anxiety he now experiences as signals that he is feeling something deeper inside of him.

Dialogue

There will always be disagreements about what actions are right and what actions are wrong. The purpose of dialogue is help people stay in relationship with each other, so that Communities of Spiritual and Universal Diversity can be co-built. Being in a relationship means that people interact in a respectful, compassionate, and loving manner, despite their differences. Here are some rules that might help guide dialogue.

RULES OF DIALOGUE

1. Each person speaks his or her own personal truth to the other.

2. Each person listens to and holds compassion for the truth of the other.

3. The highest value held by both persons is to hold mutual respect, compassion, and love for each other.

4. The goal is not intellectual agreement, although agreement may be possible in many areas.

Specific Goals of the Director-Self

The practitioner helps the client develop the seven interrelated aspects of transformational change (see Chapter 3) through work with the director-self. These include radical change, integral change, enhanced equanimity, temperance, greater ecstasy, increased capacity, here-and-now change potential, new value-based actions, and service-activism. The primary methods of transformation to develop the director-self are modeling, meditation, and action.

The practitioner *models* the aspect of change for the client. The practitioner therefore needs to work on her own spiritual development so that she can help the client see how a person might live out the aspects of change in everyday life. The practitioner helps the client understand that she is just one teacher in his life, and that the ways she practices mindfulness and activism may or may not all fit for the client. In other words, there may be practitioner traits that the client wants to follow and other traits that he chooses to reject.

The practitioner helps the client develop a *meditation practice* so that he can cultivate mindfulness. Since there are different methods of meditation, the practitioner helps fit the right methods to the client's own unique needs and situation. The practitioner helps find this unique *fit* by determining the client's interests, developmental levels, and motivation.

Finally, the practitioner also asks the client to take new actions that embody his new mindfulness. This new activity should stretch the client so that he continues to grow spiritually, but it should not add too much stress. In other words, the activity should be challenging but realistic.

CASE STUDY 5.5
OPENED-ATTENTION

A single-parent father comes to a practitioner, complaining of stress, anxiety, and dysthymia. During the assessment, the client identifies a number of aspects of transformational change that he wants to develop in his life, including equanimity, temperance, integrity, and ecstacy. The practitioner shows the client how she manifests these traits in her own life, through storytelling and personal sharing.

The practitioner describes the different kinds of meditation practices available and the client chooses to work on opened-attention methods. The practitioner then agrees to help the client develop a daily opened-attention meditation practice, in which the man takes a meditative walk early each morning before he wakes his children. After several weeks of this technique, meditating three or four times a week, the father finds that he feels less stressed, anxious, and depressed.

The practitioner follows up on this success by asking the client to initiate a new behavior that reflects his new ways of thinking. The father decides that the way he will give back to his community is through his church. He will start teaching Sunday School classes again, which will give him an opportunity to work not only with his own children but also with other children and parents in his community.

Fault versus Responsibility

The practitioner educates the client about the spiritual beliefs that can help or hinder consciousness development. Beliefs about fault and responsibility are significant in a person's spiritual maturity.

Fault, or blame, is a construct from which many clients unnecessarily suffer. Many people blame themselves, and then others, for their own pain. When people blame others, they are actually in reaction to their own self-blame. In addition, fault finding is usually associated with the avoidance of responsibility because one stays a victim of circumstance. From a spiritual perspective, there is no ultimate fault because the only cause of anything is everything. In addition, the main result of blame is that little changes; blame seems to freeze people's development. In other words, the best way to stay the same, to never grow up to be an adult, is to blame the world, to be a victim of circumstance, and thus shame the self.

In contrast, responsibility is the opposite of fault. When a person takes responsibility for her own behavior, she is no longer giving her personal power away to life's circumstances. Instead, she is taking 100 percent responsibility for her behaviors. She no longer sees herself as a victim and is thus becoming an adult. Therefore, a key cognitive shift difference between childhood and adulthood is the movement from fault to responsibility.

TABLE 5.4   Examples of Collectively Held Destructive Beliefs and Their Creative Opposites

	REACTION (DESTRUCTIVE BELIEF)	ACTIVISM (CREATIVE BELIEF)
Definition	Respond to suffering with rigidity, either-or thinking, and violence.	Respond to suffering with openness, complexity, and creativity.
Tribal affinity	Patriots love only their own nation.	Patriots love all nations.
Military action	If you support the troops, that means you also support the war.	You can support the troops without supporting the war.
Environment	If you protect the environment then you are against economic progress.	You can protect the environment in ways that support economic progress.
Biotechnology	Advances in biotechnology will harm human life.	You can create biotechnologies that enhance the Highest Good of all.
Gay/Lesbian marriage	If gays and lesbians can marry, this will harm straight marriages.	Marriage of any two consenting adults can foster the Highest Good of all.
Terrorism	You can only stop violence with more violence.	Violence never stops violence; only love can do that.

Activism and Reaction

On the local and global community levels today, there is confusion about the difference between reaction and activism. Whereas *reactions* are destructive actions that result from destructive beliefs, *activism* is creative action based on creative beliefs (see Table 5.4). The practitioner can help individuals, couples, families, or groups identify their own destructive beliefs and then replace them with more creative beliefs. Such work can help foster Mindful Daily Living.

ETHICAL-VALUE ISSUES

Implications of Outcome Studies

Mindfulness activism, like any methodology, is not effective with every client in every situation. Although Second Force, cognitive-behavioral therapy (CBT) interventions are currently the most used and thus most studied, the literature provides little evidence that CBT is overall any more effective than any other paradigm of practice. The research does show that CBT is helpful in relieving the symptoms of many kinds of "mental disorders," although the changes may not maintain or generalize over time. Cognitive-behavioral therapy does seem to often be relatively unthreatening to many clients who do not want to deal directly with emotional content or engage in deep insight work. Mindfulness-activism transformations may also be useful in helping people deal with many kinds of suffering, and further research will help us understand the relative limits and benefit of this family of methods.

Issues of Client Diversity

The social worker is aware of the formal and/or informal contract he or she has with the client. As with any paradigm of spiritual practice, the social worker selects language and behaviors that are likely to fit with the client's own family background, culture, development, and interests. Although mindfulness-activism transformations may be less threatening to some clients, the social worker still needs to assess whether the client is intellectually capable of the work and is motivated to do the challenging work of transformation.

Issues of Family and Community Diversity

As when working with any paradigm, the social worker is sensitive to the collective values, doctrines, and rituals held in the practice setting, community, and culture in which he or she works. Mindfulness activism utilizes radical approaches to question fundamental and often cherished beliefs that people have held for much of their lives. Some discomfort can therefore be expected. The social worker must be sensitive to this inevitable discomfort as well as to the level of vulnerability the client feels in relationship to family, institutions, and community. Each client may need a varying degree of support and encouragement from the social worker, depending on the degree of support and encouragement that is available from family, institutions, and community.

In addition, the social worker recognizes that she or he has a responsibility to support the Highest Good of the families and communities with which the client associates. Therefore, the social worker consistently encourages the transforming client to provide increasingly significant service to family and community.

Issues of Social Worker Diversity

The social worker evaluates her own competence to do mindfulness-activism transformations. She also constantly monitors her own needs, so that she knows that her choice of these methods are in response to the client's needs, rather than just her own. The social worker also seeks appropriate professional training and personal experience in Second Force or CBT theory and interventions, and in mindfulness-activism transformations. The social worker reads the current literature to understand the key theories, outcome studies, criticisms, and other relevant information about the methods she is using.

Issues of Ecosystem Diversity

The social worker recognizes that he has a responsibility to support the Highest Good of the ecosystems with which the client associates. Therefore, the social worker consistently encourages the client to help develop a Community of Universal Community that values all living things and the environmental systems that support life.

STUDY QUESTIONS

1. What is disciplined mindfulness? Why is it important to spiritual life?

2. To what extent do you believe that your own thoughts are disciplined? What are the obstacles that currently keep you from becoming more disciplined?

3. What are Right Actions? What makes them "right"? When there are conflicts, what are some examples of your own personal Right Actions?

4. What are spiritual lenses? How do you replace them? What personal lenses would you replace?

5. Describe the elements of dialogue. Identify someone with whom you are having a conflict. Try using dialogue methods in the conflict.

6. Why might someone want to dis-identify from a "part" of his or her personality? What parts of yourself do you want to dis-identify from? How would you do that?

RESOURCES

Bennett-Goleman, T. (2001). *Emotional alchemy: How the mind can heal the heart.* New York: Three Rivers Press.
This book describes cognitive methods of working with emotional and spiritual issues.

Friedman, M. (1983). *The confirmation of otherness in family, community, and society.* New York: Pilgrim Press.
This book describes and builds on Martin Buber's philosophy of dialogue.

Gawain, S. (2002, originally published in 1978). *Creative visualization: Use the power of your imagination to create what you want in your life.* Navato, CA: New World Library.
This book describes methods of creative visualization.

Washburn, M. (1994). *Transpersonal psychology in psychoanalytic perspective.* Albany, NY: State University of New York Press.
This book links transpersonal theory with psychoanalytic theory, and has a large reference list.

CHAPTER 6

SPIRIT WITH HEART

SPIRIT WITH HEART

The overall purpose of Spirit with Heart work is to foster a conscious heart in the here and now. In contrast to mindfulness activism, which fosters responsibility through conscious *mind*, Spirit with Heart work is about developing conscious use of Higher Self, through the awareness, cultivation, and expression of a maturing *heart*.

Just as the mind can be seen as a sacred organ and an expression of spirituality, the heart can also be seen as a sacred organ that is an expression of both Creative Spirit and Individual Spirit. Thus, we can learn more about Creative Spirit through our heart, and we can also express our soul through our maturing heart.

Spirit with Heart methods build on traditional Third Force, or humanistic-experiential, methods of practice. Those Third Force methods traditionally focused on helping people become aware of, accept, and express their emotions. These methods are mystical because they foster transformations of the heart in the *here and now*.

There is a recognition that such growth leads to an increased responsibility to support the long-range spiritual goals of radical change, integral change, enhanced equanimity, temperance, greater ecstasy, increased capacity, here-and-now change potential, new value-based actions, and service-activism.

From a spiritual perspective, the awareness and expression of feelings is a necessary developmental goal of adulthood, but not the *highest* developmental goal of emotional maturity. Spiritual maturity in the emotional dimension also includes the ability to transform unhelpful and destructive emotions into spiritual lessons and creative emotions. Such maturity also includes the ability to listen deeply to and care about the experience of other people, other living things, and ecosystems.

Listening to Spirit through the Heart

Spirit with Heart work begins when the individual learns how to listen to Creative Spirit through the language of the heart. From a spiritual perspective, the heart can know spirit in the here and now. Rather than viewing uncomfortable feelings as pathological, all feelings can be seen as soul expressions.

Conscious Use of Higher Self

The most basic method of transformation in Spirit with Heart work is the conscious use of Higher Self that the skilled professional brings to the client, community, and ecosystem. Conscious use of Higher Self is the social worker's intentional entering into a loving relationship, for the purpose of fostering the Highest Good. Conscious use of Higher Self can involve intentional use of any of the physical, emotional, cognitive, social, and spiritual developmental dimensions in spiritual partnerships.

Reopening to Support Conscious Use of Higher Self

From the perspective of Spirit with Heart, effective conscious use of Higher Self requires that the social worker open himself up to spiritual transformations and power. All spiritual transformations are collective activities that require the active participation of client, professional, and community with Creative Spirit. The professional helper thinks of himself more as a *conduit* of healing spirituality rather than as a source of that spirituality. Like any conduit, the social worker works best when he is relatively empty of obstructions.

A common potential obstruction to such openness occurs when the social worker denies or minimizes his countertransference reactions. Table 6.1 shows the major types of countertransferences that can obstruct a social worker from either assessing clearly or effectively offering transformations. Countertransferences include all the reactions that the social worker has toward the client, some of which have to do more with the social worker and some of which have more to do with the true nature of the client. Essentially, the countertransference work for the social worker is in part to determine where he ends and the client starts. As the social worker understands and accepts the true nature of his own countertransference reactions, he begins to be able to better reflect the true nature of the client back to the client.

The process of reopening does not mean that emotional and cognitive reactions necessarily go away. However, the relationship the social worker has with these reactions changes. He becomes more aware and accepting of the obstructions and, though his increased consciousness, is able to gain enough distance (or disidentify enough) from the obstructions that he can regain his ability to assess and intervene clearly.

Types of Transferences and Countertransferences

In a spiritual partnership (see page 74), transferences and countertransferences can be especially intense. Since there is a quest for spiritual growth, which is usually a profound project in most people's lives, a client's hopes and fears about the relationship can be heated up.

TABLE 6.1   Conscious Use of Higher Self across the Developmental Dimensions

DIMENSION THAT MAY OBSTRUCT SOCIAL WORKER	TRAUMA (FROM SOCIAL WORKER'S PAST) THAT MAY BE RELATED TO OBSTRUCTION	COUNTERTRANSFERENCES (CTS) THAT MAY BE RELATED TO SOCIAL WORKER'S TRAUMA	HOW CONSCIOUS USE OF HIGHER SELF CAN USE CTS AS SPIRITUAL TRANSFORMATIONS
Spiritual	Spiritual trauma (ST) suffered in family, church, community	Over- or underidentify with religious or spiritual people or with agnostics	Understand and accept the CTs so client's spirit can be reflected back
Physical	Physical trauma (PT) in auto accident, war, crime or child abuse	Over- or underidentify with victims/perpetrators of physical violence	Understand and accept the CTs so client's physical nature is reflected back
Emotional	Emotional trauma (ET) from child abuse, peer and adult bullying	Over- or underidentify with victims/perpetrators of emotional violence	Understand and accept the CTs so client's emotional nature is reflected back
Cognitive	Cognitive trauma (CT) that teaches negative views of self/Cosmos	Over- or underidentify with client's ambivalence about self/Cosmos	Understand and accept the CTs so client's cognitive nature is reflected back
Social	Social trauma (SoT) that teaches aggressive or passive behaviors	Over- or underidentify with client's inability to be socially assertive	Understand and accept the CTs so client's social nature is reflected back

Sometimes the client *idealizes* the social worker, imagining that the social worker has an unusual connection with Creative Spirit. The social worker may have such a connection, but what the client may not see is how the social worker also has a connection with Creative Spirit. The client tends to miss the imperfections of the professional helper (at least at first) and tends to miss the positive spiritual qualities of himself. The social worker's countertransference reaction in such cases may often be to be seduced by the client's projections. Thus, the social worker may start to believe that she is indeed more of a goddess than any other human being. Such a reaction may lead to the inability of the social worker to hold appropriate boundaries. This loss of boundaries commonly results in sexualized relationships, which brings unnecessary suffering to the client and social worker.

In contrast, clients sometimes have the opposite transference reaction, and *demonizes* the social worker. In these cases, instead of projecting his positive qualities onto the social worker, the client projects what he sees as the most negative qualities onto the social worker. Such a transference may develop when the client encounters difficulties in his spiritual path. Rather than confronting the difficult material, the client may simply choose to make the social worker wrong. The social worker's reaction to these kinds of cases commonly is to react defensively and/or aggressively with the client. The social worker is wise to avoid acting out such reactions with the client.

Spiritual Partnerships

Decades of research into practice outcomes suggest that social worker characteristics, particularly the ability to form effective helping relationships, are the best predictors of positive results. In spiritually based practice, the social worker also focuses on building a relationship. This relationship, however, has a basic spiritual dimension, and thus might be called a *spiritual partnership.*

In a spiritual partnership, the helping relationship always includes the presence of Creative Spirit, which means in part that a foundation of the relationship is an agreement to honor and support spiritually and all forms of human development (see Table 6.2). The social worker also recognizes that both he and the client are spiritual teachers as well as spiritual students. Since the social worker realizes that spiritual work is often transrational, the presence of Sacred Mystery is also recognized. When two people support each other's spiritual development, the outcomes of the relationship are never certain, but the intentions of the heart are held and constantly revisited.

TABLE 6.2   Examples of Social Worker Characteristics in Spiritual Partnership

DEVELOPMENTAL DIMENSION	SOCIAL WORKER'S ABILITY TO HEAR CREATIVE SPIRIT THROUGH DIMENSION	SOCIAL WORKER'S ABILITY TO USE AS A SOUL EXPRESSION OR SERVICE TOOL
Physical	Respects, listens to, and cares for her body as her unique soul expression. Can hear her body's need to rest, eat, exercise, dance, etc.	Can sing and dance how she feels. Can enjoy, discipline, exercise body. Can give therapeutic touch. Can use body for creative work.
Emotional	Respects, listens to, and cares for her heart as her unique soul expression. Can hear her heart's need to love, be loved, forgive, empathize, etc.	Can love and can show she loves. Can feel, control, and express the full range of emotions. Can sense another's emotions.
Cognitive	Respects, listens to, and cares for her mind as her unique soul expression. Can hear her mind's need for stimulation, relaxation, etc.	Can imagine another's experience. Can imagine other time and space. Can use and let go of rational mind. Can create and appreciate humor.
Social	Respects, listens to, and cares for her relatedness as her unique soul expression. Can sense her need for social contact, aloneness, etc.	Can be serious or playful socially. Can feel calm alone or with people. Notices and express what she wants and does not want from others.
Spiritual	Respects, listens to, and cares for her spirituality as her unique soul expression. Can sense her need for ecstasy, awe, connectedness, etc.	Can be in ecstatic state in both suffering and joy. Can experience and project peace of mind, forgiveness, compassion.

The relationship itself is viewed as part of the spiritual path of client and social worker, and thus all interactions are viewed with reverence, respect, and awe. Since no two people share identical spiritual landscapes, the social worker and client will sometimes have different spiritual views. In these cases, the goal of the partnership is not necessarily to find agreement but to stay in relationship through dialogue (see Chapter 5). Thus, the spiritual partnership is a place to practice the co-development of Communities of Spiritual and Universal Diversity.

In the spiritual partnership, the social worker can utilize either nondirective or directive methodologies. Most of the methodologies described in this chapter are directive. Nondirective methodologies, however, may also be useful, especially with highly motivated and autonomous clients. In such work, the social worker follows the lead of the client. In spiritual work, nondirective methods may be utilized at those times in the spiritual partnership where the social worker recognizes that the clients needs to work in an especially independent, self-motivated, and self-directive manner.

Translating Emotions into Spiritual Lessons

The social worker helps the client find the voice of Creative Spirit in her heart. Every feeling is viewed as a spiritual message that needs to be translated. In Box 6.1, examples of possible spiritual translations of the five "basic" emotions are given.

Secondary feelings may be defined as what the heart experiences when it does not want to experience its real feelings. Many clients suffer from their secondary feelings. Often they have forgotten what emotions lay underneath these secondary feelings. Box 6.2 illustrates some possible translations of secondary feelings into spiritual lessons.

BOX 6.1

EXAMPLES OF FIVE BASIC EMOTIONS AND POSSIBLE TRANSLATIONS OF FEELINGS

Sad	I am in reaction to a loss in my life, which reminds me of the impermanence of everything.
Mad	I am in reaction to some kind of hurt in my life, which is an opportunity to deal with suffering in some way.
Glad	I am in a period of joy, which I can enjoy with gratitude but without attachment.
Scared	I am being reminded that the future is always uncertain, but I will not stop reaching for my dreams.
Excited	I feel inspired by Creative Spirit, and my intent is to use my energy for the Highest Good.

■ ■ ■ ■ ■ ■

BOX 6.2

EXAMPLES OF SECONDARY EMOTIONS AND POSSIBLE TRANSLATIONS OF "SECONDARY FEELINGS"

Depressed   I went numb to avoid pain, but I ended up avoiding life. I would rather feel alive again, and take all my suffering with all my joy.

Anxious   I have been trying to avoid seeing the way things are, but the price of my detour has become too high. I will face my death so I can truly live.

Bored   I have wanted to keep things the way they are, but being on a permanent vacation has become unappealing; the greatest risk is not taking a risk.

Emotional Alchemy

Emotional alchemy may be defined as the transformation of destructive emotions into more creative emotions. The social worker helps the client move his heart into the emotional states of love, compassion, and forgiveness, using the spiritual lessons generated through the kinds of translations described in Boxes 6.1 and 6.2.

Love Alchemy

Love is the intentional desire for the Highest Good of another being. From a spiritual perspective, love is the natural state of the human heart. Thus, love is a choice that one makes to open one's self emotionally. The goal of love alchemy is to transform the social worker and client so that they both have more loving hearts.

Love benefits both the lover and the recipient of love. When caring about the other, the lover automatically moves outside of himself, and thus becomes less preoccupied with his own life drama. The other also cannot help but love herself a little more when she loves the other. Love helps the other feel less alone and more lovable. As the Dalai Lama has suggested, perhaps much of the purpose of life is to love one's self.

Why do human beings not live in a loving state all the time? Perhaps most people feel too vulnerable living with a loving heart. From a spiritual perspective, love can only exist in an open heart, which is also a heart unprotected from pain. However, people are ultimately unable to protect themselves from pain and they are no less vulnerable when they open their hearts to love.

The social worker models love for the client and also asks the client to practice bringing a loving heart to her own daily life. Love alchemy begins when the client experiences love coming into her, perhaps from Creative Spirit, from nature, or from another person. Then the social worker has the client return the love back to herself, her family, her communities, and her ecosystems.

CASE STUDY 6.1
IMAGINING LOVE

A social worker is leading a psychoeducational group for teenagers whose parents have troubled marriages. The topic of love comes up when one of the girls says that she feels in love. The teens discuss what love is and the social worker talks about how there are several kinds of love. They decide to do a guided visualization on love. The next session, the social worker has the teens all lie on their backs on the rug and close their eyes. Then she gives the following instructions:

"Imagine that you are sitting in your favorite place, outside on a long empty beach. The water is warm, big fair-weather clouds bubble up over the horizon, the sunlight is reflected on gentle waves. Now notice your heart. It is open to the warm loving energy of God, which is flowing into you from the sea, the sky, the wind, and the earth. This love fills your heart with warmth and you feel completely comfortable with your self. You begin to realize that there is limitless love available to you. You wonder why you have not experienced such love before.

"Now imagine that the love inside of you wants to move. You begin sending the loving energy back into the world. You feel love for the beautiful sea, sky, wind, and earth that has gifted you. You have so much love that you want to share it with other people too.

"Notice that the more negative and destructive emotions that you may have felt today are no longer as powerful. You feel more in control of your own emotional reactions to other people.

"Now you notice how good it feels to let your heart love yourself and other people. You wonder if there is a limit to how much you can love. As you continue to expand your love outward, you begin to realize that your love is limitless."

Compassion Alchemy

Compassion is the intentional sharing of another being's suffering or joy. Compassion always carries the loving intent to foster the Highest Good of the other. If there are few people who are able to share a person's pain, there are even fewer who can experience the other's joy. This is because compassion requires the capacity to experience and move deep feelings, and although most people can relate to having pain, probably fewer can relate to the experience of great joy.

The goal of compassion is to transform both client and social worker so that they both have more compassionate hearts. Like love, compassion benefits both the social worker and the client. When people interact with a compassionate heart, they are much more likely to live with more inner peace and creativity. The social worker can help the client practice compassion by modeling compassion.

CASE STUDY 6.2
MODELING COMPASSION

A mother is referred to a social worker by her Department of Child and Family Services (DCFS) worker. The woman had lost custody of her 6-year-old daughter after being found by DCFS to have been physically abusive with her. The mother spanked the child with a belt, leaving bruises on her legs and buttocks.

In the first session, the mother blames the child for the incident, telling the social worker that the child was out of control at home and "would not listen to anything else but the belt." Without condoning the abuse, the social worker takes a compassionate stance toward the mother. He tells her that he can see that she loves her daughter and that she has suffered considerably in life, having had an abusive childhood herself and two unhappy marriages. The mother cries, stating that "no one has cared about how hard *my* life has been."

They begin to build a spiritual partnership, in which the social worker continues to model love and compassion toward the mother, as well as to her daughter and other people. The mother starts to follow her social worker's example, and with his encouragement, starts using nonviolent and more creative parenting practices with her daughter during supervised office visits and later during overnight home visits. The mother comments that she no longer feels out of control when her daughter misbehaves: "I guess when I lost my temper I really did 'lose' something—my self-respect. Now that I have it back, I won't lose it again." Eventually, the mother goes back to court and is reunified with her daughter.

Forgiveness

Forgiveness is the intentional replacement of anger and resentment with love and compassion. Anger and resentment are usually built up inside in response to being hurt by another being.

Forgiveness is often confused with what could be called *pre-forgiveness*, which is the inability to assertively establish and defend appropriate relational boundaries. Since forgiveness is the intentional letting go of anger and resentment, a person must first be able to feel anger and assert her boundaries.

CASE STUDY 6.3
FORGIVENESS PROCESS

During an assessment, a young man, court-ordered into treatment for molesting a babysitter, tells his social worker that he had forgiven his mother, who had sexually molested him. During the first weeks of therapy, the social worker discovers that the man's mother actually had sexually molested the young man, and that the man had minimized and denied his victimization. The social worker now realizes that this young man was still in a state of pre-forgiveness with his mother.

> As the therapy continued, the man began to realize how angry he actually had been toward his mother. He had been taught that it was a sin to be angry at his parents, so he had pushed aside those feelings of anger. The social worker helped the young man put his anger where it belonged (psychologically) and then helped him finally forgive his mother. The young man started to become compassionate toward the babysitter he had molested and his heart continued to transform. The young man noticed that he is "no longer so angry at everything." He was able to stop offending again.

Forgiveness is powerful medicine that can heal hearts and relationships. As Martin Luther King once said, forgiveness is the only action you can take that can change the hearts of your enemies whether they like it or not. The social worker can help the client practice forgiveness through a creative "spirit-drama."

The wise social worker knows the importance of timing in teaching forgiveness. For example, a battered woman may need her anger to help motivate her to set a boundary of safety with her abusive boyfriend. Only later, after she has created safety in her life, may she be ready to do the forgiveness work regarding the abuse she suffered. In contrast, a man still lives with tremendous resentment toward his wife because she had an affair 20 years ago. In such a case, the social worker may appropriately suggest that he begin forgiveness work toward his wife.

CASE STUDY 6.4
HEALING TERROR WITH FORGIVENESS

After a terrorist attack in a large urban area, a social worker begins to lead a group for people who were traumatized by the attack. During the first sessions, many of the participants vocalize their anger, fear, and grief about the attack. In the following months, however, some of the clients begin to talk about their need to begin forgiveness work. One woman, for example, talked about how she did not want to become bitter, because then she would have "become as evil as the terrorists."

The social worker suggests that the group do a "spirit-drama" on their collective experiences of the trauma. In the next session, some of the group members volunteer to play various parts of the experience. Two choose to play the terrorists, two others are people who were killed, others play people who were injured or who knew someone who was hurt, and so on. After the group plays out the events, they switch roles so people have the opportunity to try out different positions.

After the spirit-dramas, the participants process the experience. Most decide that they have let go of some of their anger. Most agree that the attitude of forgiveness is healing.

CASE STUDY 6.5
FORGIVING AN AFFAIR

A 60-year-old married man comes into counseling, complaining of moderate depression and anxiety. The therapist determines that the man has been using alcohol five or six nights a week. The assessment reveals that the man's wife had an affair with a neighbor almost 20 years ago. The client states that he still thinks about the affair frequently and feels tremendous resentment. The social worker suggests that part of what is troubling the man is that he is still holding on to resentment. The man is not convinced, but agrees to do a forgiveness visualization. The social worker has the client sit comfortably and then gives the following instructions:

"First, I will examine all the feelings and thoughts I had in reaction to my wife's affair. How was I feeling about the marriage before I learned about the affair? How did I first find out? What was that experience like? What did I do or say? Why did I decide to stay with my wife? Next, I want to examine what it has been like to carry that anger all these years. How did the anger help or serve me at first? What price have I paid for staying angry over time? Has staying angry been worth it?

"Next, I want to imagine what my wife's experience might have been like. How was she feeling about the marriage before the affair? How did she feel about herself after she had the affair? How has she felt and what has she thought during the years since, particularly since I did not forgive her? Can I have compassion for her, which does not necessarily mean that I think that her behavior was acceptable?

"Now I want to imagine what it might feel like to forgive myself for my own behavior before and after the affair. Can I have compassion for how hard it was for me to have those experiences?

"Now can I imagine what it might feel like to forgive my wife for what she did or did not do during the marriage? How might it benefit me to forgive her? How might it contribute to the Highest Good of everyone involved?"

After this work, the man starts to have a transformation of the heart. He does decide to forgive himself and then to forgive his wife. He realizes that he has also been angry at his own God as well and he starts to learn to forgive God too. Then he starts to look at whether he wants to stay married or not. He realizes that if he stays with his wife, he wants to open his heart to her again.

Equanimity Alchemy

Equanimity is a general state characterized by the intentional balance, temperance, and self-control of one's emotions. In such a state of consciousness, the person is able to interact with her own self and the world with a sense of mastery over her emotions. Most people do not seem to believe that such a state of consciousness is possible, so part of the social worker's work is to model equanimity with the client. The client gradually learns to identify the creative emotions she wants to increase and the destructive emotions she wants to decrease in her life.

> **CASE STUDY 6.6**
> **EXPERIENCING SELF THROUGH ANOTHER'S EYES**
>
> A man comes to see a social worker at a community mental health center, complaining about how so many people in his life have let him down. His wife is cold and distant, he says, and his children have no appreciation for what he has given them. In addition, at the law firm where he is one of the lawyers, his boss and co-workers are competitive and cruel, and even his girlfriend has threatened to leave him. The crises occurred when a judge insisted that he get counseling after he blew up in a court room, representing a difficult client.
>
> After the first session, the social worker sees the client as hopelessly narcissistic. However, the social worker's supervisor encourages the social worker to remain hopeful, and coaches the social worker to help the client create equanimity in his life.
>
> The social worker first helps the man understand and accept his own emotions. The social worker realizes that the client does not need to "get his anger out" because the client already does that with everyone around him. So the social worker starts to help the client see how other people may emotionally react to him. They do a series of spirit-dramas, where the man role-plays his wife, mistress, children, boss, and co-workers. He begins to have compassion for his wife and children, who lived with a "rage-aholic" and selfish husband for 18 years. He has compassion for his boss and co-workers who have had to deal with his anger and competitiveness at the law firm where he works. He starts to realize how he has been using his mistress and understands why she is also furious with him.
>
> The client eventually starts to change his behaviors. After his judge-ordered counseling is completed, he continues to go to counseling voluntarily.

Fostering Deep (Multidimensional) Intimacy

In Spirit with Heart transformations, the social worker works to help the client develop intimacy along all levels of development. Such intimacy, which could be called *deep intimacy*, is both vertical (connection between all of the parts within one's self) and horizontal (between the self and another person). As illustrated in Table 6.3, each dimension of development can also be viewed as a dimension of intimacy.

The professional has a commitment to continue to develop herself along all the dimensions across her life span. The simple sharing of the helper's maturing presence can be a model and inspiration for the client. The professional also enters into a conscious relationship with client, community, and ecosystem. Decades of clinical outcome research has shown that the social worker's ability to co-create a quality helping relationship with the client is the most important factor in successful therapeutic outcomes. A helping relationship with a spiritual foundation is the most powerful relationship a professional can have with a client.

TABLE 6.3   **Dimensions of Maturity and Intimacy Available in Conscious Use of Higher Self**

DIMENSION OF DEVELOPMENT	DIMENSIONS OF DEVELOPMENTAL MATURITY IN THAT DIMENSION	DIMENSIONS OF INTIMACY IN THAT DIMENSION
Spiritual	Understanding and acceptance of the diverse spiritual landscapes of self, other people, living things, and ecosystems; leads to such states as gratitude, ecstasy, forgiveness, love, and peace	Mutual sharing and acceptance of spiritual experiences, such as awe, ecstasy, and love
Physical	Understanding and acceptance of the diverse physical landscapes of self, other people, living things, and ecosystems; leads to the ability to listen to the body and then to exercise, eat, and pleasure and rest the body as necessary	Mutual sharing and acceptance of physical expressions, such as therapeutic, sensuous, playful, and sexual touch
Emotional	Understanding and acceptance of the diverse spiritual landscapes of self, other people, living things, and ecosystems; leads to the ability to choose wisely how and when to express emotions and to include the heart's voice in decisions	Assertive mutual sharing and acceptance of the full range of feelings, including sad, mad, glad, scared, and excited
Cognitive	Understanding and acceptance of the diverse spiritual landscapes of self, other people, living things, and ecosystems; leads to mindful meditation, work, play, and transformations in self and others	Assertive mutual sharing and acceptance of mental activity, such as humor, philosophy, and beliefs
Social	Understanding and acceptance of the diverse spiritual landscapes of self, other people, living things, and ecosystems; leads to the ability to give and receive love, follow and lead in balanced ways	Mutual sharing and acceptance of such public activity as mutual silence, dance, work, and play

Inviting Mystery

Mystical spiritually-inclusive practice is mystical because interventions in spirituality typically involve here-and-now experience, are transrational in nature, have unknown outcomes, and are not easily described. (The ancient Greeks, for example, spoke of *mystos*, which was a sacred silence where spirit could be heard.)

Most people intuit on some level of awareness that the most essential nature of everything in the Cosmos is largely unknowable. (The Buddhist concept of *sunyata*, or emptiness, for example, describes the indefinable mystery behind all things.) Most people today seem uncomfortable admitting that they do not understand their world. Perhaps that is largely why we often cling so intensely to various explanations of reality. Paradoxically, however, our ability and desire to offer scientific explanations for everything may leave most people hungry for mystery in their lives. Perhaps we need mystery in our lives because when we have mystery, we welcome a state of aliveness, wonder, and awe.

The wise spiritually-inclusive social worker always invites Sacred Mystery into her practice. This does not mean that the social worker has no theories, knowledge, skills, or values to guide and inform practice. Instead, the invitation of Sacred Mystery means that the social worker makes room for mystery in her assessments and interventions, while still leaving room for the science of practice. It may be that it is at the synapse between what we know and what we are courageous enough to admit we do not know that real healing often begins. The love of mystery can empower clients because they start to realize that since no professional helper knows everything, they themselves have a response-ability in assessing and intervening in their own lives.

Ritual Co-Creation

Although every generation is challenged to create new rituals that help us meet the needs of the times, our era's acceleration of change challenges social workers to co-create rituals that address the new BPSSE (biopsychosocial–spiritual–environmental) opportunities and challenges that face us. (As Matthew Fox has said, the creation of new rituals may actually be the *most important task* of our generation.)

As described in Chapter 1, rituals combine individual or collective play with an *intent* to respond to or focus on a particular BPSSE issue. Rituals are especially useful in spiritually inclusive practice because they are largely transrational and thus compatible with the Sacred Mystery in people's lives. Although an intent for healing or transformation may be held, the outcomes of rituals are always in mystery.

The wise spiritually inclusive social worker invites the client to co-create rituals not only with his therapist but also with his communities. Rituals tend to move people immediately into community as they begin to play together.

ETHICAL-VALUE ISSUES

Implications of Outcome Studies

The literature suggests that Third Force, experiential-phenomenological interventions may not work as well with clients who lack sufficient emotional intelligence or who are unmotivated to do the work required for personal growth and development. Similarly, Spirit with Heart transformations may require motivation and emotional intelligence.

Issues of Client Diversity

The social worker asks if the client is comfortable with Spirit with Heart methodologies. The social worker also assesses whether these methodologies are likely to help the client move toward his goals. She considers whether the client is strong enough to hold the vulnerability necessary to do deep emotional work. This sense of vulnerability is inevitable, because the social worker will be asking the client to consciously give up old patterns of self-protection (such as angry outbursts or emotional withdrawal) in order to grow new patterns that foster spiritual development.

Issues of Family and Community Diversity

The social worker is careful to assess the rituals, doctrines, and values held by the client's family and community, and the extent to which these rituals, doctrines, and values may conflict with the work of Spirit with Heart. The social worker also recognizes that she has a responsibility to support the Highest Good of the families and communities with which the client associates. Therefore, the social worker consistently encourages the client to provide service to his family and community.

Issues of Social Worker Diversity

The social worker also has a responsibility to practice Spirit with Heart methodologies on himself, because he knows he cannot take the client to emotional realms where he has not gone. The social worker also constantly monitors his own needs, so that he knows that his choice of these methods are in response to the client's needs, rather than just his own. The professional helper seeks professional training and personal experience in Third Force, or experiential-phenomenological and interventions, and in Spirit with Heart transformations.

Issues of Ecosystem Diversity

The social worker also recognizes that he has a responsibility to support the Highest Good of the ecosystems that support all life. Therefore, he consistently engages in service and encourages the client to provide service to her family and community.

STUDY QUESTIONS

1. What is the goal of Spirit with Heart work?

2. What makes something sacred? How can the heart be seen as a sacred organ? What other organs in your body (such as the mind) are also sacred? What organs, if any, are not?

3. Have you ever felt that you can listen to spirit though your heart? If so, explain. Are there times when your heart is not the voice of spirit? Explain.

4. What is Conscious Use of Higher Self? How is it "more" than "conscious use of self"?

5. What are the five dimensions of development? Which of the five are you currently most developed in? Which are you currently least developed in?

6. What is a spiritual partnership? Have you ever had such a relationship with another person, in either the "social worker" or "helper" roles? How is such a relationship different from other relationships you have had with people in your life? Do you tend to use more directive or nondirective methods with your self and your clients?

7. What is emotional translation? What is emotional alchemy? How does alchemy build on translation? On what personal emotional patterns do you currently want to practice translation and alchemy?

8. Describe *deep (multidimensional) intimacy.* Do you have or want that kind of intimacy in your own life? Why or why not?

RESOURCES

Maslow, A. (1971). *The further reaches of human nature.* New York: Viking Press.
    Written by one of the pioneers of experiential theory, this book links Third Force human growth theory with transpersonalism.
Zukav, G., & Francis, L. (2001). *The heart of the soul.* New York: Simon and Schuster.
    This book describes connections between emotions and spirituality.

CHAPTER 7

RELIGIOUS SELF

RELIGIOUS SELF

The goal of this paradigm is to foster development of the Religious Self. The Religious Self is that part of the person that seeks personal spiritual development through connection with other people and that seeks to support the spiritual development of other people through the co-creation of Communities of Spiritual and Universal Diversity. Often the Religious Self seeks connection through shared rituals that have been created through a particular wisdom tradition, such as Christianity or Islam. Each person's connection with other people is manifested in both outer and inner worlds. Thus, Religious Self is represented by our social interactions with other people as well as by our interactions with the community of voices or "ego states" inside of each of us.

As the individual develops her Religious Self, she masters the ability to move purposively and fluidly between all levels of consciousness—prepersonal, personal, and transpersonal. With such mastery comes increased response-ability to bring loving consciousness into relationships with other people, living things, and ecosystems. As each individual in a religious community takes the responsibility to develop his or her own individual Religious Self, the entire religious community opens more to spiritual and universal diversity.

The purpose of developing of Religious Self is therefore not to get a person to change her religion. From the perspective of Religious Self, each religion has the capacity either to foster or to hinder the spiritual development of its members. Instead, the purpose is to help each person transform her own consciousness, so that she can help transform the collective consciousness of her local and global communities.

The person develops her Religious Self in part by learning how to choose wisely, sometimes modify, and then apply an evolving menu of techniques drawn from any of the wisdom traditions of the world. Religious Self is thus fostered through the wise development and application of a personal plan of self-discipline. The spiritually oriented social worker helps the client find the best "fit" between herself and various spiritual traditions, rituals, and beliefs. Part of the "fit" may have to do with religious preference. Some clients may want to choose traditions, rituals, and beliefs only from their own religion, and the worker always respects the client's wishes in such cases.

The wisdom traditions of the world include not only the major religions (such as Islam, Buddhism, and Hinduism) but also all other ways of knowing from both the distant and more immediate past (such as Shamanism, astrology, and science). With an increasing diversity of religions in almost every community in the country, people in the United States today have a historically unprecedented choice of spiritual traditions available to them.

From a spiritual perspective, all wisdom traditions have the potential either to support or to hinder the multidimensional development of an individual. Religions that are Communities of Spiritual and Universal Diversity are most likely to support the spiritual needs of each person, since each person is free to utilize the disciplines that best fit his or her needs, regardless of the origins of those disciplines.

Each wisdom tradition offers one or more spiritual disciplines that can be used to foster spiritual development. Since each individual has a unique spiritual landscape that may change over the years, each person may require a unique menu of one or more of these spiritual disciplines at any one time in his or her life. Some people may be satisfied with the spiritual disciplines offered in the religion of their families of origin; other people may seek out disciplines with origins in wisdom traditions foreign to their families and cultures of origin.

Disciples are literally "followers"; spiritual disciplines use rituals that are practiced by the followers of a particular wisdom tradition, with a particular meaning and intent in mind. In this chapter, selected transformational spiritual rituals are described.

CONSCIOUSNESS

As discussed in previous chapters, consciousness can be understood as ecstatic, active, and reverent awareness. Such awareness tends to be associated with increasing spiritual liberty and aliveness. These concepts are described below.

Consensus Consciousness

Consensus consciousness includes the fundamental attitudes about reality shared by a community of any size, from a family, religion, institution, and city, to a region, nation, and the entire globe. For example, people belonging to a particular church might all agree that it is best to vote for a particular political party, or people living in a particular state might believe that productivity is the highest value in adulthood. When an individual develops her consciousness, she often has experiences outside of consensus consciousness, for the simple reason that every person has his or her own unique spiritual landscape. Communities of Spiritual Diversity support the unique spiritual landscapes of each member of the community.

Ecstatic Awareness

Higher consciousness is often associated with an ecstatic state, in which the individual moves out of consensus consciousness and into a more transpersonal state of consciousness. A transpersonal state is characterized by a shift away from the child and parent-dominated ego states and into the disciplined self. The individual goes beyond both the personal and community identities to an ecstatic identity. In an ecstatic state, an individual might feel especially connected with his or her personal experience of Creative Spirit, which might take the form of his or her God, for example, or a power animal.

Reverent Awareness

Higher consciousness tends to bring unimpeded perception of the Cosmos that is accompanied by the states of equanimity, gratitude, and awe. The individual becomes more aware and appreciative of self and divine self.

Active Awareness

Higher consciousness is inseparable from social responsibility and activism. As the individual becomes more conscious, she or he has greater sensitivity and ability to respond to the needs of other people, other living things, and the ecosystems that support all life. Thus, individual spiritual development is understood as being related to increasing spiritual activism.

Spiritual Liberty

Higher consciousness is both a cause and effect of Spiritual Liberty. Spiritual Liberty is an internal state in which the individual is personally free to see things the way they really are and then act responsibly to support the Highest Good.

Spiritual Aliveness

Spiritual aliveness is also related to higher consciousness and spiritual liberty. A spiritually alive individual is open to experience and expresses all the emotions, thoughts, and other sensations available to her or his body–mind–spirit. Spiritual aliveness is accompanied with the intent to express emotions, thoughts, and other sensations in such a way as to foster the Highest Good.

Full-Range Consciousness

Full-range consciousness is the ability to move wisely, fluidly, and with integrity between all levels of consciousness. A person with full-range consciousness is aware of and accepts all the parts of her or his own self, as well as the parts of other people in her or his world.

The Levels of Consciousness

When a client is able to function on all the levels of consciousness and move between them freely based on each social circumstance, then that client is able to use his Religious Self effectively in his or her relationships with other people. As described in Chapter 1, transpersonal theory suggests that most individuals can function at any of three levels of consciousness: the prepersonal, personal, and transpersonal levels. (The term *transpersonal* is therefore used in this chapter and in the literature in at least two different ways. First, transpersonal can be understood as theory that describes a branch of psychology that studies the spiritual development. Second, transpersonal also means the third level of consciousness, which is described in this paragraph.) The three primary levels of human consciousness are described by the major religious and spiritual traditions of the world and are increasingly confirmed by scientific research..

Prepersonal consciousness is characterized by a childlike view of the Cosmos that emphasizes impulses over reason or intellect, but that also allows for the experience of pleasure. Prepersonal consciousness also enables adolescents to begin to individuate from their families. With *personal consciousness,* there is a greater focus on the needs of other people, communities, and ecosystems; more responsibility in using reason; and the ability to postpone pleasure to examine one's own shadow and accomplish goals. Personal consciousness enables adults to cooperate with others for the community's greater good. Finally, *transpersonal consciousness* is characterized by an increasing focus on the supervisory self, from which the individual observes and oversees the child and parent with equanimity and temperance. Transpersonal consciousness enables the elders in a community to model the highest levels of well-being—such as equanimity, forgiveness, and compassion—for the younger people. Across the lifetime, the individual gradually develops his or her ability to operate in each of the three levels of consciousness.

None of these levels of consciousness should be viewed as necessarily more healthy or unhealthy than any other. The following case study illustrates how a person with full-range consciousenss might utilize all the levels of consciousness in a typical day of her life.

CASE STUDY 7.1
A DAY IN THE LIFE OF A PERSON WITH FULL-RANGE CONSCIOUSNESS

It's Sunday morning, and Tami is sleeping soundly when her alarm clock goes off at 6:45 A.M. She goes into her *personal* level of consciousness and responsibly turns off her alarm and gets out of bed. As Tami gets out her floor mat and does her breathing and stretching exercises, she notices a sense of calmness and focus (*transpersonal* level). She then prepares whole-grain waffles (her *personal* level wants to eat healthy) for breakfast. She sits down with her waffles and then her *prepersonal* level enjoys eating them with maple syrup and a little butter.

On the way to church, Tami drives in the middle lane, refusing to go into reaction to the pods of speeding cars competing to race downtown (*transpersonal*). When she gets to church, she stops and lets an old man walk across the parking lane in front of her (*personal*). She arrives in time to begin her Sunday School class with sixth-graders from her church (*personal*). Then she sits with her friends to listen to the minister's sermon, and she feels a sense of oneness with God (*transpersonal*). Afterwards, being a member of the church board, she attends a meeting with the pastor and other members in which she expresses her concerns about the Sunday School curriculum (*personal*). Later, she takes a leisurely stroll with a friend and they trade jokes and enjoy the weather (*prepersonal*).

Developmental Indicators of Levels of Consciousness

Most children and adolescents operate primarily at the *prepersonal* level of consciousness. They are most concerned with their own pleasure and self-importance in the world. When adults get "stuck" operating primarily at this level, the psychologist might say that they have "Axis II" traits, such as seen in the so-called narcissistic, borderline, or antisocial disorders. When people lose the ability to operate at the prepersonal level (such as when they are "stuck" at the personal level, as described next), then they may seem to have lost their ability to experience play, pleasure, and spontaneity, and we may call them anxious or depressed.

Hopefully, most young adults begin to develop the ability to live at the *personal* level of consciousness. At this level, people begin to take more responsibility for the welfare of other people, other life forms, and the health of the ecosystems. When people get stuck at this level, they might say they have "responsibilititus" or "guilt-aholism" and psychologists might say they have dysthymia or anxiety. The inability to operate at this level tends to lead to some of the symptoms described under Axis I.

Finally, by middle age, most adults develop their *transpersonal* consciousness. At this level, the people are able to operate primarily in the disciplinary self ego state. They are able to stop living in reaction to their pain and suffering, and they seek such higher levels of well-being as peace of mind, compassion, temperance, and equanimity. People stuck at the transpersonal level may be withdrawing from the world to avoid the suffering in their lives or in some other way may have lost a purity of motivation. The inability to operate at this level can trap a person into a pattern of reaction to every life event.

Developing Full-Range Consciousness

How can a social worker help a client develop full-range consciousness? In general, the worker is to help the client see where she is primarily functioning at and then help her move to the next step of spiritual development. When the client has been able to experience all the levels of consciousness, she can intentionally begin to move between them. At any time in life, the client may be at one of three "transformations" of change: the prepersonal–personal transformation, the personal–transpersonal transformation, or the transpersonal–prepersonal transformation. At such transformations, the client becomes motivated to move out of place of being "stuck" primarily at one level of consciousness.

Facilitating the Prepersonal–Personal Transformation

At a prepersonal–personal transformation, the client is challenged to begin or continue the process of creating an adult identity. Whereas the child's identity is inseparable from his family, culture, and community, the adult has created a personal identity through his own thoughts and actions. As adult identity is created, the person takes increasing responsibility for her own thoughts, feelings, and actions. In most cultures, people create their identity out of the elements listed in Box 7.1 One of the most challenging parts of identity making is *shadow work*, which is the uncovering of aspects of self that are hidden, covered by shame, and/or underdeveloped. For example, if a client grew up feeling shame about her sexuality, part of her shadow work may be to become aware of and express her sexuality.

The social worker helps the client across the transformation between prepersonal and personal functioning in a number of ways. On the *cognitive* level (level 2), the social worker can first explain transpersonal theory to the motivated client. The social worker helps the client understand that, just like in any other dimension of development, there is step-by-step progression in spiritual development. The social worker explains what the different levels of consciousness are, and how they all are equally valuable. By providing this cognitive map, the social worker helps the client see where she is at in her spiritual journey and then what her next steps might be. The element of mystery is also introduced, in that consciousness itself can also evolve, and that humanity may be currently co-developing new path-

---

BOX 7.1
TYPICAL ELEMENTS AND EXAMPLES OF ADULT IDENTITY

Possessions	Home, vehicle, clothing
Finances	Income, wealth, valuables
Roles	Parent, child, worker, boss, lover, spouse, student
Beliefs	Political, religious, scientific, philosophic
Power	Level of authority at work, church, home, community
People	History, family, friends, community, culture, fame
Emotions	Past and current feelings, *DSM* symptoms
Body	Gender, race, strength, beauty, sexuality, illness

ways of spiritual development. Any unhelpful beliefs that are obstacles to spiritual growth are also identified and replaced.

Additionally, the social worker can help the client think about what elements of identity she wants to develop next in her life. The source of these elements come from inside the client herself, specifically from the "dreams" or hopes she has about her future. From a spiritual perspective, the dreams people have about what they want to be in their lives come from Creative Spirit and thus they need to be attended to. Obviously, people do not always realize their dreams completely, but dreams can be understood as signals that come through the soul. They are compass headings to give us direction in our lives toward the essence of who we are meant to become. (See also Level 1 interventions in Chapter 4; the paradigms or levels are first described in Table 3.2.)

On the *emotional level* (Level 3), the social worker can help the client identify emotional responses that may be either helpful or unhelpful to the client's current spiritual growth process. For example, feelings of fear and shame can motivate a person to avoid taking steps to grow and instead to seek safety. On the *physical level* (level 5), the social worker might suggest that the client engage in a some kind of body work that enhances concentration, mindfulness, and body–mind–spirit connection.

CASE STUDY 7.2
PREPERSONAL–PERSONAL TRANSFORMATION

A social worker is running a support group for high school seniors who live in families with dysfunctional marriages. In the group discussions, the teens decide that they would like to explore their future plans. The social worker realizes that this is an opportunity to do some prepersonal–personal transformation work, since most of these teens operate primarily on the prepersonal level of consciousness. She explains the theory of transpersonal consciousness development, telling them, "You are at a time in your lives when you are creating a personal identity. This may go on for years or even decades. Eventually all of us will have the opportunity to go beyond personal consciousness too and dis-identify from the personal identity each of us has created."

The social worker invites the teen participants to write down a list of their dreams in each of the categories in Table 7.1 and prioritize them in order of current importance. By the end of the eight-week group, each teen has identified a few goals and related tasks to work toward.

Methods of Working with the Prepersonal Religious Self

What methods of Religious Self can be used to support the development of the Religious Self of clients who operate primarily at prepersonal levels of consciousness? The prepersonal level is characterized by an overemphasis on a self-centered identity. The general goal is to help the client gradually replace her overinflated sense of self-importance with a social identity. A person with such a social identity

TABLE 7.1   Examples of Goals and Methods in Work with Typical Prepersonal Issues

TYPICAL ISSUE	GOAL	METHODS
Client has underlying shame (sense of inferiority, lack of self-love, disconnection from Creative Spirit) compensated by an exaggerated sense that she can and should get all of her needs met by the world	Client becomes more of who she was meant to be and loves that person more; in particular, client accepts her own need for self-discipline and spiritual development	Use meditation (see Level 2) and body work (see Level 5) to increase awareness and acceptance of client's body–mind–spirit self
Client deals with her shame through *personal narcissism* (measuring my value by how much I can take) and thus can justify individual and collective violence	Client no longer sees herself as a victim and thus no longer justifies any violence perpetuated by herself or her religious community	Provide client with meaningful and satisfying service opportunities modeled and supported by members of a religious Community of Universal Diversity
Client has overdeveloped child ego state and underdeveloped parent ego state	Client develops a healthy parental introject who will care for and control the inner child.	Client becomes a disciple of a social worker who will help her develop inner control

takes increasing responsibility for her religious community and helps transform her religion into a Community of Universal Diversity. These methods typically provide structure, encourage self-control and social responsibility, and provide modeling for empathy and compassion (see Table 7.1).

Facilitating the Personal–Transpersonal Transformation

During life's personal–transpersonal transformations, the transformational work focuses on purposefully *dis-identifying* from elements of identity that the client has created. Dis-idenification does not mean that the client necessarily has to give up any of the elements of adult identity, nor does it mean that the client has "forgotten" how to enjoy herself on a prepersonal level. Dis-identification does mean that the client realizes she is "more" than any of the parts of herself with which she has previously identified.

The process of dis-identification is intentional, although (as is true in all transformational work) the ultimate outcome is always unknown. The social worker supports the client's desire to do this work and provides a cognitive map for the process. The motivations for change are reviewed. At some point in a person's life, the individual may begin to feel that the fruits of her labors are no longer deeply satisfying. This dissatisfaction is often the catalyst for change from personal to transpersonal consciousness.

Sometimes the client has experienced significant losses in her life, such as the loss of a loved one or job or health, that she wants to deal with through the development of transpersonal consciousness. Sometimes the social worker can also facilitate the personal–transpersonal transformation by doing a dis-identification exercise in the office. In either case, the goal is to help the client make a more permanent shift, so that transpersonal consciousness is available to her in any moment. The client may need to engage in new spiritual disciplines to help her resist the tendency to return to the familiar personal level of consciousness. For example, Level 2, mindfulness work, might help the client focus on what is most important to her now and what is not.

Methods of Working with the Personal Religious Self

The work with clients who operate primarily at the personal level of consciousness is essentially to replace an overemphasis on social identity with a spiritual identity. The social identity, which is focused on the expectations of other people, is gradually replaced with the spiritual identity, which is focused on the spiritual growth. The general goal is to help heal the client's shame so that he can calm his inflated social importance and thus ultimately help his religious community become a Community of Universal Diversity (see Table 7.2).

TABLE 7.2   Examples of Goals and Methods in Work with Typical Personal Issues

TYPICAL ISSUE	GOAL	METHODS
Client has underlying shame (compensated by an exaggerated sense that she can take care of the world without getting most of her own needs met)	Client becomes more of who she was meant to be and loves that person more; in particular, client accepts her own need for play, love, enjoyment, and expression	Help client experience ecstatic states through such methods as journey work, sweats, circle dances, and time-space travel work
Client deals with her shame through *social narcissism* (measuring my value by how much I can give and give up to others) and thus can justify violence perpetuated on herself, either by self or others	Client no longer sees herself as a martyr and a caretaker for others and thus no longer justifies any violence perpetuated by herself or her religious community	Support client in developing prayers or positive intentions in which she can affirm her own boundaries and needs, thus better balancing what she gives to and takes back from the world
Client has overdeveloped adult ego state and underdeveloped child and disciplined self	Client finds adults (including her social worker) whom she wants to follow (be a disciple of) to develop inner control	Client learns to develop disciplined self through mindful activism and mystical heart work

CASE STUDY 7.3
PERSONAL–TRANSPERSONAL TRANSFORMATION

A 55-year-old man comes to the social worker complaining of depression. "I don't know why I am so down, I have everything I want" says the client, "I am a CEO of a big corporation, I have a 4,000 square foot house, 2 forest green SUVs, a lawn with no dandelions, a daughter who is a cheerleader, a son who is the school quarterback, and a beautiful new wife." As the client explores his life with the social worker, he begins to realize that the things he has no longer satisfy him. Something has changed, although the change has been gradual and even subtle. The social worker realizes that this man is on the edge of a personal–transpersonal transformation and has the potential to have a transformational experience. The social worker explains transpersonal theory to the client, and says, "The pain you now feel actually is a gift—you are not mentally ill but actually on the verge of becoming more alive. But in order to have what you most want, you might have to let go of some things you no longer want." "What do I want?" asks the client. They explore that question over several weeks, and eventually come to the realization that the client wants peace of mind and a sense of connectedness.

The client agrees to go through a dis-identification exercise. He sits in a comfortable chair and closes his eyes. The social worker then works down the list of elements of adult identity, starting with possessions. The social worker says, "Imagine in your mind's eye all the possessions with which you most identify. Good. Now ask yourself, 'What is left of me if all my possessions were gone?'" Then the social worker repeats the same process with each of the other elements—finances, roles, beliefs, power, people, emotions, and body. Then the social worker asks the client to notice his experience of dis-identification and imagine how he would live his life differently if he was in this state of consciousness more often. The social worker finishes up the exercise by asking the client to recollect each of the dis-identified elements with the statement, "Now imagine welcoming the next element back into your personality."

The social worker encourages the client to follow up on this exercise by making changes in the way he thinks and acts. The man decides eventually to change his career and to live his life more simply. He spends more time with his children and begins to reevaluate who he really is and what kind of marriage he really wants.

Facilitating the Transpersonal–Prepersonal Transformation

Although transpersonal consciousness could be called the most advanced level, since it must follow the emergence of the personal out of the prepersonal states, individuals can also become "stuck" here. The client may focus so much on spiritual growth that he withdraws from the world of relationships, community, and ecosystems. As a result, the client may have forgotten how to enjoy and appreciate life and also may be neglecting his responsibility to other people, life forms, and ecosystems. Therefore, this kind of transformation is called *transpersonal–prepersonal*, because the client may need to shift his overemphasis on spiritual identity with a renewal of interest in self-identity and social identity.

Methods of Working with the Transpersonal Religious Self

In work with clients who operate primarily at the transpersonal level of consciousness, the general goal is to help heal the client's shame so that he can calm his inflated spiritual importance and thus ultimately help his religious community become a Community of Universal Diversity. Table 7.3 illustrates common themes in work with the Transpersonal Religious Self..

Why There Is No Prepersonal–Transpersonal Transformation

Of concern to the social worker is the today's common confusion between prepersonal and transpersonal states, which parallels our confusion between the false self-love of narcissism and true self-love (see resource Wilber, 1977). Many people, wishing to avoid the difficulties and pain of developing the social responsibility and self-awareness of Personal Consciousness, try to "skip" that level and go straight from prepersonal to transpersonal levels of consciousness. The prepersonal state of consciousness often is associated with narcissistic self-love, which is actually a com-

TABLE 7.3   Examples of Goals and Methods in Work with Typical Transpersonal Issues

TYPICAL ISSUE	GOAL	METHODS
Client has underlying shame compensated through an exaggerated sense that she has already reached the highest levels of spiritual growth being and thus no longer needs to interact with the world	Client becomes more of who she was meant to be and loves that person more; in particular, client accepts her own spiritual limitations and her own responsibility to be of service to the world	Client receives individualized help from an advanced social worker who can help her dis-identify from her spiritual achievements
Client deals with her shame through *transpersonal narcissism* (measuring my value by how spiritually developed I am) and thus can justify individual and collective violence	Client no longer sees herself as a victim and thus no longer justifies any violence perpetuated by herself or her religious community	Help client to re-enter her outer world (for example into relationships within a couple, family, or community) for the purpose of providing service to other people, living things, or ecosystems
Client has disconnection from her child and parent ego states	Client finds adults (including her social worker) whom she wants to follow (be a disciple of) to develop inner control	Help client re-enter, enjoy, and appreciate her life in the Cosmos (for example by exploring feelings through mystical heart methods)

pensation for low self-esteem through overinflation of self. In such cases, the individual is also at risk to further disempower himself and join (or help create) a religious community that is not accepting and compassionate toward spiritual and universal diversity. Overinflation is seen in the often grandiose attitudes of the prepersonally oriented leaders of such communities, which is reinforced by the faith of their prepersonally oriented followers. Overinflation is also seen in the attitudes of the followers, who think they can achieve spiritual maturity without doing any personal work. Often abuses of power can occur in these prepersonal religious communities, resulting sometimes in emotional, physical, financial, or sexual abuse.

States and Stages of Consciousness

Transpersonal theory also suggests that, in addition to the levels of consciousness, there are also states and stages of human consciousness (see resource Wilber and Cohen, 2004). The *states of consciousness* can occur spontaneously to anyone on a given day or night in their life. They are states that do not require work to develop because they are natural to each human being.

In contrast, the *stages of consciousness* are intentionally developed by each person. Like other developmental stages, the stages of consciousness evolve in order, step by step. The *egocentric* stage of consciousness, the beginning stage, is focused on the immediate desires and feelings of the individual. *Ethnocentric* consciousness expands from the individual focus of the egocentric stage to a focus on the tribe the individual belongs to. Although ethnocentric consciousness is more mature than egocentric, the danger is that tribal focus can lead to exclusion of other tribes and often even violence directed toward other tribes. At the *worldcentric* stage, consciousness continues to expand to now embrace a planetary focus. Although the worldcentric can end violence toward other people, people can still remain disconnected from and abusive to other living things and ecosystems. Finally, the most expansive focus is the *Kosmoscentric* stage, which embraces all of creation. Any of the states of consciousness can occur at any of the stages, as illustrated in Table 7.4.

Finding the Best "Fit" between Client and Spiritual Discipline

With the increasing number of choices of spiritual disciplines that the individual has today, social workers may feel challenged to find the discipline that best fits a client's current needs and spiritual path. The best place to start is to ask the client what disciplines appeal to her. Although religions are social institutions, spiritual work is individual work and spiritual disciplines reflect the individual interests of each person.

There may be times in a person's life when he or she experiments with using many different spiritual disciplines. Then the social worker supports the client's need to explore new ways of thinking and acting. At other times, the client may make a commitment to one particular commitment. The social worker then supports the client's need for focus and progress.

TABLE 7.4   **Examples of Relationship between the States and Stages of Consciousness (see Wilber, 1977)**

	WAKING STATE (GROSS/EGO)	DREAMING STATE (SUBTLE/SOUL)	DEEP SLEEP STATE (CAUSAL/ABSOLUTE)
Egocentric stage	I want food. I want sex.	I find myself inside a body with desires.	I do not experience myself as separate from other people and the Kosmos.
Ethnocentric stage	Only my tribe is right. My tribe is at war.	I find myself in a tribe at war with another tribe.	I do not experience my tribe as separate from other tribes and the Kosmos.
Worldcentric	Earth is the most important planet.	I find myself on the planet Earth.	I do not experience my planet as separate from other planets and the Kosmos.
Kosmoscentric stage	I am happy to be part of the Kosmos.	I find myself an alive being in the Kosmos.	I do not experience the Kosmos as separate from Creative Spirit.

ETHICAL-VALUE ISSUES

Implications of Outcome Studies and Transpersonal Theory

There is still relatively little information on the efficacy of transpersonal interventions in the literature. However, there is growing evidence that religiosity tends to be associated with many physical and mental health indicators. Such research as the relatively well-publicized prayer studies suggest that Religious Self methodologies can facilitate healing. Transpersonal theory suggests that individuals can work on aspects of their spiritual paths across their entire life spans, and that such work is developmental in nature. For example, individuals who operate primarily at the prepersonal level, many of whom are in the first decades of life, will generally not be ready to do dis-identification work.

Issues of Client Diversity

The spiritually oriented social worker is committed to supporting the spiritual maturity of the client. However, the social worker also recognizes that each client has a unique spiritual landscape and needs to have personal reasons for doing transformational work.

In addition, all issues of religious diversity are respected. Some clients will be willing to explore rituals drawn from all wisdom traditions, whereas others will be open to only one religious tradition or perhaps none at all. All such perspectives should be honored.

The social worker is especially challenged to be aware of religious and spiritual transferences and countertransferences, since they are indicators of client and social worker characteristics. The spiritually oriented social worker is committed to become aware of her or his own spiritual and religious biases as well, and may benefit greatly from seeing another spiritually oriented therapist or supervisor from time to time.

Issues of Family and Community Diversity

The social worker is careful to assess the rituals, doctrines, and values held by the client's family and community, and the extent to which these rituals, doctrines, and values may fit or conflict with the work of Religious Self. The social worker also recognizes that he or she has a responsibility to support the Highest Good of the families and communities with which the client associates. Therefore, the social worker consistently encourages the client to provide service to family and community.

Issues of Social Worker Diversity

A client who wants to work on developing a particular level of consciousness will most likely want to find a social worker who has mastered this level herself or himself. Thus, the wise social worker continues to work on his or her own spiritual path. Some social workers will be uncomfortable using rituals drawn from particular wisdom traditions because of their own religious perspectives; such beliefs should be respected

Issues of Ecosystem Diversity

The social worker also recognizes that she or he has a responsibility to support the Highest Good of the ecosystems that support all life. Therefore, the social worker consistently engages in service and encourages the client to provide service to family and community.

STUDY QUESTIONS

1. What is the Religious Self? How important is the social dimension in your spiritual life?

2. What wisdom tradition(s) have you been most drawn to in your life? Has your interest changed over time? Why do you think that is?

3. Which level of consciousness—prepersonal, personal, or transpersonal—do you primarily operate in?

4. What is full range consciousness? How many people do you know who seem to have such consciousness? How would you describe them?

5. Which of the transformations in consciousness seem to be the most difficult to you? Which if any have you already gone through? What was your experience of your change?

RESOURCES

Moore, T. (2002). *The soul's religion: Cultivating a profoundly spiritual way of life*. New York: HarperCollins Publishers.
    This is one of a number of useful books by Moore that describe elements of spiritual growth. In this one, Moore talks about the relationship between the soul and religiosity.
Wilber, K. (1977). *The spectrum of consciousness*. Wheaton, IL: Quest.
    Wilber describes his theory of consciousness development in this text.
Wilber, K., & Cohen, A. (2004). Following the grain of the Kosmos. *What Is Enlightenment?* May–July, 44–53.
    Wilber and Cohen discuss elements of consciousness.

CHAPTER 8

BIOCONSCIOUSNESS

These methods foster consciousness by developing the body–mind–spirit connection, listening to Creative Spirit (or God) speak through the body, and embodying Creative Spirit (or God's will) in daily life.

FOSTERING THE BODY–MIND–SPIRIT (BMS) CONNECTION

From a spiritual perspective, the body, mind, and spirit of each individual is interconnected at birth. Since there is always a reciprocity between the processes of the three dimensions, the functioning at one level can be viewed as both a cause and an effect of the functioning at the other two levels. As people navigate through childhood and adolescence, they often feel they have to give up parts of their body, mind, or spirit because these parts are not acceptable to family, friends, institutions, community, or culture. In the second column of Table 8.1, there are examples of some elements of body, mind, and spirit.

The social worker helps the client foster the BMS connection, which means that the client welcomes back and reintegrates the parts of herself or himself that were discarded. A combination of methods can be used to foster these transformations. The process may include the following five steps.

STEPS IN FOSTERING BMS CONNECTION

1. Increase the client's awareness of what elements of body, mind, and spirit have been discarded by the client's family, institutions, communities, and culture.

2. Increase the client's awareness of what elements of body, mind, and spirit he has discarded because of his family, institutions, communities, and culture.

3. Increase the client's awareness of how these losses have negatively impacted the Highest Good of himself, other people, other life forms, and ecosystems.

4. Enhance the client's commitment to recovering the elements he has lost.

5. Support new thoughts and behaviors that help embody that commitment.

TABLE 8.1   Examples of Elements in Body, Mind, and Spirit and Healthy Related Actions

DIMENSION	ELEMENTS	RELATED ACTIONS
Body	Skeletal system	Daily posture
	Muscular system	Physical skills
	Circulatory system	Aerobic exercise
	Respiratory system	Breath work
	Digestive system	Dietary habits
	Reproductive system	Sexual behavior
Mind	Beliefs	Openness
	Values	Moral maturity
	Intelligence	Thinking
	Creativity	Synthesizing
	Knowledge	Learning
	Awareness	Mindful patience
Spirit	Compassion	Sensitivity to suffering
	Forgiveness	Letting go of anger
	Peace of mind	Living in moment
	Equanimity	Letting go of reaction
	Temperance	Right mix at right time
	Love	Letting go of fear

Increase the Client's Awareness of What Elements of Body, Mind, and Spirit Have Been Discarded by the Client's Family, Institutions, Communities, and Culture

The social worker is a student of the contexts in which the client lives. She helps the client see that he is not alone and that he shares the loss of elements of his BMS connection with many other people. The client also begins to understand why most people in most cultures discard elements of themselves as they grow up, and how it is still possible to reclaim the elements that have been lost. These understandings may help the client become hopeful and more accepting of his current developmental process.

Increase the Client's Awareness of What Elements of Body, Mind, and Spirit He Has Discarded Because of Family, Institutions, Communities, and Culture

In general, a transformational strategy for work with the BMS might begin on the *cognitive* level. Much of the work of developing the BMS connection is in the increasing of the client's awareness and acceptance of the elements in the each of the three dimensions. The social worker can explain that, from a spiritual perspective, health is wholeness, the integration of all the "parts" that make up a person. Similarly, she can share her belief with the client that illness is the state of being disconnected (or in "dis-ease") with various parts of the self.

The social worker tries to assess which parts of her client are most integrated and which are least integrated. She usually discovers that there are historical and environmental factors associated with this integration process. Familial or cultural experiences may have created unnecessary shame or guilt about elements of the body, mind, or spirit. The social worker helps the client become aware of any parts of his self that have been discarded over time.

On the *emotional* level, the social worker can explore with the client how the client feels about his body, mind, and spirit. Many people are not emotionally ready to accept parts of themselves. There may be, for example, feelings of disgust and shame about some of these parts of self. Such feelings may interfere with the healing process, because the client does not want to accept the parts that need to be integrated. These feelings may be associated with past trauma that will need to be explored before they can be healed.

The social worker also understands that many of her clients may confuse glamorization with awareness and acceptance when they think about the elements of body, mind, and spirit. As illustrated by the examples in Table 8.2, glamorization is illusionary, whereas acceptance is based on what really is. The client may start to realize that glamorization has been a very poor substitute for self-awareness and self-acceptance in his life.

Increase the Client's Awareness of How These Losses Have Negatively Impacted the Highest Good of Himself, Other People, Other Life Forms, and Ecosystems

In one sense, the social worker's job is to notice the arrows sticking out of the client and then twist those arrows until the client can feel again how he is wounded. The purpose of such work is not to cause the client more pain, of course, although the client may at times feel that way. The purpose is instead to help the client become more aware again of who he is and of what he has lost. The social worker can twist those arrows by asking the right questions or by simply pointing out what the wounds might be.

TABLE 8.2   Examples of Glamorization Contrasted with Awareness and Acceptance

DIMENSION	GLAMORIZATION OF ELEMENT	AWARENESS AND ACCEPTANCE OF ELEMENT
Body	I want the perfect body. I want you to have the perfect body. People *are* their bodies.	I accept my body the way it is today. I accept your body the way it is today. You and I are more than our bodies.
Mind	I want to be smart. I am my mind.	I accept my mind the way it is. I am more than my mind.
Spirit	I have trendy spirituality. I am my trendy spirituality.	I accept my spiritual landscape today. I am more than my spiritual landscape.

The spiritually oriented social worker might also use transrational methods to help the client work with his losses. The social worker uses the term *transrational* rather than *irrational* because nonverbal methods are not inferior to talk therapy and can be equally effective. Transrational methods might include such activities as movement, painting, sculpture, and psychodrama. For example, the client might be asked to draw a picture of his body, mind, and spirit and show the relationship between them on the same sheet of paper. Then he might be asked to draw the location where the "holes" are in his full being. The social worker could also, for example, have clients do a movement that expresses their current "wounded" selves and then do a movement representing their healed or whole selves.

Enhance the Client's Commitment to Recovering the Elements He Has Lost

After the client becomes aware of the importance of the BMS connection, and increases his awareness of how and why parts of his BMS are still discarded and need healing, his desire to change often is often enhanced. The social worker encourages the client's commitment to recover the lost elements.

Support New Thoughts and Behaviors That Help Embody That Commitment

All of the awareness-building work just discussed can be followed up with changes in thinking and more action oriented, behavioral change work. The social worker may help the client replace unhelpful thoughts with new ways of thinking, as illustrated in Table 8.2.

The client may want to reintegrate the discarded parts through the use of new behaviors. Examples of such related actions are in the third column of Table 8.1. For example, if he lives primarily "in his head," the client may want to practice daily meditations during which he listens to what his body "says" about issues in his everyday life.

Hopefully, the client will also become more active in service to other people, other living things, and ecosystems as he heals his own BMS connection. For example, as people become more familiar with the state of their own physical well-being, they may also become more aware of the well-being of other living things and the Earth itself. Such awareness can be the growing basis for new behaviors.

Body Reintegration: Fostering Reintegration of Discarded Elements of the Body

On the community level, although the mainstream culture in the United States seems to glamorize the body, the same culture devalues elements of the body that are thought to be unappealing. An obvious example of glamorization is in how the marketing and media industries commonly use the display of "perfect" bodies to make money. In contrast, normal functions and attributes of the body—such as aging, elimination, sexuality, and death—seem to make many people uncomfort-able. The culture substitutes glamorization instead of acceptance.

On the individual level, social workers often notice that their clients have dis-carded significant elements of their bodies. From a bioconsciousness perspective, many people living today live largely above their neck, meaning that they prefer to navigate through the world using only outer cortexes. Although the brain is an incredibly useful organ, the body has many other parts, and each part can provide a way of knowing. People can have a "gut" feeling in their intestines, for example, or a "heartfelt" feeling about a decision in their chest. Another way to express this tendency to live in the head is to say that the individual has given up her or his connection with her or his animal or savage nature.

Many so-called mental disorders can be reframed as disruptions in the BMS connection. From this perspective, for example, such common symptoms as anxi-ety and depression are actually symptoms of health, since the soul is still alive, try-ing to speak through the symptoms, that reintegration is necessary. Depression and anxiety could therefore be understood as symptoms associated with a ten-dency to live chiefly in the mind—a mind disconnected from body and spirit. Per-haps such imbalances often begin in childhood, when a young person tries to avoid pain and control his or her environment by anticipating everything mentally. Later in life, this coping mechanism becomes a long-term imbalance. Body work, then, is transformational work that can help the client recover those elements of self that have been discarded and thus restore her natural BMS connection.

Clients in a state of physical suffering may benefit from a reframing of their suf-fering, using a spiritual perspective. When a client has some kind of physical suffer-ing, the social worker often notices that the client is angry at her illness or disease, and even at her body. Such anger, although understandable, can inhibit the client's ability to pay attention to her physical pain and make meaning out of her illness. The desire to fight the illness is perhaps related to the current culture's bias that everyone needs to take pain and symptom medication when ill and then get back to work as soon as possible. An alternative to this "fast-food recovery" philosophy would be to allow the body to have the illness and to make meaning out of the suffering.

CASE STUDY 8.1
AN EXAMPLE OF BODY REINTEGRATION

A 20-year-old man visits the student counseling center at his community college. He complains to the social worker, "My life is a never-ending series of misfortunes." The social worker learns that in the last month, the young man has had a bad ankle sprain, the flu, and a case of food poisoning. His football coach sent him to the coun-selor because he was concerned about the client's attitude.

In the session, the young man refers to his ankle as my "—— ankle." The thera-pist says, "What if you looked at your sore ankle as blessing?" The client answers, "How the —— is a sprained ankle a blessing?" The therapist replies, "That is something for you to discover, but you might begin by noticing that someday your body will probably age and surely will die. So if all you are is this beautiful body that you now have, then you may always be in fear of losing it." The young man rolls his eyes but is quiet.

In the next sessions, the young man starts to talk about how he has always looked at his body as a perfect machine that is supposed to work all the time. He also realizes how much he identifies with having a strong youthful body, and how he looks for such perfection in the women he dates. The social worker has the client do simple meditations, where the client just sits with his injury and notices his body and mind. When the client just notices his injury and stops wishing it would go away, he starts to realize that when his body breaks down, he becomes angry because he feels helpless and worthless. The client starts to work on feeling acceptance and even gratitude, for the first time in his life, for the way his body and world are.

Body Reintegration: Healing the Sacred Connection between Sexuality and Spirituality

Sexuality is an element of the body that is often at least partially discarded. From the bioconsciousness perspective, sexuality and spirituality are interconnected elements of every person. A person's spiritual development has an ongoing impact on his or her sexual development. For example, a client who operates primarily on the prepersonal level of consciousness will probably tend to relate sexually in a prepersonal style, putting personal needs and immediate gratification first. Similarly, a person's sexual development has an ongoing impact on his or her spiritual development. As a person understands, accepts, and expresses her or his sexuality, the person can increasingly understand, accept, and express her or his spirituality through that sexuality.

From the bioconsciousness perspective, sexuality and spirituality are not only interrelated but are also similar processes. Both sexuality and spirituality are connecting forces that can bring people closer to other people and to their own souls. Every person has a unique sexual and spiritual landscape. Sexuality and spirituality are also powerful forces that can motivate people to be independent and unpredictable in the way they think and act. Finally, since both forces are fundamental to human nature, when either sexuality or spirituality is suppressed, the individual's fundamental nature is also suppressed to the same degree.

Both spirituality and sexuality are often regulated and even suppressed by families, institutions, and communities. Such regulation is understandable, because the powerful forces of spirituality and sexuality probably frighten well-meaning parents, clergy, and community leaders. However, since people who are free to become mature sexual and spiritual beings also tend to be free in their thoughts and behaviors, the regulation of sexuality can also be viewed as oppressive, particularly to sexual, cultural, or political minorities.

Social workers can work to help their clients understand that the focus on sexuality in mainstream culture substitutes glamorization for acceptance. This glamorization is characterized by shelves in bookstores of self-help titles on sex, monthly "secrets" revealed in popular magazines about sex, and the ongoing use of sexuality as a marketing tool in many industries. The social worker also works to help clients understand and accept their own unique sexuality, and to reconnect their sexuality with their bodies, minds, and spirits so that the clients' sexuality fosters the Highest Good in themselves and others.

CASE STUDY 8.2
AN EXAMPLE OF REINTEGRATION OF SEXUALITY

Two young women in a year-long relationship are referred by their pastor to see a social worker for couple counseling. The social worker works at a church-sponsored agency that does psychotherapy from a spiritual perspective. One of the main complaints that the couple brings to therapy is that their sexual intimacy is not satisfying, although they are still strongly attracted to one another.

The couple agrees to explore their BMS histories. Both of them deny any sexual traumas in their past. However, the social worker pushes further and they co-discover that both of them grew up in families, institutions, and communities that suppressed sexuality, particular female sexuality, and even more so same-sex attraction. Neither woman was taught the names of her genital body parts, and both women learned that females are supposed to act shy and modest. They realize that, although their church officially supports Lesbian relationships, they both discarded major parts of their sexuality early in their lives. They realize that, in their words, deep down they "still believe it is a sin to love each other."

The social worker works with them both, helping them to rediscover their sexuality. They do a visualization together, for example, where they both allow themselves to imagine their sexual fantasies, and then they share them with each other. Their sexual relationship starts to become more creative and satisfying as the work goes on.

Mind Reintegration: Fostering Reintegration of Discarded Elements of the Mind

Just like the body, in mainstream culture in the United States, the mind is typically either overvalued and idealized or devalued and discarded by the culture. On the one hand, the culture tends to overvalue and idealize the importance of mind in self-identity and self-worth. People tend to think that they *are* their minds. Despite the easy access of information on the Internet, knowledge is still emphasized over creativity and wisdom in most classrooms. When people feel bad, professional helpers say that they have *mental* health issues, rather than body–mind–spirit issues.

On the other hand, the culture tends to devalue the importance of *mindfulness*, which is the ability to see things the way they really are, without needing them to be necessarily different. Young people are taught to fill their minds up with knowledge, but are not taught how to understand and discipline their minds. The social worker helps the client understand that knowledge is a poor substitute for the wisdom of mindfulness.

How can a social worker foster the reintegration of the mind in a client? The work begins on the cognitive level. The social worker helps the client understand how her or his family, institutions, culture, and communities may have influenced the loss of elements of mind. The social worker also might have to help the client see that such elements not only exist but are desirable and obtainable. As illustrated in here, some people can spend most of their lives misunderstanding what mental maturity is.

CASE STUDY 8.3
AN EXAMPLE OF MIND REINTEGRATION

A 76-year-old woman is referred to a social worker at a neighborhood adult day health center in an economically poor neighborhood. She has a reputation in the center of being one of the most intelligent seniors at the center, as well as a natural leader. She likes to greet everyone when they arrive, and she has her favorite table where she likes to sit and play cards. She seldom loses a game, and always prides herself on her quick wit. Lately, however, she has seemed depressed.

The Center Director asked the woman to talk to the social worker. At first she refused, but then relented when her depression got worse. The social worker learned that the woman was told by one of the other women during a game that she was losing her memory. "I realized that she might be right, my memory has been slipping. I never thought that would happen to me," she told the social worker. The social worker talked with her about the idea that mental maturity is not about intelligence or memory but about mental discipline.

The social worker "sold" the client on the idea that she could still be a special person in her community, but that what would be most special about her was changing. Instead of being smarter than everyone else, she could be a model of mental maturity, a woman who was compassionate and wise. As they met over the weeks, the woman decided that mental discipline and maturity consist of her attitudes about herself and other people.

Spirit Reintegration: Fostering Reintegration of Discarded Elements of the Spirit

Like body and mind, U.S. culture also seems to have an ambivalent attitude about spirit. On the one hand, the concept is everywhere. The best-seller lists usually seem to have at least one book with the words *soul* or *spirit* or *religion* in the title. Many popular films deal with aspects of spirituality, including consideration of witches, angels, and of course "may the force be with you." Magazines carry pages of advertisements for workshops where one can study anything from the spirituality of food to yoga, astrology, and chanting.

On the other hand, content on spiritual development and maturity remains missing from public education. Many people reach adulthood having never discussed their own unique spiritual experiences in a safe environment. The spiritual dimension is still largely ignored and sometimes openly ridiculed in academic research and teaching.

Just like body and mind, spirituality is often glamorized in our culture rather than understood and accepted. As a result, people may substitute spirituality as a glamorous commodity for spiritual development and maturation. For example, since being "New Age" is very trendy in many social circles, people may be tempted to compete to be the most spiritual person who does the most recent spiritual techniques. Or in a particular church, there may be a competition to see who is the most spiritual, based on behaviors or appearances.

The reintegration of spirit, then, begins with a growing awareness of what has been lost and what might be gained by reintegration. The social worker helps enhance the client's awareness, and supports the client's growing need to make changes in his life. Just like in the body and mind dimensions, each story of spiritual loss and reintegration is unique to each individual. The social worker may use this basic principle, but also adapts to the individual circumstances of each case.

CASE STUDY 8.4
AN EXAMPLE OF SPIRIT REINTEGRATION

A 40-year-old woman is referred to a social worker by the court, following her second DUI (driving under the influence of alcohol) in six months. The woman at first denies she has a drinking problem. It turns out that she is married to a prominent lawyer in town and that she is a prominent member of the XYZ Church. When the social worker reads the court papers to her, she says, "I have always been a good citizen, I am a very religious person, and I do not deserve to be treated this way." The social worker talks about the difference between religiosity and spirituality, and then asks about the woman's spiritual life. At first, the woman describes her spiritual life as very rich, but over several weeks of sessions it becomes increasing clear to her that she is living in spiritual poverty. She has no peace of mind, little compassion for herself or others, and feels that there is little if any meaning in her life. Further discussions reveal that her marriage to her husband is very empty for her as well. The social worker helps her explore her spirituality and the woman eventually realizes that she would like very much to change her consciousness, but without using alcohol or other drugs. She joins a meditation course and continues to attend her church. She decides to confront her husband about his affairs.

BMS DIALOGUE: HEARING CREATIVE SPIRIT
SPEAK THROUGH THE BODY

The body can be viewed as a voice of Creative and Individual Spirit. From this perspective, when an individual listens to what her body is "telling" her, she can learn more about her soul's journey. The social worker supports the client as she finds significance and meaning in the many experiences she has as a spiritual being in a human body.

Making Meaning Out of Genetics

Today, Western medicine generally views diseases of the soul as biogenetic in origin. Thus, for example, if a young man is depressed, it is because he has a "chemical imbalance" which arose out of his "genetic predisposition." The bio-consciousness perspective does not deny that such linkages exist, but it also proposes that the causal direction goes in both directions. In other words, so-called chemical imbalances and genetic predispositions can also be viewed as expressions of spirit and soul. Indeed, all inherited characteristics can be viewed from a spiritual perspective.

For example, the social worker can work with the often-more-obvious genetically based characteristics. A client can be supported in making spiritual significance out of the gender, sexual preferences, ethnicity, body type, and other characteristics with which she was born. Such significances would of course always be personal and unique to each client. Many different techniques can be used. The client can simply be asked to reflect on the meanings that come to mind. The social worker can ask the client to draw a picture of herself as a spiritual being inside a body. The client can make up a birth story in which she imagines that she chose her gender, ethnicity, and so on before she was born for particular spiritual reasons.

Making Meaning Out of Dis-Ease

When a client has uncomfortable physical symptoms, the social worker can also help the client find spiritual meanings in these experiences as well. For example, if a client gets a cold every winter, the social worker may work with the client to find the meaning of this pattern. Although the client may choose to go to a traditional or nontraditional physician for diagnosis and treatment of her illness, the social worker helps the client discover spiritual meaning in the illness.

In order to assist in this significance-making process, the effective social worker may work closely with other helping professionals. The typical clinic of the future may well have a spiritually oriented social worker in partnership with other health care social workers, such as nurse social workers, homeopathic professionals, body-workers, and physicians. The multidisciplinary team works together to provide body, mind, and spiritual services to each client. Although each professional has a speciality, all are familiar with the perspectives of the other disciplines. In such a clinic, the spiritually oriented social worker focuses on the significance-making process.

CASE STUDY 8.5
HEARING SPIRIT THROUGH THE BODY

A 44-year-old woman goes to for an assessment at the new body–mind–spirit clinic downtown. The intake worker sits down with her and learns that she has been suffering from several ongoing illnesses. She has had outbreaks of shingles, chronic back pain, and a sprained shoulder, all on her left side. The intake worker refers the woman for treatment from the clinic nurse social worker, as well as schedules a session for her with the Licensed Clinical Social Worker (LCSW), who is a spiritual social worker as well. During the first meeting with the LCSW, the client also talks about her frustrations with mothering. She is a single mother with two adolescent girls. Both are now dating, and the household has become more conflictual. Neither girl is doing well in school, although they both were good students before they were in high school. The LCSW asks the woman how she makes sense out of all the things in her life right now. "I was hoping *you* would tell me," the woman replies.

The LCSW has the client lie on the floor on a large piece of paper and she draws the outline of her body on the paper. When the client first sees the drawing she says, "Ugh, am I getting that fat?" They discuss the idea that physical development in adulthood is about learning to accept and love and care for one's own body as it ages. The client cries during this discussion and talks about how unattractive she feels. "From a spiritual perspective," says the social worker, "you were given the perfect body right now to help you learn what you need to learn."

Using the body outline, the social worker has the client draw in the body parts that she most likes and most dislikes or the parts that are dis-eased, using different crayon colors (she picks red for pain, blue for relaxation, yellow for tension, etc.). Then the client is asked to use different colored marker pens to write in the emotional and spiritual processes she thinks might be associated with each body "part" she has drawn in. This process may take several weeks, and the associations may change over time. For example, she draws her shingles red across the side of her body. She then writes down that the emotions associated with the shingles seems to be "fear" and "anxiety." The woman writes down that the spiritual processes involves with the shingles seems to be "a call to pay more attention to how I am stressed out way too much and wasting my life." The social worker works with the client on each of these associations. She asks the client to make a commitment to herself to take action steps to foster her own Highest Good. In relation to her shingles, the client decides that much of her fear and anxiety and stress have been an unnecessary reaction to her children. "I have been too involved in their lives," she says.

EMBODYING CREATIVE SPIRIT IN DAILY, "EVERY BODY" LIFE

A person embodies spirit when he intentionally uses his body to experience and express Creative Spirit. From this perspective, "every body" experience has a spiritual basis. After healing the BMS connection and learning to dialogue with the body, the client can learn to embody spirit in her life.

Embodying the Natural Rhythms of Creative Spirit

Just like the world has its own rhythms, so does the human body. The social worker can help the client accept all these natural rhythms, through awareness and intentional actions. The social worker can help the client find associations between her own rhythms (including those of sleep, energy level, menstruation, hunger, well-being, and illness) and rhythms in her local ecosystem (including those of the seasons, day and night, the weather, and animal behavior). These associations might take any form. As the client embodies spirit, deep healing can take place.

CASE STUDY 8.6
MAKING ASSOCIATIONS BETWEEN BODY EXPERIENCES AND NATURE

A social worker is working with one of her clients in her private practice, a 35-year-old married mother of three. Her presenting problem is mild depression. She reports that "I get bummed every month when I get PMS because it really bothers my husband and children." When asked, she reports that she seems to feel more "irritable" before and during her period each month: "I wish those darn periods would go away," complained the woman. The social worker answered, "Another way to look at them is that they are a blessing." The client laughs sarcastically, "Tell that to my husband," she said. "Perhaps eventually you will be saying that to him," the social worker replied.

The worker and client start to look at the woman's body from a more spiritual perspective. Instead of viewing her body–mind–spirit experience each month as an illness, the social worker invites the client to view her periods as a spiritual process. The client finds associations in nature for her period, in the thunderstorms that come over the mountains in the desert town she lives in. She starts to see her irritation not as a problem, but as "bolts of lightning and thunder" that must come down from the clouds every once in a while. She starts to realize some of the resentments she has about the marriage that she has kept bundled up inside of her. She starts to talk with her husband more assertively about what she wants and does not want. She realizes that her depression is a friend also, just like her periods, through which spirit can communicate with her.

Embodying Dis-Ease, and Recuperation

From a spiritual perspective, all physical suffering can lead to spiritual growth. In U.S. culture, people are often expected to need little or no recuperation from disease or illness. Instead, many people take medicines that reduce the symptoms of their illness (such as fatigue, headache, body ache) and return to work or school as soon as possible. Another way to think about such symptoms is that they are opportunities for embodiment of spirit. The social worker does not diagnose or treat the illness unless she has the appropriate medical license. However, the social worker can work with enhance client's body–mind–spirit perspective on his disease and help him embody what he feels his spirit is "telling" him through his body. Clients often discover that part of the message of spirit is to take better care of themselves and to live more balanced lives.

CASE STUDY 8.7
EMBODYING DIS-EASE AND RECUPERATION

A social worker is visited by a 45-year-old man who is a surgeon at the local hospital. The client, also a strong marathon runner, has become depressed and anxious after a series of minor injuries have kept him away from his running all summer. The surgeon's wife insisted that he go to a counselor because she was "sick of hearing him whine all the time." The social worker asks the client what he wants to get out of counseling. The surgeon says, somewhat insincerely, "Well, maybe you can give me one of your psychological explanations about why I keep getting hurt." The social worker says, "Yes, and maybe we can expand your work from just the psyche to issues of body, mind, *and* spirit—and maybe it is better if *you* do the explanatory work, not the counselor."

The social worker has the client do a series of role-plays in which the client plays each of his injuries. The therapist sits in a chair opposite the client and tells the client that she will play *him* in the role-plays. She asks, "Knee sprain, why are you in my life?" "To make you miserable," says the sprain. "Why do you want to do that?" "Oh I don't know—maybe so that you will learn to do something else besides work and run." The surgeon chokes back a tear: "Ever since my father died last year I keep thinking about my own death. These little injuries are like little deaths—I'm not ready to die." "I wonder how you would live your life if you knew you only had a year left," the social worker states. The work had begun.

Issues of Client Diversity

Every client has a unique body–mind–spirit connection that the social worker helps strengthen. The social worker respects the language that each client uses to describe the body, mind, and spirit. She respects the fact that people view the BMS connection differently. All views are respected.

The social worker realizes that some clients will feel very uncomfortable with BMS work. Perhaps they have become disconnected from their body in large part because they were molested as a child or because they have a physical disability. Some people have been raised in families, religions, or communities that teach that a separation of body, mind, and spirit is the desirable goal. The social worker respects the client's cultural and religious roots and always is sensitive to the motivation and openness of the client to BMS work.

Issues of Family and Community Diversity

The social worker realizes that many cultures across the world teach people from childhood to think of their bodies, minds, and spirits as interconnected, and that some cultures, such as the dominant culture of the United States, teach that there is a separation of these elements. Therefore, the social worker needs to be respectful of the differences between clients as she does her healing work. Her goal is not to change people's religions or cultures, but to help them heal their BMS connection.

Issues of Social Worker Diversity

The effective social worker is committed to developing her own BMS connection so that she can model this connection for her clients. She recognizes the elements that she has discarded and strives to reintegrate them.

Not all social workers are comfortable with BMS work. Some may have strong cultural or religious beliefs about sexuality, for example, that make such work difficult for them. All social workers can explore their value systems and determine what biases they may have in working with BMS issues.

Issues of Ecosystem Diversity

The social worker realizes that BMS work can increase a client's sensitivity to the well-being of other people, living things, and ecosystems. The social worker uses BMS work to support the Highest Good of the ecosystems that support all life.

STUDY QUESTIONS

1. What is the BMS connection? Why is it important? Is the BMS connection in your life important to your well-being? Explain.

2. What are some examples of elements of body, mind, and spirit that you have discarded because of various life experiences, perhaps in relation to your family, institutions, or culture?

3. Continuing from question (2), how would you go about reintegrating these elements back into your self? What obstacles might get in the way of this process? How would you overcome them?

4. What are the three methods discussed in this chapter? Why are they described in the order they appear? Which method(s) appeal to you the most? Why?

RESOURCES

Murphy, M. (1992). *The future of the body: Explorations into the further evolution of human nature.* New York: Jeremy Tarcher/Putman/Penguin.
   This book is a wonderful resource for those who want to study what scientists think may be possible in humanity's long-term future.
QI: The Journal of Traditional Eastern Medicine
   This journal has many interesting articles about body–mind–spirit healing practices drawn from many cultures and wisdom traditions.

CHAPTER 9

COLLECTIVE CONSCIOUSNESS

From the perspective of collective consciousness, when human beings are in conflict, the best source of knowledge and wisdom is always collective. People who are in conflict always have the opportunity to use methods of collective consciousness to co-discover and co-create the Highest Good.

Much of the work described in the first chapters of this book involves methods of individual transformation. The rationale for such methods is that individual transformation can lead to the development of collective transformation. In this chapter, methods of working directly with collective transformation are described. The rationale for these methods is that collective transformation can also lead to individual transformation. These two rationales are not mutually exclusive, because, from a spiritual perspective, individual and collective consciousness are always interconnected. Thus, collective-consciousness methods help co-create Communities of Spiritual Diversity that in turn support the development of Individual Consciousness.

Methods of collective consciousness include conscious intimacy, conscious dialogue, conscious service, and conscious activism designed to support the development of Communities of Spiritual Diversity.

CONSCIOUS INTIMACY

Conscious intimacy is nonviolent sharing on all the dimensions of human intimacy, including the physical, emotional, cognitive, social, and spiritual, with the intent of fostering the Highest Good of all participants (see Box 9.1).

From a spiritual perspective, when two or more people develop conscious intimacy between them, they are able to co-create a *collective consciousness* that is greater than the consciousness either individual can have alone. Such collective consciousness can be useful in helping discover and then support the Highest Good. For example, parents with conscious intimacy can make wise decisions that support the Highest Good of their children, their marriage, their family, and their communities.

Conscious intimacy is horizontal, in that it is *between* people. In contrast, *vertical* intimacy is the connection a person has between all of his or her own dimensions

■ ■ ■ ■ ■

BOX 9.1

DIMENSIONS AND EXAMPLES OF INTIMACY

Physical	Dancing together (circle dancing)
	Making music together (singing, drumming)
	Sharing work project (planting trees, building home)
	Sharing creative project (making a mural)
	Sensuality and sexuality
Emotional	Sharing feelings verbally
	Expressing feelings nonverbally
	Listening or attending to feelings
Cognitive	Sharing ideas
	Listening to ideas
	Sharing humor and laughing together
	Reading poetry
	Telling stories
Social	Taking relationship(s) out in public setting (at restaurant)
	Sharing relationship(s) with other people (at a party)
	Taking relationship(s) out in nature (on a quiet hike)
Spiritual	Sharing one's soul with another
	Attending to another's soul
	Experiencing Creative Spirit together
	Praying together
	Doing a sacred ritual together

of intimacy. Vertical intimacy is therefore related to the body–mind–spirit connection, and is the ability to experience all the dimensions of intimacy in the here and now. Conscious intimacy is also *intentional,* in that people develop closeness of body, mind, and spirit with another person with the aim of fostering each other's Highest Good.

The more a person develops his or her vertical intimacy, the more that person is able to develop conscious (and horizontal) intimacy in his or her life. Thus, the work of developing conscious intimacy begins and remains concurrent with the work of developing vertical intimacy.

The social worker helps foster the development of vertical intimacy in the client through the building of awareness and intent. The client is taught about what vertical intimacy is and then is helped to understand what dimensions of intimacy remain disconnected from herself. Then the social worker helps the client become more familiar with and accepting of these dimensions. The client develops an intent to develop her vertical intimacy on an ongoing basis, because every person has a lifetime of learning opportunities about themselves.

The development of conscious intimacy builds on the work of vertical intimacy. The social worker helps the client become more aware and accepting of the dimensions of intimacy that she still does not have with the significant other(s) in her life. Although she will not, of course, want to have the same intensity or level of intimacy with every person in her life, she may want to experience all the levels as deeply as she is capable of in the here and now with at least one significant other. Many people do not believe that such intimacy is possible, and have given up, so the social worker provides encouragement. The social worker also helps the client identify ways to create more intimacy in her life, and then follow through and do her creating. Although the following case study focuses on romantic, heterosexual love, conscious intimacy methods can be used to foster closeness between people in all kinds of relationships.

CASE STUDY 9.1
DEVELOPING VERTICAL AND CONSCIOUS (AND HORIZONTAL) INTIMACY

A spiritually oriented social worker at a local mental health clinic is visited by a 30-year-old man who has just moved to the suburb where the clinic is. His presenting problem is that he is diagnosed with attention-deficit hyperactivity disorder (ADHD), and has been on and off medication since his adolescence. The social worker asks permission to speak with the psychiatrist (who also works at the same clinic). (The clinic requires that clients who receive psychiatric care must also receive concurrent counseling.) The psychiatrist is also spiritually oriented and tells the social worker that although the man does have some of the classic symptoms of ADHD, she suspects that his deeper issue is that he is more alone than he wants to be in his life. She adds, "And as we know, they haven't made a pill yet for loneliness."

The social worker had the same impression as the psychiatrist. He asks the client about his love life, defining the term broadly to include all people that the client may care about. "What love life?" responds the client, with a little drama. It turns out that the client's career is going well. He is a successful computer programmer who was just transferred to a new division in the suburbs by his corporation. The social worker gets to work.

First, they discuss vertical intimacy. The social worker convinces the client that it is in his best interests to develop his vertical intimacy. Together they determine that he is most disconnected from his emotional and spiritual and social dimensions. They co-develop a plan in which the client will investigate his emotional, spiritual, and social dimensions. He will keep a journal to write down his emotional and spiritual experiences every morning and evening. He will start to attend two social events every week to overcome some of his fear of being in social situations.

About four months later, the client meets a young woman to whom he is attracted. The social worker then starts to work on conscious intimacy with the client. The client has become aware that he wants a relationship with a woman in which he has all the dimensions of intimacy. For most of his life he did not believe that such a relationship was possible, but in the past months he has become more optimistic. The social worker works with the client as he takes more risks each week to share more of himself with the woman with whom he is spending time.

The last time the social worker heard from the client was a year later. The client sent a postcard to the social worker, stating briefly that he had moved in with the woman and they were talking about getting married. The front of the postcard said "Happily ever after."

CONSCIOUS DIALOGUE

Conscious dialogue is a method of nonviolent intimacy with an agreed intent between the participants to help co-discover and help co-create the Highest Good of all participants, other people, other living things, and the ecosystems that support all life.

BOX 9.2

ELEMENTS AND EXAMPLES OF CONSCIOUS DIALOGUE

Participants agree on initial intent, location, and time of meeting.	Following several incidents of religious-inspired violence, the dialogue will be between people representing two different religions. The first weekly meeting will be at a "neutral" location on a weekday evening. It is agreed that the goal is to help heal the divide between the two religions and support the Highest Good of the community.
Simple group norms are established	The facilitator(s) or leader(s) asks group members to discuss norms. Participants agree that there is no violence or threats, that people should speak one at a time, that different views are respected, and that no one can make anyone else wrong.
Rituals are shared.	The meeting begins with two prayers, one offered from each religion. Everyone goes around and introduces themselves. One week people share what their favorite breakfast is. Another week they share a travel fantasy. Simple food and drink is provided on a rotating basis.
Each week the work of dialogue is fostered with agreed-upon group structures.	The first week, people from the XYZ religion sit in the middle of the group (in a circle in a circle) and talk about their experiences while people from the ABC religion sit quietly on the outside and listen. Then they switch. Then the whole group dialogues.
Each week, collective consciousness is used to plan and carry out action steps for the coming week.	The first week, a consensus builds that the group liked getting into how people really feel and think and that the next meeting should be designed so that participants can go into more depth on the same topics. Small groups will be used again but this time both religions will be represented in each group.
Collective consciousness is used to plan and implement community Spiritual Activism.	One week the group decides that they need to start teaching youth in the community about dialogue. A subgroup composed of representatives from both religions is identified that will do focus groups with the youth from both religions to find out what kind of projects youth might want.
Periodic evaluations are done and "mid-course corrections" made.	During one meeting, the group evaluates what has happened so far. A consensus emerges that progress has been made but that much remains to be done. The group schedules a meeting with the mayor's office to suggest a series of public events during the year that will foster more interactions between people from both religions.

From a spiritual perspective, when people get together with the shared intent to have conscious dialogue, they can develop a collective consciousness that is more powerful and useful than consciousness on an individual level. Such consciousness can be used to help solve the challenges that local and global communities now face (see Box 9.2).

Dialogue is a term used often in U.S. culture to describe intellectual interactions between people. However, conscious dialogue is not just an intellectual exercise, but involves *all* the dimensions of conscious intimacy. Communication is more than just words; it is also an energetic mosaic of body, mind, and spirit that is expressed and sensed. Conscious dialogue is *intentional* communication of body, mind, and spirit, with the aim to co-discover and help foster the Highest Good of not only the participants but of other people, living things, and ecosystems.

The spiritually oriented social worker is committed to understanding and practicing conscious dialogue because she realizes how important it is that people learn to communicate and cooperate in today's world. With increasing mass-casualty terrorism, ecological destruction, and other global survival threats, humanity must learn to dialogue across differences if we hope to mitigate and solve these challenges.

In order for conscious dialogue to truly work, each group member must take responsibility to "co-hold" the intent of the group and to focus on discovering and supporting the Highest Good. Each participant must also strive to relate to other people with compassion, forgiveness, and love. The social worker models this kind of responsibility. She helps the group start to dialogue and then her most important task is often to get out of the way so that the group can develop its own collective consciousness.

CONSCIOUS SERVICE

Conscious service is the intentional use of the whole body–mind–spirit—which includes the physical, emotional, cognitive, social, and spiritual dimensions of development—to promote the Highest Good of other people, other living things, and the ecosystems that support all life. From a spiritual perspective, everything in the Cosmos is a part of one *really big* body–mind–spirit system. From such a perspective, all service is actually self-care.

The ultimate goal of conscious service is to foster a collective consciousness that includes all of humanity. Such a consciousness would enable humankind to develop the wisdom and cooperation necessary to reduce unnecessary suffering, provide basic needs for everyone, and co-create a global Community of Universal Diversity.

Thus, conscious service is not just a motivation of the helping professions, but it is also a *goal* of the helping professions. The social worker models conscious service so that his clients will follow his example and live more in service to others as well. A person does not have to be a social worker or a nurse to live the path of service. Any profession and any life provides ample daily opportunities for service to others.

■ ■ ■ ■ ■ ■

BOX 9.3

ELEMENTS AND EXAMPLES IN CONSCIOUS SERVICE

Awareness of another's suffering	I see that Bill, someone in the office, is in distress.
Compassion for that suffering	I wish that Bill had peace of mind.
Right actions that relieve suffering	I offer Bill a smile and a compliment, even though he is struggling.
Evaluation of the results	Bill smiles back and seems to feel a little better.

Conscious service can be thought of as helping on the personal level. Everyone has opportunities for individual service. The social worker encourages the client to take advantage of such opportunities to help others (see Box 9.3). For example, if a client is a college student, the social worker might ask him if there is another student who is too alone, or who needs some kind of support, or who requires other assistance. If the client is an elderly person, the social worker might ask her how she could be a model for the younger people in her family, or how she could teach everyone in the family something important about love or life.

CONSCIOUS ACTIVISM

Conscious activism is service that intentionally strives to change the structure of families, institutions, and communities for the purpose of fostering the Highest Good. It is based on the wisdom of collective consciousness, because collective consciousness is often more likely to discover the Highest Good than any single person's individual consciousness (see Box 9.4).

■ ■ ■ ■ ■ ■

BOX 9.4

ELEMENTS AND EXAMPLES IN CONSCIOUS ACTIVISM

The group forms around a shared intent.	A group of people agree to engage in conscious dialogue in response to concerns that a gay man was murdered in the community, following a series of violent attacks on gay men. Although about half the participants believe that homosexuality is a sin, everyone shares the intent to stop the escalating violence.
The Highest Good is identified through collective consciousness.	The group of people begin a process of conscious dialogue. They reach a consensus that the community is deeply split over this issue and that the Highest Good would be to offer, promote, and model alternatives to violence.

The right actions that will foster the Highest Good are identified through collective consciousness.	Through continuing conscious dialogue, the group of people agree that the local churches will sponsor a series of dialogues in the community, at which various people in conflict will engage in conscious dialogue with each other and the audience.
The community collectively implements right actions.	The group initiates the "Bridges across Differences" program. The meetings are rotated each month between different churches. Each month, the sponsoring church provides advertising, room, and light refreshments.
The community collectively evaluates the results.	At the end of the year, violence toward sexual minorities is down by over 50 percent. Interestingly, overall violent crimes have also decreased, although the causes of these changes remains unclear.

Conscious activism is an opportunity for a group of people to work together to better understand and support the Highest Good. It can be challenging because the group functions best when it learns conscious dialogue. It can also be very rewarding because new friends and new community can be created, and the collective consciousness of many people can lead to more effective service in a community.

TRANSFORMATIONS OF COUPLES, FAMILIES, INSTITUTIONS, AND COMMUNITIES

Conscious intimacy, dialogue, service, and activism can help foster the collective consciousness that can help transform families, institutions, and communities.

Couple Transformations

The social worker can help couples develop conscious intimacy and conscious dialogue in their relationship. These methods can help foster simultaneous transformations both in the relationship and in the individual lives of each partner. When transformations occur in couples, both partners become more accepting and loving of each other as their relationship becomes a small but vital Community of Spiritual Diversity.

CASE STUDY 9.2
COUPLE TRANSFORMATION

A couple comes to see the social worker at the Family Therapy Clinic. They have been living together for six years. One woman says that although there was excitement and closeness at first, now all they seem to do is fight. Her partner agrees and adds that she has been considering leaving the relationship but wanted to give counseling a try first. The social worker has the women talk about their expectations for the relationship. Although both expected physical and emotional intimacy, they had not talked about developing cognitive, social, and spiritual intimacy. They discuss the meanings of all these terms and then engage in office work and homework.

The couple starts to develop cognitive intimacy by practicing talking in front of the social worker about what they both want and do not want in the relationship. The social worker gives them a homework assignment to spend two different kinds of social time together during the next week. They are to take a walk in nature without talking at all and they are to spend a night out with friends. Then they are to discuss their experiences with each other before the next session.

The couple begins to develop spiritual intimacy by each sharing in front of the social worker the story of their own spiritual history with each other. Then, during the week, they are to co-design a spiritual ritual that symbolizes their dream of their relationship, practice the ritual, and then share it with the social worker at the next session.

The social worker discovers there still are unresolved conflicts in the relationship. One of the women wants to have children and the other does not. In later sessions, the social worker has the couple practice conscious dialogue, in which they share their emotional, cognitive, and spiritual processes about this issue with each other.

Family Transformations

The social worker can also work with families to foster their conscious intimacy and dialogue. Here, the focus may be on transforming parent–child relationships and intergenerational patterns. The social worker strives to help the family become a Community of Spiritual Diversity.

CASE STUDY 9.3
FAMILY TRANSFORMATION

The Green family comes to the Family Center with the presenting problem that Billy was caught with marijuana at his junior high. The social worker determines that, like most families, the Greens have not yet co-created a Community of Spiritual Diversity. The father has been carrying on a secret affair and the mother is secretly addicted to prescription drugs. Billy's older sister, Marcia, is a straight-A student in high school, but she is silently bulemic and depressed. Billy's younger sister, Jane, who just turned 13, is very quiet and socially withdrawn. Billy seems in some ways the healthiest member of the family, a kind of "ugly duckling" who has given up trying to be a duck because he is not one.

The social worker talks about how often people feel like they are ugly ducklings or misfits in their own families. She asks each family member to talk about his or her own loneliness. The conversation begins on the cognitive realm of intimacy, but soon moves into the realms of emotional and spiritual intimacy. The family is beginning to be more "real" with each other as they practice conscious intimacy.

The father and mother are anxious that their three children become successful, which seems to mean that Billy develop a career that makes a lot of money and that the girls attract handsome well-off husbands. The social worker has each family member consider what his or her own value hierarchy is, and then they practice conscious dialogue, sharing these hierarchies with each other. This process seems to help reduce some of the underlying tension at home, as real thoughts and feelings are honestly shared and heard for the first time.

The family also practices conscious dialogue around the topic of personal strengths, limitations, and addictions. This is a difficult topic, and the parents decide to move into couple counseling when the material gets into subjects that they do not want to share with their children.

Institutional Transformations

The social worker sometimes works with institutions to help them become true Communities of Spiritual Diversity. The work is similar to the work with couples and families, but because there are more people involved, the social worker structures the process back and forth between large and small sized subgroupings.

CASE STUDY 9.4
INSTITUTIONAL TRANSFORMATION

The social worker is asked to facilitate a group of faculty at the Department of Counseling at Purple College. The President of Purple College, Dr. Orange, is concerned about all the intradepartmental bickering that is going on in the department. At the first meeting, the social worker sits with the faculty and starts to explain what conscious dialogue is. Unfortunately, some of the more outspoken members argue with her about definitions and other intellectual issues.

The social worker notices her own countertransference, which is an underidentification with the most outspoken faculty. She works with the dean of the troubled department to choose six faculty who are capable of conscious dialogue and she sets up a "circle in a circle" format in which these six talk with each other while the rest of the faculty sit silently and watch (often a difficult task for academics). She does not try to work with conscious intimacy because she realizes that such closeness is not a goal for most faculty in the department, nor is it a goal of President Orange's administration that is paying her. Luckily, the technique works. The six faculty, representing a cross-section of the faculty, are able to model conscious dialogue for the rest of their colleagues (with a little guidance from the facilitator).

The rest is history. The department became more collegial, their publishing then increased, and the school became one of the top ten schools listed in the next year's popular magazines. Dr. Orange's salary was increased by a thankful Board of Trustees.

Community Transformations

Increasingly, skilled spiritually oriented social workers will also be asked to help facilitate conflicts and other challenges between large groups of people in local and even global communities. Like transformational work with institutions, this work will focus on teaching and leading conscious dialogue. Multiple structures will also be used, such as the small and large group formats, as well as multiple methods of communication, including television, radio, and the Internet. In many large-scale situations, a team of facilitators may be required to do the job.

CASE STUDY 9.5
COMMUNITY TRANSFORMATION

The state has been polarized over environmental issues. Both sides have recently escalated their attacks on each other, not only in the media but also out in the wild lands. The latest incident turned violent as an old mining road closed to off highway vehicles (OHV) by a judge was reopened illegally by a group of angry ranchers and OHV enthusiasts. Fistfights erupted at the gate and someone fired shots into the crowd. Three people were wounded, including a small boy.

The social worker and her team of facilitators were called in by the governor's office to work with the various parties to help stop the violence and find reasonable compromises. The facilitation team travels down to the area of the state where the most intense conflicts have occurred.

A dozen leaders representing each viewpoint are identified through meetings with local authorities. All 24 people attend a weekend retreat in which they learn and practice the skills of conscious dialogue. The various events are scheduled. The "dirty two-dozen," as the media starts to call them, do a two-hour conscious dialogue for a local TV station. Then they break up into four facilitation teams and they go out and help lead dialogues in the various local communities, each group accompanied by at least one professional facilitator for the first few times.

Gradually, the violence decreases and the model seems to be working. Each small community develops its own conscious dialogue group and most people in the troubled area of the state seem to feel that a "win-win" compromise is possible. Eventually, areas for OHVs and areas that are OHV-free are set up. Education and enforcement of the new regulations are done by a committee with representatives from both sides of the issue.

RELIGIOUS, SPIRITUAL, AND SCIENTIFIC FUNDAMENTALISM

The Threat of Traditional Fundamentalism

The spiritually oriented social worker is aware of how fundamentalism threatens the well-being of people at the family, community, and global levels. For example, an individual takes a fundamentalist view when she identifies with the rituals, beliefs, and doctrines that she has held, and does not tolerate (is blind to the divinity of) people who hold other doctrines, rituals, and beliefs. From a spiritual perspective, fundamentalism is thus an imbalance of consciousness in which the individual operates primarily at the personal level. From a psychological perspective (see

TABLE 9.1   Examples of Fundamentalist Views in Religion, Spirituality, Science

	VIEW OF SELF	VIEW OF THE OTHER
Religion	My religion's God is the only God.	Your religion's God is untrue.
Spirituality	My beliefs are the only true belief.	Your beliefs are wrong.
Science	My school of thought is the only truth.	Your school of thought is wrong.

Chapter 7), such consciousness is "ruled" by the parental ego state (or "super-ego") that in part regulates behavior, judges what is right or wrong, and takes ownership of the outside world. A person can hold fundamental views about anything. As shown in Table 9.1, the social worker may see clients with fundamentalist views about religion, spirituality, or science.

Fundamentalist views may lead to violence and oppression for several reasons. First, the belief in an ultimate truth can seem to justify any behavior in defense of that truth, including violent verbal and physical expressions. Second, when one believes in an ultimate truth, one also tends to devalue people who do not hold that belief, which can seem to justify the use of violence against them. Third, fundamentalism tends to create theocractic families and communities with power in the hands of a ruling elite, putting people with less power at increased risk of oppression and other maltreatment. Fourth, within the larger community, there is a tendency for people with fundamentalist views to isolate themselves and their families from people who have different views, and social isolation is associated with higher rates of domestic violence and child maltreatment.

From a spiritual perspective, the extent to which a person's views are "extreme" is not necessarily as dangerous as *how* the person expresses those extreme views. The social worker becomes concerned when fundamentalism leads to the oppression or maltreatment of other people.

Conscious Fundamentalism

The social worker has an alternative vision of fundamentalism, *conscious fundamentalism*, that can provide the sense of safety, community, and shared values, traditions, rituals, and doctrines that many people want, but that is also a democratic and nonviolent Community of Spiritual and Universal Diversity. Table 9.2 supplies some examples of the differences between traditional fundamentalism and this alternative fundamentalism for which the spiritually oriented social worker advocates. As the fundamentalist client becomes more conscious, she does not necessarily give up her beliefs but rather she changes how she relates with other people.

The social worker uses all the techniques of the collective consciousness paradigm to work with fundamentalism. She strives to help people become more mindful of their reactions to the rapid change that is characteristic of this era of

TABLE 9.2   Re-Visioning Fundamentalism: Examples of How Characteristics Might Change as Traditional Fundamentalism Is Replaced with Conscious Fundamentalism

CHARACTERISTIC	TRADITIONAL FUNDAMENTALISM	CONSCIOUS FUNDAMENTALISM
Consciousness	Mostly personal consciousness	All levels of consciousness
Relating style	Judgment, control	Kindness, forgiveness
Governing style	Theocracy	Democracy
Leaders	Patriarchal leadership	Women and men as equal partners
Safety	Safety through war	Safety through peace
Response to change	Fear, rigidity, control	Openness, acceptance, creativity
Communication	Condemn opposing viewpoints	Dialogue opposing viewpoints
My truth	My truth is the only truth	My truth is sacred to me; respect me
Other truths	Your truths are false	I respect your truth as sacred to you
Community	Limited acceptance of diversity	Spiritual and Universal Diversity
Nature	We own and use the Earth	We share and protect the Earth

human history. She gives families and communities alternative ways to respond to rapid change so that their fundamentalism can be more conscious and result in the co-creation of Communities of Spiritual and Universal Diversity. She refuses to be hostile toward fundamentalistic individuals and communities, whether she finds them in the university, the church, or the New Age organization. However, she is also just as strongly committed to helping them become democratic and nonviolent organizations. She is willing to work on the individual, couple, family, group, and community levels to move traditional fundamentalism to conscious fundamentalism.

Issues of Social Worker Diversity

The effective social worker recognizes that collective-consciousness methods are challenging, and that he must do his own personal "homework" if he stays in the field. Such homework might include attendance at workshops where he studies his own issues and values and practices conscious intimacy and dialogue. Many social workers of collective consciousness may also consult with spiritually oriented therapists of their own so that they stay aware of their own inner processes.

Not all communities are open to doing this work. Some, especially fundamentalist communities, may view any spiritually oriented interventions as hostile, evil, or even "satanic." The spiritually oriented social worker strives to be forgiving and compassionate toward individuals and groups that are hostile toward his work. He does this because he believes that, as Martin Luther King once said, forgiveness is the only attitude that can change the hearts of one's enemies, whether they like it or not.

Issues of Ecosystem Diversity

The social worker realizes that collective-conscious work can increase a client's sensitivity to the well-being of other people, living things, and ecosystems. The social worker uses the work to support the Highest Good of the ecosystems that support all life.

STUDY QUESTIONS

1. What is collective consciousness? How is it different from individual consciousness? How are the two related? Have you ever had a personal experience of collective consciousness, where you felt that many minds were able to identify and help co-create the Highest Good? If so, describe it.

2. What is conscious intimacy? How is it different from intimacy?

3. Do you believe that conscious intimacy is possible in your life? In everyone's life? What areas of intimacy (e.g., emotional, spiritual) are you the most comfortable with? In which areas are you the least comfortable?

4. What is conscious dialogue? How is it different from dialogue? Why is it important today? What local or global issues do you think most require conscious dialogue to resolve?

5. What is traditional fundamentalism? What are the dangers of such thinking? What groups or communities do you know have fundamental characteristics?

6. How is conscious fundamentalism different from traditional fundamentalism? How can a social worker help foster conscious fundamentalism?

RESOURCES

Dalai Lama. (1999). *Ethics for the new millennium.* New York: Riverhead Books.
    The Dalai Lama offers his ethics, which can help inform the spiritually oriented social worker in his or her challenging work in fostering collective consciousness.
Friedman, M. (1974). *The confirmation of otherness in family, community, and society.* New York: Pilgrim.
    This text describes the rationale and characteristics of dialogue, which the author calls "confirmation of otherness."

CHAPTER 10

ECO-CONSCIOUSNESS

ECO-CONSCIOUSNESS

Just as methods drawn from the spirit-embodied paradigm help foster the body–mind–spirit connection in all human beings, eco-consciousness methods help foster the body–mind–spirit–environment connection in all living things. Methods of transformations are used that support the natural healing that occurs in human interaction with other living and life-supporting things in the ecosystems. Eco-consciousness also is used to transform human families, institutions, and communities into Communities of Universal Diversity that support the Highest Good of all living things and the ecosystems that support them. In this text, the word *environment* is used inclusively, to contain not only the natural ecosystem but also human-made or human-modified structures (parks, buildings, cities, etc.) and human communities.

There are five kinds of transformational methods in eco-consciousness described in this chapter:

1. Healing the body–mind–spirit-environment connection

2. Eco-dialogue

3. Nature as spiritual teacher

4. Creating Communities of Universal Diversity

5. Service to environment

All these methods work with living and life-supporting things, which include everything in an ecosystem that a scientist would say is not alive. These methods might include visualizations involving animals, plants, and landscapes; experiences that combine therapy with interactions with nature; and activism in the service of other living and life-supporting things.

HEALING THE BODY–MIND–SPIRIT ENVIRONMENT CONNECTION

The social worker is aware of her own body–mind–spirit–environment (BMSE) connection, and works to heal that connection in her life. Her own personal transformations increase her sensitivity to the health of the BMSE connection in other people. She realizes that many if not most people today spend relatively little time in nature, have little awareness of the plants and animals that live in their local ecosystem, and no longer have sacred plants, animals, and landscapes that they use for healing. She knows that from an eco-consciousness perspective, such disconnections are unhealthy for people.

The social worker assesses the health (wholeness) of the client's BMSE connection, using indicators such as those illustrated in Table 10.1. Since every person has a unique landscape of elements in his or her own BMSE connection, the social worker needs to be open to different kinds of indicators of well-being.

The social worker helps heal the BMSE connection in her client through transformation methods that build awareness and co-create new rituals (see the case study on page 135). Awareness-building methods help the client become aware of the health of his own BMSE connection. The social worker can build such awareness through work in the office or through experiential work with plants and animals or out in more wild environments.

TABLE 10.1   Some Indicators Used in Assessing the Body–Mind–Spirit–Environment Connection

DIMENSION	SOME INDICATORS THAT ELEMENTS OF THE DIMENSION HAVE BECOME DISCONNECTED (SPLIT-OFF OR LOST)	SOME INDICATORS THAT ELEMENTS OF THE DIMENSION HAVE BEEN RECONNECTED (HEALED)
Body	Lack of exercise Poor dietary care of the body Inability to hear what the body needs	Balanced exercise and rest Well-balanced diet Ability to hear body's needs
Mind	Little mental self-discipline Predominance of negative thoughts Little loving intent to self and world	Ability to discipline mind Predominance of positive thoughts Great loving intent to self and world
Spirit	Reacts negatively to pain Uses addiction to avoid pain Stuck in one level of consciousness	Reacts with equanimity to experiences Uses mindfulness in dealing with pain Can intentionally shift consciousness
Environment	No sacred landscapes, animals, plants Harms ecosystem more than helps Cannot dialogue with plants, animals	Has sacred landscapes, animals, plants Helps ecosystem more than harms Loving dialogue with plants, animals

Cross-Dimensional Interactions

The social worker appreciates how there are always cross-dimensional interactions between any dimension and the other three dimensions. He helps the client understand and take responsibility for how the client takes care of her body, mind, spirit, and environment. From an eco-consciousness perspective, all people are responsible for their own individual impact on themselves, other people, other living things, and ecosystems. Every thought a person thinks, every meal a person eats, every interaction a person has with his or her environment has an impact on the well-being of the BMSE connection (see Table 10.2).

Building Awareness through Methods in the Office

In the office, the social worker can explain to the client what the BMSE connection is and why it is important. The social worker can also help increase awareness through transrational methods. For example, a client might be asked to draw a picture of his BMSE connection, in which he illustrates, without using words, which elements are most and least integrated.

TABLE 10.2 Examples of Cross-Dimensional Interactions in Healing the Body–Mind–Spirit–Environment Connection

DIMENSION	EXAMPLES OF HARMFUL CONNECTIONS	EXAMPLES OF HEALING CONNECTIONS
Body	*Mind:* No sleep reduces mental clarity. *Spirit:* Sexual denial can be dispiriting. *Environ:* Heavy meat diet increases food industry that stresses environment.	*Mind:* Exercise improves mental clarity. *Spirit:* Good posture assists meditation. *Environ:* Eating more raw local vegetables reduces wasteful food transportation.
Mind	*Body:* Worry gives me headaches. *Spirit:* Denial can fuel addiction. *Environ:* Devaluing nonhuman life fosters cruel farming methods.	*Body:* Affirmations help athletic output. *Spirit:* Awareness supports compassion. *Environ:* Belief in BMSE connection supports protection of wild ecosystems.
Spirit	*Body:* Lack of faith fosters distress. *Mind:* Resentments foster bitterness. *Environ:* Blindness to spirit in all things leads to harm to ecosystems.	*Body:* Prayer can help heal my body. *Mind:* Meditation brings peace of mind. *Environ:* Reverence for sacred landscapes fosters protection of resources.
Environment	*Body:* Artificial climates impact my body. *Mind:* Avoiding nature is depressing. *Spirit:* Living indoors is dispiriting.	*Body:* Tending garden centers my body. *Mind:* Animals and plants offer wisdom. *Spirit:* Nature is the great healer.

Biophilia and Ecophilia

The term *biophilia* (see Wilson, 2002, reference at end of chapter) was invented to describe the innate affiliation each person has with other living things. Biophilia explains why people love gardens, sunsets, pets, and homes next to beautiful forests.

From the eco-consciousness perspective, people also have an innate affiliation with and love for natural ecosystems, which we could call *ecophilia* (see Wilson, 2002, reference at end of chapter). Thus, ecophilia is a more inclusive term that suggests that people have an affinity to everything in the Cosmos. Ecophilia explains why people all over the world have wisdom traditions that incorporate interactions with natural, sacred landscapes. In the United States, many people have tried to affiliate with the beautiful landscapes by buying homes in the suburbs, an effort based on the misguided theory that it is possible to carve out a piece of nature to live on without impacting the whole ecosystem. Perhaps if the landscapes we loved were sacred to us, we would not be destroying them to such an extent. The social worker educates the client about biophilia and ecophilia and asks the client to explore whether these qualities apply to him.

Biognosis and Ecognosis

The term *biognosis* (see Wilson, 2002, reference at end of chapter) was invented to describe the working knowledge that informs the wise use of plants, animals, and ecosystems as sacred medicines. Here, the word *medicine* is meant to be inclusive of all substances and energies that may foster health and healing. Prior to the historical movement away from nature and "rural" living into permanent city life, all of our ancestors depended on biognosis in their diets and health care.

From the eco-consciousness perspective, people also have a need for knowledge of how to use the Earth and its sacred landscapes as medicine, which we could call *geognosis*. *Geognosis* is a more inclusive term than *biognosis*, because it suggests the importance of knowledge of everything in the Cosmos as potential medicine. Such knowledge informs people's wise use of minerals, soil, water, air, landscapes, and other resources in the ecosystem for health and healing. The social worker educates the client about biognosis and ecognosis and asks the client to explore how these qualities might apply to him.

Sacred Internal and External Landscapes

From the perspective of eco-consciousness, in today's world most human beings have lost their connection with their animal nature. A person's animal nature can be thought of as the elements of her body that she shares with other nonhuman animals. Our animal nature can also be thought of as a voice and expression of Creative Spirit. Similarly, most human beings have also lost their connection with the external, natural world, and our natural environments can also be seen as voices and expressions of Creative Spirit.

When a person makes her or his animal nature or the natural world sacred, the person holds an attitude of respect and reverence for them. When the client decides to make her body and her natural world sacred, she uses her body and nature as bridges to Creative Spirit. For example, if a client sees her body as sacred, then she listens to and respects the wisdom of her body. Whether her body is tired, excited, sad, or ill, she responds as if Creative Spirit is talking to her. Similarly, if a client sees nature as sacred, then mountains, seasons, storms, and stars are all expressions to use to make spiritual meaning.

Building Awareness with Plants, Animals, and Ecosystems

Another way to foster awareness of the BMSE connection is to take the client, with her permission, on a field trip. Field trips can go to any location where there are other living and life-supporting things with which she can interact. The social worker can ask the client to go on a walking meditation in the park or on a canyon trail, for example. Or the client can go to visit a horse ranch or the city animal shelter.

CASE STUDY 10.1
HEALING THE BMSE CONNECTION

Eight people signed up for the social worker's new spirituality group called "Exploring the Body–Mind–Spirit–Environment Connection." The social worker begins the group by asking each person to do an imaginative journey in which each person watches again the earliest memory he or she has of nature. Then each client is asked to share his or her story with the group. Most of the stories came from early childhood. Most of the clients shared very positive memories; some even called their experiences magical. The social worker then asked the group to talk about how these childhood experiences are similar or different from the experiences they now have as adults in nature. Most of the clients said that they have lost that sense of wonder and magic about nature. One woman expressed the opinion that "school beats any sense of wonder and imagination out of you." Another said, "It's not cool in adolescence to have a sense of wonder; you're supposed to be cool."

The group takes a field trip to a canyon near town in their next session. It is springtime and the social worker has everyone find a comfortable spot to lie on the grass. Then she asks them to take a gentle walk and reflect on springtime. They are asked to be mindful about how springtime impacts the way their bodies feel, the way their minds think, and the way their souls experience the world. The discussion reveals that there are both individual differences and similarities. Most of the clients say they tend to feel more energy in their bodies, they become more optimistic and extroverted, and their souls open up to new growth.

The next session, the social worker has everyone stand in a circle in the group room with their shoes off. After a movement warmup, the social worker asks each client to spend 15 minutes creating a series of movements that describes the current state of his or her, personal body–mind–spirit–environment connection. Then each client dances in front of the group. After each individual dance, the group circles the person who just danced and does a spontaneous healing dance, during which each person holds the intent of health and healing for the dancer.

ECO-DIALOGUE

Conscious dialogue between people was described in Chapter 9. *Eco-dialogue* is communication between a person or persons and another living thing or a part of an ecosystem. Eco-dialogue, like conscious dialogue, involves many ways of "talking" and "listening." However, nonverbal and transrational communications may be more prevalent in eco-dialogue. Such communications might include sensory, emotional, or intestinal ("gut") intuitions. From the eco-consciousness perspective, the collective consciousness that can arise from eco-dialogue is most likely to co-create the wisdom needed to resolve conflicts between the intentions of people and the needs and well-being of other living and life-supporting things.

Many people might ask, How is any communication with trees and mountains possible, much less a dialogue that can create wisdom? Our ancestors not only believed that such communications were possible, many of them had such conversations on a daily basis. They believed that everything in the Cosmos was an expression of Creative Spirit, and they listened to what the animals, plants, rocks, mountains, and stars had to say to them. Western civilized people gave up that viewpoint as we came to believe in the scientific view that the Cosmos is more like a giant machine than a complex, living organism.

The wise social worker knows that many of her clients would prefer living in a Cosmos that is an expression of spirit with which they can interact and communicate. The social worker also realizes that the scientific and spiritual models of the Cosmos are not mutually exclusive. None of the leading theories of physics—including M Theory, String Theory, Loop Quantum Gravity, Quantum Mechanics, or General Relativity—rule out the possibility that all matter and energy in fact have a Spiritual dimension or basis. Our reality often appears to have many seeming dualities that defy our rational minds. The social worker does not necessarily feel it is her job to resolve these mysteries for herself or her client.

CASE STUDY 10.2
ECO-DIALOGUE

One client has been working on his spiritual development with his social worker for years. He came in for an individual session and told his social worker about an experience he had while on a camping trip in the high desert. It turns out that he was hiking with his girlfriend when he stopped by an unusually large juniper tree. He closed his eyes spontaneously and touched the trunk of the giant tree. To his surprise, he saw in his mind's eye an image of a long black scar on the tree. When he walked around the tree a minute later, he saw a scar on the other side of the trunk, apparently from a fire or lightning strike. "I told my girlfriend," he explained to the social worker, "that I think I felt the tree's suffering." "You are becoming more open to spirit," replied the social worker. "Yes, and I think that by feeling the tree's pain, and caring about the tree, I somehow helped it," said the client.

Rather, the social worker tries to help the client find meaning in and appreciation of the mysteries that we are given in our lives.

Eco-dialogue involves two processes: "talking" and "listening." Talking to other animals, plants, and nonliving things may be easy, since people seem to do it all the time. The social worker sees her clients talk to their pets, their flowers, the clouds, and their cars, for example. Listening may be what is most difficult to us uppity-humans, who believe we are so much smarter than everything else.

The first step in listening to nonhuman entities is to have the intent to become open to listening. Being open to listening means that the client is willing to look at his own projections, prejudices, and expectations about what other living and non-living beings might "say." The next step is to listen, with body, mind, and spirit.

CASE STUDY 10.3
ECO-DIALOGUE II (CONTINUATION OF CASE STUDY 10.1)

In another session, the social worker took her group out for a weekend in the wilderness. They camped in a broad canyon with many side canyons of slick rock filled with stands of ponderosa trees. The social worker asked each client to set up his or her sleeping bag at a location that felt like a "power spot." Later, at sunset, the group gathered by the social worker's sleeping spot. "Now I want you each to tell me what it was about your spot that drew you to it," began the social worker. "Try to describe how your body, mind, and spirit reacted to the spot. Try to give the spot a voice, and talk about what you hear." The first volunteer said, "I picked a spot on a flat rock right below a red cliff. It felt to me that it was the place where the rock was slowly dissolving into sand. I am dissolving slowly also, my 'old self' is being replaced with something bigger that I still do not understand."

NATURE AS SPIRITUAL TEACHER

From the eco-consciousness perspective, everything in nature has a spiritual basis and everything can thus be a spiritual teacher. The term *nature* is used in an inclusive sense here to include all natural and human-influenced ecosystems. There are few, if any, locations on Earth that have not been influenced by the activities of people.

Journeying into Nature

The social worker can work with clients to not only listen to other living and life-supporting things but also to imagine *being* other living and life-supporting things. When a client is suffering, often there is something in nature that is comforting and healing for her. The client is asked to notice what things most attract her, or what things have appeared in her environment recently. Box 10.1 illustrates four steps that can be used to do an imaginative journey into nature. The same steps can be used with a mountain or a stream.

BOX 10.1

JOURNEYING IN NATURE: FOUR STEPS AND EXAMPLES

Begin with my intent.	I saw a hawk on my walk this morning. I want to learn what kind of medicine the hawk has for me today.
Open and let go.	I am aware of my own patterns. I have not dealt with stress well this month. Today I am in a hurry and worried about work.
Focus and imagine.	I relax and close my eyes. I imagine the hawk flying as I saw it this morning. I imagine I am the hawk flying.
Be aware and imitate.	I notice how the hawk seems to think and feel about stress. As a hawk I can see the big picture. All the little things will be taken care of. As a hawk I do not hang on to self-importance. I am part of everything, living in the moment, soaring. I like the medicine.

CREATING COMMUNITIES OF UNIVERSAL DIVERSITY

The social worker feels a responsibility to help foster Communities of Universal Diversity in which people value all life forms and work to enhance the well-being of all life and the ecosystems that support them. The social worker can play many helping roles, including that of therapist, educator, and advocate, when he works toward helping families, institutions, and communities become Communities of Universal Diversity. The process begins with conscious dialogue around the issues in the community, during which awareness of problems and possible solutions is increased. After consensus is reached about the Highest Good, a project is initiated and then evaluated.

CASE STUDY 10.4
A FAMILY BECOMES A COMMUNITY OF UNIVERSAL DIVERSITY

The Blue family came for family therapy at the Pleasant Valley Counseling Center. Like most families in Pleasant Valley, the Blues are affluent and live in a 4500 square foot home on the edge of the foothills in the exclusive Very Pleasant Valley Estates. The presenting problem is that the Blues are blue. Both parents seem to be moderately depressed, as is their only child, Beatrice. The family psychiatrist recommended they see a counselor in addition to the psychotropic medications they all take.

The social worker finds no suicidal ideation in the family. He determines that the family has little conscious intimacy with each other—much more time is spent with the television than with each other. The father is very successful financially, but still works 50 to 60 hours a week. The mother drinks by herself and abuses prescription drugs every evening before she goes to bed. The daughter gets good grades in Pleasant Valley Intermediate School, but she is socially withdrawn and has chronic stomach pain and headaches.

The social worker gives each family member a chart that contains the five methods of eco-consciousness work (see page 131) and another identical chart with empty cells. She asks each member to write down his or her own indicators of body, mind, spirit, and environment on the empty chart. Then they discuss the results. It turns out that everyone in the family identified split off elements of their body, mind, spirit, and environment. They are all struck with the similarities in their charts: Most of the cells are full of indicators of missing elements.

Next, the social worker begins to offer the family ways to reintegrate the missing elements. On the body level, everyone in the family begins an aerobic exercise program and a healthy diet heavy on raw vegetables. On the mind level, the family begins taking lessons from the social worker in simple mindfulness exercises. On the spirit level, the social worker talks with the family about the healing that can come from practicing mindful service in their home and community. Each member is asked to identify and complete some kind of service each week. Finally, on the environment level, the social worker asks the family how they would like to reconnect with the beauty that is literally in their backyard. Combining their spiritual and environmental levels into a service project, they decide to build a public access sidewalk from the street to the land behind their house. They then help organize the building of a trail up into the foothills above the house. They end up meeting and working with their neighbors and larger community in related service projects.

In evaluating his cases a year later, the social worker finds that his additional use of a BMSE connection approach with his families was more successful than his use of only traditional family therapy approaches.

CASE STUDY 10.5
AN INSTITUTION AND COMMUNITY BECOME A COMMUNITY
OF UNIVERSAL DIVERSITY

A new school counselor is hired to begin work at the Gray Concrete High School (GCHS). The new social worker discovers that the youth in this school have some of the lowest test scores in the entire city and state. Families in the area served by GCHS generally have low income; many are below the poverty line. There is also a pattern of racial tension in the neighborhood.

The social worker decides to invest half of her time developing and working with groups of parents and children from the community. She is able to get donations of food from local businesses and she opens up the school for the first Community Night. Using conscious dialogue, the social worker asks the attending families to talk about what they need in order to improve the GCHS neighborhood. The priorities that emerge are crime control, better education, and more quality public space.

Next, the social worker initiates focus groups, using conscious dialogue, with students at GCHS and discovers that students want to help the neighborhood achieve its goals. She sets up a voluntary program where all students can, with parental permission, get school credit for doing volunteer work and then writing about it. Student response is enthusiastic. One of the most popular activities has to do with co-creating a more beautiful and "green" environment. Students create a community garden, plant trees, and help repair and improve the grounds around the school. The community follows the students' lead and soon increasing numbers of adults and younger children get involved.

In evaluating the project a year later, the social worker and school administrators and teachers discover grades and test scores have gone up and local crime has dropped. People have also noticed a drop in littering and an increase in public use of the parks and school grounds.

SERVICE TO ENVIRONMENT

From the perspective of eco-consciousness, when a person lives a commitment to service to the environment in which she lives, the individual herself, her community, and the entire ecosystem all benefit. As the individual gets involved in activities that go beyond her own immediate problems and desires, she often discovers that her own life satisfaction and well-being have been enhanced. The well-being of other human and nonhuman living things is also enhanced when the individual works to enhance environmental health.

Family Values

The social worker models and teaches spiritual values with respect to every part of the body–mind–spirit–environment. These values might include respect, gratitude, connectedness, Sacred Mystery, meaning making, imagination, and compassion. The social worker has *respect* for all living and life-supporting things and he sees them all as expressions of Creative Spirit. *Gratitude* is a thankful perspective that the social worker can choose to have toward reality. The social worker also values his *connectedness*, or relatedness, with every living and life-supporting thing. There is an appreciation for the *Sacred Mystery* in the beauty and transverbal language of nature. The social worker uses his *imagination* in working to create *meanings* in his experience of nature and the environment. And, he practices *compassion* for all living and life-supporting things, believing that his sensitivity to suffering helps heal the Earth.

These values are *family values* when the idea of "family" is expanded to include our biggest family, which is all human and nonhuman life on the planet, as well as the ecosystems that support life. The social worker strives to help the client expand notions of family, because a more inclusive definition of family supports the Highest Good of all people on earth.

Local Community Activism

Local community activism is directed toward challenges in the social worker's proximate living area. Since the work is often done with people in the social worker's own neighborhood, county, or city, this kind of activism may build on existing relationships and organizations that the social worker already has. Eco-dialogue is an integral part of this kind of activism, from this perspective, since the spiritual power of many people is greater than of few. The social worker first strives to help people identify social policy changes that are needed to foster the BMSE connection in all people in the local community. The action steps are collectively planned and implemented.

Radical Forgiveness

In any form of spiritually based activism, one of the biggest action tools is *radical forgiveness*. Rather than using bullets or bombs, radical forgiveness utilizes many of the methods of transformation described in this text, including mindfulness, compassion, love, and service. Radical forgiveness is used to combat the unwise use of power, such as when people fail to respect and protect the well-being of living and life-supporting things.

Radical forgiveness is radical because it is not only nonviolent but it is also forgiving, and can therefore get at the roots of violence and heal them. The spiritually oriented social worker appreciates that forgiveness can change the hearts of other people. Perhaps forgiveness is one of the most important, perhaps the most important, choice a person can make in his or her life. Radical forgiveness not only transforms other people's hearts but it also transforms the person who forgives. Radical forgiveness is a body–mind–spirit–environment process. Much like conscious dialogue, radical forgiveness involves respect for other people, regardless of what they have or have not done.

CASE STUDY 10.6
RADICAL FORGIVENESS AND CONSCIOUS DIALOGUE
IN LOCAL COMMUNITY ACTIVISM

The social worker is invited to join a task force set up by the mayor to help heal the religious tension in the city. Like many communities, the city has a dominant religion, the XYZ Church, which enjoys powerful political and social advantages. Many people affiliated with other religious groups, as well as many unaffiliated with religion, have resentments toward members of the XYZ Church. In turn, many members of the XYZ Church carry resentments toward people outside their faith.

The social worker suggests that the membership of the mayor's task force include not just religious diversity but also diversity of ethnicity, economic and political power, and sexual orientation. The mayor agrees. The social worker also suggested that the task force first hold public meetings where people can engage in conscious dialogue around the issue of religious diversity. The task force learned at these public meetings that people have become more concerned about learning how to live with religious diversity since a series of recent terrorist attacks, which seemed to highlight to people how religious hatred can lead to violence.

Then the task force decides to set up a "seed" Dialogue Training Group (DTG). This first DTG is composed of local religious leaders, communication experts, and civic leaders. The DTG meets twice a month for six months, rotating responsibilities for facilitation around its own membership, until members feel they are ready to help train others. In these groups, members practice conscious dialogue and radical forgiveness.

Next, members of the first seed DTG begin meeting with other groups of people. One DTG member, for example, meets with groups of high school students. Some of these students begin to form their own DTGs. Some local churches also develop DTGs of their own.

Global Community Activism

Global community activism employs methods of transformation used in local community activism, but applies them to small groups of people selected from different socioeconomic groupings, cultures, religions, and/or nations.

CASE STUDY 10.7
RADICAL FORGIVENESS AND CONSCIOUS DIALOGUE
IN GLOBAL COMMUNITY ACTIVISM

The social worker, along with professional friends, form a nonprofit group. This group's mission is to "foster radical forgiveness and conscious dialogue between global populations." Their first work is in the Middle East, where they invite 24 local leaders from a divided nation, half Muslim and half Christian, to a week-long "Forward" (rather than retreat) on the Mediterranean coast of North Africa.

The first few days are spent preparing meals together and sharing music, dance, and other rituals. Then the group begins practicing conscious dialogue and radical forgiveness. By the end of the week, the participants have made friendships across religious lines.

On the last day of the Forward meeting, participants identify projects in which each of them wants to participate to co-create positive change in their country. They stay in contact and assist each other in their projects.

Issues of Client Diversity

Not every client will be open to working with methods from the eco-consciousness paradigm. For example, some clients might believe that there is insufficient scientific evidence to support these methods. Others might object on religious grounds, perhaps believing that their God does not want them to view other animals or plants or life-supporting things as being equal to human beings. As always, the spiritually oriented social worker is respectful of these attitudes. However, the social worker is also willing to advocate for the well-being of all living and life-supporting things because she believes that it is in the Highest Good of everyone when people are good stewards of the Earth.

Issues of Social Worker Diversity

Eco-consciousness methods demand that the effective social worker be mindful of his own biases and prejudices. Just as in mindful-activism, there is a recognition in eco-consciousness that human beings seem to often have unwelcomed thoughts that can lead to destructive or self-destructive behavior. Thus, instead of trying to stop such thoughts, the wise social worker models *awareness of such thoughts, holding the intention* to promote the Highest Good, and self-discipline in *practicing right actions.* Every individual social worker will have his own unique cognitive challenges.

Issues of Ecosystem Diversity

Each group that the social worker works with will have its own unique character-istics. The social worker always practices with the attitudes of conscious intimacy and dialogue. He is also aware that there are seldom "good guys" and "bad guys" in any conflict, including environmental conflicts. Therefore, the social worker works with the intent to support the Highest Good for all living and life-support-ing things.

STUDY QUESTIONS

1. What is the body–mind–spirit–environment connection? To what extent do you think you are disconnected from the environment you live in? If a disconnect did develop, how did that occur? How does such a disconnect impact your overall well-being? What do you think you want to do about the disconnect?

2. What is eco-dialogue? Have you ever experienced eco-dialogue in your life? For example, do you think cats and dogs have emotions? What about other mammals? If so, can you sense their emotions? Can they sense yours?

3. How, if at all, has nature been a spiritual teacher for you in your life? In what ways are the teachings of nature different from the teachings you may have received from human beings?

4. Do you see an importance in creating Communities of Universal Diversity? Have you ever be-longed to such a community? Would you like to? Why or why not?

5. How might a person's service to the environment help promote the Highest Good of that per-son? Can you see a benefit in encouraging all young people to practice such service?

RESOURCES

Buhner, S. H. (2002). *The lost language of plants: The ecological importance of plant medicines to life on Earth.* White River Junction, VT: Chelsea Green Publishing.
    This book presents an interesting discussion of how natural medicines have developed for the benefit of all life on Earth.

Ingerman, S. (2000). *Medicine for the Earth: How to transform personal and environmental toxins.* New York: Harper & Row.

    This text offers suggestions on how to do healings for the Earth and ourselves.

Tompkins, P. (1973). *The secret life of plants.* New York: Harper & Row.

    An interesting exploration of the physical, emotional, and spiritual connections between plants and humans is featured.

Wilson, E. O. (2002). *The future of life.* New York: Alfred A. Knopf.

    Wilson introduced such terms as *biophilia* and *ecophilia.* Wilson is one of the leading voices supporting the new environmentalism for this new century.

CHAPTER 11

SPIRITUALLY ORIENTED PRACTICE WITH CHILDREN, YOUTH, AND FAMILIES

From a spiritual perspective, the root purpose of the family is to support the spiritual development of all family members. The traditional definition of family is expanded to include not only the people who share a common roof or ancestry (residential family) but also all other people in their local and global communities (community family) and other living and life-supporting things (ecosystem family).

From a spiritual perspective, children and youth are seen as generally more open to spiritual experience in the here and now than adults and as more self-centered and concerned with their immediate gratification and pleasure (see Table 11.1). From a transpersonal perspective, people typically change their identifications as they mature spiritually across their life spans. Children, who are born with a connection with Creative Spirit, are gradually socialized away from their common experiences of awe, magic, and mystery. They identify with nature and the family until they reach adolescence, when they identify more with their peer groups. Awe, magic, and mystery become "uncool" in the peer group, and are often replaced with the desire to experience sexuality and altered states of consciousness through the use of alcohol and other drugs.

On the one hand, then, children are seen as spiritual beings who have not yet been as socialized, as most adults are, into suppressing their natural spiritual experiences and expressions. Most families, institutions, and cultures are viewed as communities that, though often well-intentioned, nevertheless are often relatively unsafe places for children and youth to explore their spirituality. Many adults have forgotten what it is like to be young and open to Creative Spirit, and therefore may lack understanding and compassion for the spiritual curiosity and creativity of children and youth. Instead, some adults may view the spirituality of children and youth as rebellious or even as potential threats to the social order and current power structures.

On the other hand, however, children and youth have generally not yet developed a sense of identity and are not yet taking on adult-like responsibility for

TABLE 11.1   Selected Indicators of Life-Span Spiritual Development

INDICATOR	CHILDHOOD (0–12 YEARS)	ADOLESCENCE (13–19 YEARS)	EXTENDED ADOLESCENCE (20+ YEARS)	MID-ADOLESCENCE (OFTEN IN 30S OR 40S)	ADULTHOOD (HOPEFULLY BEGINS LATER)
Primary level of conscious-ness	Prepersonal	Synapse from prepersonal to personal	Personal	Synapse from personal to transpersonal	Transpersonal
Developing connection with external environment	Connection with Creative Spirit lost	Dis-identify from nature and family	Dis-identify from peers	Dis-identify from roles	Dis-identify from service, self-discipline
	Identify with nature and family	Identify with peer group	Identify with family and work roles	Identify with self-discipline and service	Identify again with Creative Spirit
Developing connection with internal environment	Connection with Creative Spirit lost	Dis-identify from magic, awe, mystery	Dis-identify from sex and intoxication	Dis-identify from wealth, beauty, fame	Dis-identify from ecstatic experience
	Identify with awe, magic, mystery	Identify with sex and intoxication	Identify with wealth, beauty, fame	Identify with ecstatic experience	Identify again with Creative Spirit

the well-being and Highest Good of their families, communities, and ecosystems. Thus, the social worker strives to prepare the child or teen to move toward increased adult-like responsibility for other living and nonliving things without losing their natural child-like ability to experience and express Creative Spirit in the here and now.

RELIGIOUS AND SPIRITUAL EDUCATION IN THE FAMILY

Education is, from a spiritual perspective, the process of *drawing out* such expressions as knowledge, wisdom, and right behaviors from a person's soul. Two ways of fostering spiritual development in the family is through religious education and spiritual education. The social worker utilizes both methods, since both are equally useful to children and each can be complementary with the other (see Table 11.2).

Religious education in the family can be seen as a process of fostering spiritual development through the interaction of the child's Religious Self with Com-

TABLE 11.2   Some Complementary Goals of Religious and Spiritual Education in the Family

RELIGIOUS EDUCATION	SPIRITUAL EDUCATION
The child is introduced to and participates in the beliefs, doctrines, and rituals of the family's religion.	The child is supported in his own natural search for, creation of, and participation in the beliefs, values, and rituals that best fit him.
The child is introduced to and explores the sacred texts and other sacred symbols of the family's religion.	The child is supported in her natural search for, creation of, and exploration of her own personal sacred symbols of spirituality.
The child learns to value and learn from a wise and loving religious Community of Spiritual and Universal Diversity.	The child learns to value and learn from a wise and loving spiritual teacher who supports his spiritual development.
The child develops her Religious Self, which includes the social skills necessary to support the Highest Good through community action.	The child develops Conscious Use of Higher Self, including compassion, wisdom, and love necessary for service in the Highest Good.

munities of Spiritual and Universal Diversity. The child may be introduced to any religion of his or her family, without any pressure to have to accept any doctrine, belief, or ritual. From this perspective, children and youth do need to know about the spiritual and religious beliefs of their parents and other family members. When children have this information, it helps them understand the behaviors of the people around them, they receive a foundation that they can use to compare themselves to as they grow, and they learn to accept spiritual and religious diversity. If children do not receive religious education, they may not develop the skills of their Religious Self enough to help co-create religious Communities of Spiritual and Universal Diversity when they are adults. The religious educator is supportive of the spiritual education that the child also receives.

In spiritual education, the child begins to explore her or his own spiritual experiences and shares them either with a mentor or teacher or in a safe community setting. Children and youth are seen as spiritual beings, generally at least as capable as adults of developing their spirituality and often much open to new spiritual experiences. The parent or mentor is accepting of the unique spiritual landscapes that each individual child discovers. The mentor also encourages the child and helps the child find meaning in her or his experiences.

Sustaining Relationship

When two people sustain a relationship, they co-create an interconnection between them that is essentially a small-sized Community of Universal Diversity. Both people strive to respect and support each other's individual and collective well-being.

There is mutual respect for each other's spirituality and religiosity. In the case of a caretaker–child relationship, the caretaker provides the child with a religious and spiritual education, but also understands that ultimately the child's spiritual and religious path may be quite different from that of the caretaker. If the family does not identify with a particular religion, then the practitioner might help the parent or caretaker educate the child about other religions that exist in his or her local and global communities.

The role of the social worker in part is to help families sustain their relationships over time. His or her role is also to support the development of the child's Religious Self, so that the child acquires the skills and values that will enable him or her to eventually help co-create Communities of Spiritual and Universal Diversity as an adult. Ideally, children learn from their caretakers how to co-create sustaining relationships with other people, regardless of each person's religious and spiritual beliefs. The social worker also encourages parents and caretakers to sustain a relationship with the child regardless of where the child might be at in his or her spiritual and religious journey, even when a child makes decisions that appear to contradict the religious beliefs and practices of the caretakers.

RELIGIOUS AND SPIRITUAL MALTREATMENT

Social workers have traditionally been involved in protecting children, youth, and vulnerable adults from various forms of maltreatment, including physical, emotional, and sexual abuse and neglect. The spiritually oriented worker also has a responsibility to protect people from religious and spiritual maltreatment, which can have a profound impact on a person's spiritual development. The social worker respects the right of every individual, family, and community to freely choose and practice the religion of their choice. The social worker also recognizes that the leaders of the majority of religions are opposed to abusive practices. The need to protect people from religious and spiritual maltreatment is not used by the worker to justify efforts to change any person or group's religion.

Just as with definitions of other forms of maltreatment, definitions of religious and spiritual maltreatment are most effective when they leave room for interpretation by the expert social worker, who can assess the unique circumstances in each case (see Boxes 11.1 and 11.2) and then intervene to help the caretakers parent more effectively. Such definitions can also be used to inform prevention programs. The spiritually oriented social worker prefers to use prevention strategies to reduce religious maltreatment rather than to have to respond to serious cases of maltreatment after children have already been traumatized. In the most serious cases of religious maltreatment, most children have probably also suffered psychological abuse and perhaps other forms of abuse as well.

Although religious and spiritual maltreatment may occasionally be the presenting problem in a case, usually the social worker uncovers such maltreatment in the process of assessing an individual, couple, family, or group. The social

---

BOX 11.1

ELEMENTS OF RELIGIOUS MALTREATMENT

1. Child, youth, or vulnerable adult is threatened with or is punished with physical or emotional violence in order to influence or control her views of and participation in any religion.
2. Child, youth, or vulnerable adult is denied religious education, regarding either his own family's religion or other religions he is drawn to in his local and global communities.
3. The religious teacher of a child, youth, or vulnerable adult abuses the unequal power in that helping relationship for economic, sexual, psychological, or other kinds of gain.
4. In the name of her God or religion, a child, youth, or vulnerable adult is taught to hate another person, family, religion, culture, race, or other group of people.
5. In the name of his God or religion, a child, youth, or vulnerable adult is taught to hate any aspect of himself, including any elements of his body-mind-spirit-environment.
6. In the name of her God or religion, a child, youth, or vulnerable adult is encouraged to use any kind of violence against herself, other people, other living things, or the ecosystems that support all life.
7. In the name of his God or religion, a child, youth, or vulnerable adult is sexually abused or otherwise traumatized.
8. In the name of her God or religion, a child, youth, or vulnerable adult is denied a spiritual education.

BOX 11.2

ELEMENTS OF SPIRITUAL MALTREATMENT

1. Child, youth, or vulnerable adult is threatened with or is punished with physical or emotional violence in order to influence or control her spiritual experiences and expressions.
2. Child, youth, or vulnerable adult is denied a spiritual education.
3. The spiritual teacher of a child, youth, or vulnerable adult abuses the unequal power in that helping relationship for economic, sexual, psychological, or other kinds of gain.
4. The spiritual teacher of a child, youth, or vulnerable adult denies his student a religious education.

---

worker may first use education as the least intrusive and aggressive method of transformation. The worker recognizes that caretakers usually do not intend to harm, and therefore first works to help deepen the caretakers' awareness of the unintended impact of their behaviors on the child, youth, or vulnerable adult. If education does not work, the social worker may need to confront the caretaker more assertively. If physical, emotional, or sexual abuse or neglect accompanies the spiritual maltreatment, the social worker is mandated, of course, to contact Child Protective Services and/or law enforcement.

CASE STUDY 11.1
TRANSFORMING RELIGIOUS AND SPIRITUAL MALTREATMENT IN A FAMILY

A mother calls a social worker at a child guidance clinic. She has three children, but is concerned about her middle child, a daughter. The mother had read the child's diary (without her permission) and discovered that she had been having suicidal ideation. The social worker asks that the whole family come to therapy. The father is unenthusiastic (he says, "It is our daughter who has the problem, not everyone in the family") but finally agrees to come in for a family session on a Tuesday evening. In the assessment, the worker uncovers a number of issues. The oldest daughter, Debi, age 19, has an alcohol and cocaine problem, the middle daughter, Susie, age 17, is at risk of developing bulimia nervosa, and the youngest son, Billy, age 14, is depressed and anxious. The marriage between the parents is distant and cold.

The social worker is not concerned that the father is religiously conservative and wants the children attend the XYZ Church. Unfortunately, the father is also verbally and occasionally physically abusive with his wife. He explains that, in his opinion, in the XYZ Church, they believe that God wants the husband to run the household and the wife should follow his leadership. He further justifies his behavior by saying that, although his wife is not allowed to work outside the home, "she has the most important job in the home," which is to parent the children. His wife is no longer willing to conform to his wishes and the abusive behavior and threats have escalated.

When the father discovered a book on evolution that he did not approve of in Susie's room, he spanked her and grounded her. The social worker assessed that all the members of this family are at risk, but that Susie has been especially scapegoated by the father for years. Since there is a risk, Susie signs the standard "suicide contract" with the therapist, agreeing to talk with her or someone else before she would ever start to act out her suicidal feelings.

The worker realizes that she needs to reach the father since he has so much power in the family. She sells the idea of family therapy to the father, saying, "I really appreciate you caring so much about your family to come to these meetings and to do all the things you do to promote your children's religious education. You seem exhausted in fact from working so hard. Do you feel that way?" The father is relieved that the worker is not hostile to him or to his religion and he starts to relax his guard a bit. With their permission, the worker meets with the father and mother and a male clergy member from the XYZ Church that the worker knows. They discuss how the XYZ Church leaders urge men to share equal power with their wives.

Over the next months, the worker helps deepen the family's awareness of the mental, emotional, and then spiritual state of each family member. As the father starts to open up, he gradually is able to hear the truth from each person in the family, including his wife's truth. Although he experiences a sense of greater failure and increased vulnerability, he also starts to realize that if he loses control, he actually "wins" in terms of reduced stress and more intimacy. Once the father has this transformation, every other part of the family system also starts to shift. Susie no longer seems to need to binge and purge and she openly goes with her mother to a New Age festival downtown. Her father is still hard for her to relate to, but she no longer feels as scared of him. The father initiates an effort to get Debi into a drug and alcohol treatment center. At the social worker's request, he also spends more quality time with Billy. The father discovers in a session that Billy feels most spiritual out in nature. They decide to take more time out of each week to spend together.

CELEBRATING THE MIRACULOUS SPIRITUALITY OF THE CHILD

Miracles can be viewed as transformations in our experience of our body–mind–spirit–environment connection. By that definition, many children live miraculous lives in which they periodically experience a state of "oneness" with their world. The prepersonal consciousness of an infant does not have the mind-dominance of personal consciousness; since the mind does not rule her, the infant is thus likely to be very aware of her body, spirit, and environment. In the "altered" state of childhood, people may feel they have "magical" powers that connect the body, mind, spirit, and environment and that can influence events in ways that most adults do not think are possible. For the child, life is seldom painless, but is often wondrous.

However, there are adults who believe in the magic connections that many children naturally sense, and many of them are brilliant physicists. Currently popular ideas drawn from quantum mechanics, String Theory, and "M" Theory, for example, all suggest that there are probably profound connections between consciousness and matter. In fact, some physicists now think that consciousness not only influences matter but also *creates* matter. Perhaps most children still posses a intuitive way of knowing through which they sense the connections between all things.

The social worker strives to help the child develop such adult functions as self-discipline, a Religious Self, and a balanced commitment of service to self, other people, living things, and ecosystems without losing the childlike sense of openness, wonder, mystery and awe.

Perhaps it is in adolescence when such spiritual expressions as wonder, mystery, and awe are most under attack. This is because peer pressure usually discourages *enthusiasm* (literally "to be inspired by God"), which is often viewed as too childlike. Growing up thus requires in part that the teen hide the natural spirituality of childhood. After losing their enthusiasm, many teens and adults only feel comfortable revisiting their childlike spiritual nature when using alcohol or other drugs. An important task of the practitioner is to help adolescents retain their spiritual nature as they mature, so that they have access to both prepersonal and personal consciousness as they prepare to enter adulthood (see Table 11.1).

Most children and adolescents are not ready to develop transpersonal consciousness, simply because most have not yet developed a Personal Self. However, all children and adolescents are spiritual beings, and thus may still benefit from methods of transformation (such as those described in Chapter 7).

Some practitioners may choose to develop courses that combine aspects of both religious and spiritual education. Such a class can include the best elements of both kinds of education: the historical background and cultural perspectives of religious education and the immediate, personal, and mystical experiences of spiritual education. Such a class can also be designed for children, adolescents, and/or adults.

For example, a class can be designed that focuses on the experience of the miraculous in everyday life. The content of such a class might include some or all of the areas of interest and exercises described in Table 11.3. The "Background"

TABLE 11.3   Outline of Class Content: Opening to the Miraculous

MIRACLES IN THE PAST, PRESENT, AND FUTURE (5 MEETINGS)	MIRACLES IN THE MIND, BODY, SPIRIT, AND IN OUR LOCAL AND GLOBAL FAMILIES AND COMMUNITIES (5 MEETINGS)
1. What are miracles?	**5. Miracles in my individual future (my self)**
Background	*Background*
1. Summarize the literature on miracles, using stories and simple metaphors.	1. Describe the relevant literature.
2. Describe the history of miracles, as viewed by different religions across time.	*Activities*
Activities	1. Students discuss what miracles they each want in their future.
1. Each student describes what he wants out of this class.	2. Evaluate course and make mid-course corrections.
2. Each student describes what is miraculous to her.	
2. Childhood miracles	**6. Miracles related to our bodies**
Background	*Background*
1. Describe relevant literature on the miraculous in childhood, with illustrations from a multimedia program.	1. Describe the current literature on miracles in physical health and healing.
Activities	*Activities*
1. Recall an event in your childhood when you experienced the miraculous.	1. Class discusses the process of creating physical health.
2. Draw a picture of that event.	2. Students give examples of physical healing in their own lives.
3. Share your picture with a partner or class.	
3. Miracles in adolescence	**7. Miracles in our minds**
Background	*Background*
1. Describe relevant literature on the miraculous in adolescence, illustrated with appropriate multimedia.	1. Describe the literature on mind and healing and engage the students.
Activities	*Activities*
1. How did your sense of the miraculous change for you in adolescence?	1. Students discuss how the mind creates suffering.
2. Lead a guided imagery in which students recall a miraculous adolescent experience.	2. Students discuss how the mind can also create miracles.
4. Miracles in adulthood	**8. Miracles in spirit**
Background	*Background*
1. Describe relevant literature on miracles in adult life, illustrated with appropriate multimedia.	1. Describe the literature on miracles of spiritual healing
Activities	*Activities*
1. Students discuss: "If you could have a miracle this week, what would you wish for?"	1. Students discuss what the purpose of miracles may be in most religious traditions.
2. In small groups, students describe the most miraculous thing in their current life.	2. Students discuss what the purpose of miracles in their own lives might be.

9. Miracles in local and global families and communities

Background

1. Describe relevant literature on miracles in families and communities.

Activities

1. Students write down miracles they wish for in their families and communities.
2. Students share these descriptions with each other and find common themes.

10. Miracles in my shared future (the world)

Activities

1. Students work to co-create miracles in their individual, collective, and global lives.
2. Students co-create ritual(s) in support of these miracles.
3. Evaluate and close.

---

segments are opportunities for religious education, and the "Activities" segments are opportunities for spiritual education. These areas and exercises can be modified to fit the developmental needs of each group being served.

SPIRITUALITY AS A SOURCE OF FAMILY STRENGTH

Social workers often serve multiproblem families that are under considerable stress because of such interrelated issues as underemployment, oppression, racism, poverty, lack of housing, hunger, family maltreatment, legal problems, poor transportation, and other factors. In such cases, the social worker can help family members identify their spiritual and religious beliefs and rituals and use them as a source of strength. The social worker knows that some families and cultures have religious traditions that they draw strength from during difficult times, and the worker may begin by building on these traditions. If the worker is less religious than the client or family, or is unfamiliar with their religion, she or he can still learn about the family's beliefs and rituals by listening with respect and interest.

All of these religious and spiritual sources of strength could also be thought of as factors of individual and family resiliency. The social worker can take a complete spiritual and religious history of the family that goes back several generations to help uncover the family's traditions. The worker then can ask the family to describe what their beliefs teach them about suffering, faith, and life challenges. They can explore together if individuals feel as ease with their own God (if they have a God) and to explore what they need to do to feel more at ease.

SACRED PLAY

Any play can be sacred play, in the sense that the enjoyment and spontaneity of play can lead to spiritual transformation. People often do best what they enjoy doing, and children's abilities to play enable them to experiment with new ways of

TABLE 11.4 Spiritual Transition Groups with Children, Adolescents, and Families

KEY TRANSITIONS OF CHILDHOOD AND ADOLESCENCE	SPIRITUAL TRANSITION GROUPS
Entering material world through birth	**Sibling group** In this child-centered group, siblings of the new baby explore the spiritual dimension of having a new baby in their families. This group focuses on the spiritual meaning and opportunities available in the transition from "only child" to "older child." The practitioner attempts to group members in age-similar categories. Content for siblings younger than 10 years will be activity focused, and might include the use of stories, puppets, films, paintings, and other mediums to help the children own and express their emotional and spiritual experiences. Older children and adolescents may be able to verbally address such topics as (1) what I have lost and gained since the birth, (2) the spiritual gifts that may come from these losses and gains, and (3) how to rediscover my own value as a member of this family. **Parents' and other caretakers' group** Caretakers explore the spiritual dimension of birthing a child. This parent group may at first meet weekly during the pregnancy and then gradually meet less frequently across the parenting life span, as the children move through the various stages of childhood and adolescence and become adult children. There are "open-topic" meetings when participants can discuss the spiritual lessons, challenges, and rewards of parenting. When meetings are structured, topics might include (1) what the spiritual meaning and purpose of parenting is for each participant, (2) re-experiencing the spiritual journey of their own childhoods, and (3) exploring hopes and fears for the future.
Entering preschool and verbal-social world	**Preschoolers group** In this child-centered group, the focus is on the suffering and joy children experience when leaving home and going to school. The spiritual opportunities of the child's growing ability to communicate and interact socially are also explored. Since the children are typically about 5 or 6 years old, meetings are structured with such activities as nature walks, art projects, movement exercises, and group games.
Entering puberty, junior high school	**Girls' group** In this child-centered group, girls and their mothers (and other caretakers) meet to explore the spiritual dimension of the puberty transition. Weekly topics may include (1) what spirituality means to each participant, (2) what the spiritual "purposes" of adolescence are to each participant, (3) sacred sexuality, (4) co-creating rituals, (5) spiritual dimension of friendship, (6) practicing dialogue about spiritual and religious diversity, (7) fostering the group's collective intelligence, and (8) planning service projects. **Boys' group** The boys group has similar structure and content to the girls group. Boys and their fathers (and other caretakers) are the participants.

Entering adulthood, leaving home	**Young adults' group** Adult children meet for the purpose of fostering each other's spiritual development and service to others. Topics might include (1) what the spiritual purpose and meaning of adulthood is to each participant, (2) mourning the loss of childhood and revisiting its spiritual meaning, and (3) exploring individual and collective dreams about the future.

feeling, thinking, and being. Play also gives people opportunities to try on new roles, interact with a diverse group of people, and visit transforming environments. For example, most children seem to especially enjoy outdoor play, which brings them in contact with the mystery and healing power of the natural world.

From a spiritual perspective, play is synonymous with freedom. Sacred play both requires and creates more spiritual freedom. When a child is allowed to freely follow his or her own natural interests, play can be an expression of soul and Creative Spirit. Social workers are generally concerned that so many children do not engage in creative play. When play is limited to only a few themes, growth and transformation may be inhibited. For example, visit any family home in the United States and you are likely to see young boys playing war and combat games with toys and electronic devices, and young girls playing with electronic games and other toys that emphasize dating, personal beauty, and mothering. In excess, such play may not only limit creativity but can also put girls and boys into gender-oriented boxes too small for their souls.

Although there is of course a need for warriors and mothers in society, the definitions of warrior and mother have become narrowly defined. Although warriors today are "good guys" who fight "bad guys," warriors could also be thought of as the use of a "masculine" expression of both men and women who "fight" for personal transformation and the development of Communities of Universal Diversity. Although mothers today are usually thought of as women who nurture and support children and adolescents, mothering could also be thought of as a "feminine" expression of both men and women who care for the Highest Good of all living things and the ecosystems that support all life.

SPIRITUAL TRANSITION GROUPS

From a spiritual perspective, many children and adolescents today have to travel too alone and too far in their spiritual journeys. Most young people do not belong to Communities of Spiritual or Universal Diversity in which they can safely explore, experience, and share their spirituality with other people. Often young people have to navigate through life changes without any interaction with or support from caring adults. These life transitions of children and adolescents are opportunities for growth and transformation. Content of some selected spiritual transition groups are described in Table 11.4.

STUDY QUESTIONS

1. As you review your own childhood and adolescence, examine what kind of religious and spiritual education you received (if any). Describe the ways your religious and spiritual education was helpful and/or unhelpful to your spiritual development.

2. Review how your family of origin, religion, and other communities dealt with religiosity and spirituality when you were growing up. What would you change, if anything, in how you would lead a family, religion, or community?

3. In what ways, if any, have you experienced or observed spiritual or religious maltreatment? What were the causes and impact of such maltreatment?

4. What do you think about miracles? What is your own personal sense of the miraculous in life? Why do you think you feel the way you do? What do you want to change, if anything, about how you approach the miraculous in life?

5. What spiritual transitions in your own childhood and adolescence were most significant to you? Explain.

RESOURCES

Coles, R. (1990). *The spiritual life of children.* Boston: Houghton Mifflin.
    This book describes the author's pioneering research into the spirituality of young people.
Walsh, F. (Ed.). (1999). *Spiritual resources in family therapy.* New York: Guilford Press.
    This book includes a series of chapters on interesting topics related to spirituality and family therapy.

CHAPTER 12

SPIRITUALLY ORIENTED PRACTICE WITH ADULT AND AGING CLIENTS

From a spiritual perspective, the purpose of adulthood is to give the soul time to develop multidimensional developmental maturity, which involves ongoing, life-long work on all the interrelated dimensions of development: physical, emotional, cognitive, social, and spiritual. Since every person is recognized as a body–mind–environmental being, adult maturation is seen as a process that must address the body–mind–spirit–environment connection at every life stage.

Multidimensional developmental maturity is associated with individual transformations. The maturing adult increasingly has access to all of her developmental "parts," which means that she is aware and accepting of the dimensions of development. In addition, she increasingly uses those parts with integrity or wholeness for the Highest Good of her self and divine self, which means that her heart, mind, body, and soul are able to find agreement about how to live.

Thus, multidimensional developmental maturity is also associated with collective transformations. As adults in a community foster their maturity, they become increasingly able to transform their community into a Community of Spiritual and Universal Diversity. The maturing adult recognizes that as he develops, he becomes more responsible for the well-being of other people, living things, and ecosystems.

There are many potential life obstacles to multidimensional developmental maturity. From a spiritual perspective, the social worker views such obstacles as opportunities for the client to learn to grow. For example, as illustrated in Table 12.1, the family, institution, and culture often put gender-related limitations on people's development. The social worker helps the client become aware of these obstacles and encourages the client to view them as opportunities themselves for spiritual growth can be overcome in a client's lifetime.

From a spiritual perspective, the developmental expectations held for adults today are very conservative. For example, as illustrated in the gender-related limitations in Table 12.1, as long as they become wealthy or powerful, we often expect only male adults to be angry and competitive and narcissistic and concrete ("black and white") thinkers (which is what can be observed in most 8-year-old

TABLE 12.1   Gender-Related Limitations to and Key Elements of Multidimensional Developmental Maturity

DIMENSION	LIMITATIONS OFTEN PUT ON WOMEN	LIMITATIONS OFTEN PUT ON MEN	ELEMENTS OF DEVELOPMENTAL MATURITY FOR WOMEN AND MEN
Physical	Body cannot age after puberty No wrinkles or fat	Must always be virile No baldness	Acceptance of the body across life Listen to and care for body Use body to foster spirituality
Emotional	Anger not OK Sadness is feminine Must be vulnerable	Sadness not OK Anger is masculine No vulnerability	Can feel, express, control emotions Learn to love self and universe Use heart to foster spirituality
Cognitive	Black and white thinking only Never act too smart	Black and white thinking only Always act smart	See complexity through "gray" thinking and transrational wisdom Use mind to foster spirituality
Social	Must win contests with other women to be most popular and attractive	Must win contests with other men for wealth, power and fame, status	Able to be alone or with people Give back through spiritual service Use relationships to foster spirituality
Spiritual	Purpose of life is to serve husband and children	Purpose of life is personal success, defeat the enemy	Purpose of life is spiritual development and spiritual service Use soul to foster spirituality

boys). Similarly, as long as they become beautiful and popular, we often expect only female adults to be beautiful, popular, sad, vulnerable, and concrete thinkers (which is what can be observed in most 14-year-old girls).

The argument could thus be made that if "successful" men grow up to be about 8 developmental years old, and "successful" women to about 14 developmental years old, then family and society is generally pleased. This does not mean that to be competitive or angry, for example, is "bad" or even always "dysfunctional." Nor is it "bad" or always "dysfunctional" to want to be beautiful or popular. The problem with these limitations is that they so often can become inflexible restrictions. Thus, both men and women can find themselves in "boxes" too small for their souls.

The spiritually oriented social worker who works with adults can often be guided by a knowledge of the highest levels of adult maturity. Key elements of developmental maturity for women and men, some of which are illustrated in Table 12.1, are described next.

The Ecstatic State

A goal of adult spiritual maturity is the ability to relate to each of the five dimensions of development from an ecstatic state. The ecstatic state is a meditative state in which the adult watches the body, mind, heart, or soul. For example, a mature adult is capable of observing her emotions, thoughts, or body without identifying with those emotions, thoughts, or body sensations. This state is associated with the Observing Self or transpersonal state of consciousness (see Chapter 7). In such a state, the adult can observe her self and the universe with acceptance, love, and compassion.

PHYSICAL MATURITY

Viewing the Body from a Spiritual Perspective

The maturing adult understands that he is not just his body, but rather a spiritual being that inhabits a physical body. This dis-identification from the body is not a disconnection from the body. Rather, the adult becomes more connected to his body as he learns to observe, discipline, and surrender to his body from an ecstatic state. In contrast to the child, who naturally still believes that she *is* her body, and thus must identify with all the perceived imperfections and illnesses she may have, the adult is free to experience all the suffering and joy that having a body brings to a spiritual being. The body is viewed as a sacred voice of Creative Spirit.

Acceptance of the Body

The maturing adult accepts his body. Such acceptance means that the adult is at ease with the way he looks, with his body's strengths and limitations, and even with the illnesses he may have. This does not mean that the person does not take care of his body and strive to improve his health, but such efforts are based on a love-based relationship with the body, rather than a shame-based relationship. The social worker helps the adult client realize that shame about the body does not lead to health, but rather to a state of "dis-ease" characterized by an often endless series of attempts to change the body into an ideal form.

Listening and Responding to the Body

Sometimes the body needs rest. The mature adult is willing to take care of her body and get enough relaxation, nutrition, and care. In an era when people expect their bodies to continue functioning, often with the help of medication that does not heal as much as mask pain, even the word *recuperation* is now seldom used.

Sometimes the body needs exercise. The mature adult engages in a regular exercise program that fits with her body's ability, limitations, and needs. The adult may consult with experts to determine what kind of exercise program would best meet those needs. Such a program might include aerobic exercise, weight training, and stretching work.

Sometimes the body is sick. When the mature adult has an injury or illness, she does not curse her body or diseased body part. Rather, she accepts her disease, she strives to find the meaning in her disease, and she takes care of her body so she can heal. She may seek help from other people as she works to accept, find meaning, and heal.

Ability and Wisdom to Express Spirit through the Body in a Disciplined Way

The maturing adult expresses spirit through a physical practice. Such control and discipline may be in an organized and established form, including a tradition of dance, music, fasting, martial art, or yoga, conducted under the supervision of a teacher. Control and discipline may also be in a more individual and spontaneous form, such as personal rituals of movement, exercise, or other physical expression. The adult views such expressions as opportunities to care for her soul as well as her body. She seeks personal and often social meanings in these expressions.

For example, a woman might decide to study a martial art. Her spiritually oriented counselor helps her find a teacher who is not just proficient in a discipline but who also believes in instructing the student that the purpose of her art-form is not to practice violence but peace.

Another way to express spirit through the disciplined body is through service. The maturing adult uses the body to serve others. For example, a person might shovel the snow off a neighbor's driveway or help an elderly person carry water.

Ability and Wisdom to Express Spirit through the Body by Way of Surrender and Enjoyment

The maturing adult also expresses spirit by letting go of her body and enjoying it. Such enjoyment can occur in many ways. When an adult plays a game, whether it is an athletic sport, a computer game, or a card game, today we might say she is in a "zone" or in "flow," which means she is in the ecstatic state. When an adult enjoys a good meal, a sexual experience, or a beautiful sunset, a transpersonalist might say she is operating at a prepersonal level of consciousness, which means she is experiencing pleasure while in the ecstatic state.

EMOTIONAL MATURITY

Viewing the Heart from a Spiritual Perspective

The maturing adult has disidentified from his heart, which means that he no longer believes he is just his feelings. Instead, he views himself as a spiritual being who lives with a heart. The person has become free to experience and express his emotions from the ecstatic state. He views his heart as a sacred voice of Creative Spirit.

Acceptance of the Full Range of Emotions

The maturing adult is comfortable with and respects all of his emotions. He understands that every emotion is a teacher that can help him learn more about himself, his world, and Creative Spirit. He prefers to feel at ease with his emotions, viewing them as soul expressions rather than as signs of illness.

The adult realizes that he will at times experience emotions that are very uncomfortable, such as fear, anger, and sadness. At other times he knows he will experience very pleasant emotions, such as joy and relaxation. He strives to experience all these emotions, comfortable and uncomfortable, from the ecstatic state, standing beside himself with his God, in his joy and pain.

Wise Expression of the Full Range of Emotions

The maturing adult realizes that it is in her Highest Good to control her emotions in certain situations and to express her emotions spontaneously in other situations. Thus, for example, anger may serve a battered woman who needs the motivation and energy to end an abusive relationship. However, at some point, perhaps years after the abuse has stopped, she might decide to let go of her anger because it no longer serves her as she strives to begin a new relationship. The maturing adult works toward developing the wisdom to know when and how to express emotion.

Ability to Express Spirit by Showing Love from the Heart

The maturing adult not only loves other people, living things, and the world but he also shows that love. Maturity thus also involves the development of a loving, compassionate, and forgiving heart. From a spiritual perspective, such a heart is expressing Creative Spirit. The adult also serves other people, living things, and ecosystems with his disciplined heart by fostering such feelings as love, compassion, and forgiveness toward other people, particularly those who have caused him pain.

COGNITIVE MATURITY

Viewing the Mind from a Spiritual Perspective

The maturing adult has dis-identified from her mind and views her mind from an ecstatic state of consciousness. She is free to view all of her thoughts as interesting opportunities for learning and growth. She views the mind as a sacred voice of Creative Spirit.

Acceptance of Thoughts

The maturing adult is at ease with all of his thoughts. Although he is aware of his thoughts, he is not willing to let them control him anymore than he lets his emotions control him. He prefers thinking about his thoughts as messages from his soul, rather than as signs of mental illness.

Faith

Although she may not understand the nature of the universe, the maturing adult has faith that the universe is friendly and operates in the Highest Good. The adult thus refuses to believe in her fears and anxieties, because she does not want to believe in a unfriendly world that will only harm her. She does not deny that there is tremendous suffering in the world, and prays for the relief of suffering, but she also believes that all suffering can lead to spiritual growth.

Ability to Express Spirit through the Mind

The maturing adult strives to express Creative Spirit though his thoughts and words. He endeavors to avoid judgmental, blaming, hostile, or destructive thoughts and words toward himself or other people. Instead, he fosters loving, forgiving, compassionate, and healing thoughts and words toward himself and others. He cultivates an attitude of gratitude in his life.

SOCIAL MATURITY

Viewing People, Living Things, and Ecosystems as Sacred Expressions of Creative Spirit

The maturing adult has dis-identified from her relationships with other people, living things, and ecosystems, so that she is free to be connected to everything in the Multiuniverse. She no longer thinks that she is just her friendships, her family, tribe, or nation, and she has replaced the identifications of the child with a deep sense of respect for the sacredness of everything.

Ability to Live in Nonreaction Rather Than in Reaction to Pain

The maturing adult has learned to control his initial reaction when other people, other living things, or ecosystems cause him pain. He realizes that his initial reaction is usually to hurt back and/or to hurt himself. Instead of fostering his frightened and angry feelings, he feels his pain and sadness but holds an intent of nonreaction. Nonreaction is neither social withdrawal nor aggression, but is characterized by a state of awareness and calmness and by kind actions toward other people, living things, and ecosystems.

Contemplative Time

The maturing adult sets aside regular contemplative time, during which she can do her own spiritual practice. She may choose to do such practice alone and/or in a social (religious) context. The ability to be alone, in contemplation, frees the adult so that she is not afraid of her deepest self and gives her awareness of her inner world.

Purity

The maturing adult strives to act out of pure motive when interacting with other people, living things, and the ecosystems that support all life. Pure motive occurs when the body, mind, and spirit all share the same motivation and intent. She notices other motivations that arise in herself (such as desire for fame, fortune, or power) and gently lets go of them as they surface.

SPIRITUAL MATURITY

Viewing the Development of Consciousness from a Spiritual Perspective

The maturing adult is dis-identifing from her level of consciousness, and increasingly views her spiritual development from an ecstatic state of consciousness. She refuses to compensate for her feelings of shame and inadequacy by inflating herself through her spiritual or religious achievements, beliefs, and behaviors. Instead, she looks at all experiences as opportunities for her to heal her shame and to love herself more.

Cultivating a Sense of Connection

The adult also fosters an increasing sense of connection with everything else in the Multiuniverse. There is a sense in the adult that other people are not only similar to him, but that he shares a common identity with all people. Similarly, the adult feels a connection with other living and life-supporting things. This sense of connection, felt deeply, helps foster compassion, love, and forgiveness.

Cultivating Peace of Body–Mind–Spirit

Increasingly, the maturing adult experiences a sense of peace in her life. Such peace is not just an absence of internal conflict between body, mind, and spirit but it is also a sense of tranquility, calmness, and ecstasy. Such internal peace is associated with the deep peace that many people now want to co-create on earth, between nations, religions, and peoples.

Ability to Express Spirit through the Soul

The maturing adult strives to express Creative Spirit though his spiritual work. He believes that his body–mind–spirit is already "good enough," so he feels no need to pretend to be better or more special than any other person, living or life-supporting thing. However, he never ceases to look for opportunities to grow spiritually.

PRACTICE IN SUPPORTING ADULT MATURITY

Inclusive Strategies

In the work of adult development, the effective spiritually oriented social worker utilizes interventions drawn from all seven paradigms of spiritual transformation outlined in Chapters 1 through 10. Examples of interventions, drawn from each of the paradigms, are given here.

Spiritual Momentum

Transformations of adult development can be lonely journeys during which the client can have crises of faith. During such crises of faith, the client may question why she is going through so much suffering, and she may be tempted to avoid growth and choose familiar and safe options instead.

The spiritual perspective, which is also often the biggest perspective, can help the client strengthen her faith in the developmental process. The social worker may ask the client to imagine the most significant life transformations that she will go through across her entire lifetime. As the client does this work, she may better see how her current challenges fit into the biggest issues of her life.

Similarly, the social worker may also ask the client to imagine the most significant life transformations that her intergenerational family has gone through. Such work can help the client see her own life challenges from a different, bigger, and thus more spiritual perspective. She may appreciate how her current challenges fit into the development of collective consciousness in her family and culture over many lifetimes of change.

CASE STUDY 12.1
USING SPIRITUAL MOMENTUM TO FOSTER MATURITY

A 30-year-old man with moderate dysthymia and anxiety has been working on himself for about six months with the help of his social worker. During the work, the client discovered that he had been focused primarily on the goal of social popularity. He complains that, since he has been getting better, most of his friendships have been disappearing. In one session, the worker has the client do an imaginative journey in which he first looks at the transformations that his parents and grandparents made in their own adult lives. Then he looks at the transformations that he will make in his own life. He sees how important it has been to all his family members to eventually shift from the goal of achieving social popularity to the goal of finding a true vocation and finding a life partner. With this perspective, the client realizes that, just like a snake has to shed its skin to grow, he may have to give up some friendships before he can have the new kinds of relationships he now needs.

Mindful Daily Living

The social worker knows that his clients may need to express and enhance their spirituality through service to other people. The worker helps the client become aware of what her developmental intentions are. Then the worker supports the client in changing her beliefs and behaviors in order to move toward achieving those intentions.

> **CASE STUDY 12.2**
> **USING INTENTIONS TO FOSTER MATURITY**
>
> The social worker starts to see a 66-year-old woman whose husband died several years ago. The client has become depressed and has lost her interest in life. The social worker helps the client explore what her developmental intentions are, and the woman starts to talk about wanting to "do something for somebody else." The worker supports the client's intention, and shows her how her desire for service fits into multidimensional developmental theory. The client decides she wants to work with children and the worker refers her to several locations where such service is possible. The woman starts to volunteer in a receiving home for maltreated children. She reports that the work has given new meaning and purpose to her life.

The social worker also sees himself as a warrior who will fight many battles with each client over the view of the client. The client often first presents with a very negative view of herself. The worker strives to help the client view herself as a lovable being who has a divine place and purpose in the Multiuniverse. Often, when the client is suffering, she will create new reasons to deny her divinity.

> **CASE STUDY 12.3**
> **USING REFRAMING TO FOSTER MATURITY**
>
> The social worker has being seeing a 45-year-old single man, never married, for about a year. The man has made tremendous progress in changing his life. He has cleaned his home, once filled with clutter, and starting dating women he liked. One day he walked into therapy and said, "I have never been as bummed in my whole life!" As they start to talk about the week, there appears to be no obvious or even subtle causes for the client to feel so badly. The worker realizes that her client may again be feeling "allergic to feeling worthy." When the social worker reveals her opinion, the client first laughs. Then he bursts into tears and finally says, "I think it is true. I still must believe that I do not deserve to be this happy."

Spirit with Heart

The worker knows that perhaps the most common complaint her adult clients make is that people have caused them pain. She sees these situations as opportunities for her clients to love themselves and other people more. The social worker gives love, compassion, and forgiveness to the client, and in doing so helps the client love and forgive himself and other people.

CASE STUDY 12.4
USING EMOTIONS TO FOSTER MATURITY

One of the social worker's clients comes in, complaining that everyone at work has been difficult to work with, all the men on the Internet that she has been talking to are unhealthy, and everyone in her family has been unfairly hostile to her. The client then frowns at her social worker and says, "And don't you dare tell me again that this is an opportunity for me to love myself!" The worker sits quietly for a few moments. Then the worker says, "You look very sad today." They are both silent for another minute and then the client starts to talk about how hurt and sad she is. The therapist listens as the client processes her pain. Then the client says, "OK, now I am ready to talk about how all of these people are my teachers." "Yes, I think they are," says the worker. "They are challenging you to love yourself more and more, and I will keep telling you that until you start to feel it down deep in your heart. You have experienced maybe a thousand times that you are not lovable. It is OK for your therapist to love you a few hundred times until you get it."

Religious Self

The social worker recognizes that most people seek religious experiences or practices to assist them in their multidimensional development. Like any other life events, religious experiences can foster the physical, emotional, cognitive, social, and spiritual dimensions. The worker helps people consciously select, navigate through, and benefit from their religious experiences.

CASE STUDY 12.5
USING THE RELIGIOUS SELF TO FOSTER MATURITY

A social worker who practices at a large military hospital setting is called on to see a new client who is recovering from a war wound. The physician who made the referral is concerned that the man may be at risk for substance abuse and other self-destructive behavior. In the assessment, the worker determines that the man is indeed at risk for such behavior, and is suffering many of the symptoms of post-traumatic stress disorder. The client also tells the worker that he "used to be religious but no longer believes in God, after what I have seen." The worker listens to the man's war stories, all of which are indeed potentially traumatizing. After several sessions, during which the client tells his stories, the worker normalizes the client's angry feelings about God and then talks to the client about the many different kinds of spiritually based programs that are available in the hospital and surrounding community. The worker helps the client find some programs that fit well with his needs. The client attends several of the groups, some of which he continues with, including a prayer group run by other veterans and a class taught by a woman at the local Yoga Center. The social worker follows up and supports the client as he attends meetings and makes new friends.

Bioconsciousness

The worker also looks for opportunities to help clients become more aware of the current quality of their own body–mind–spirit connection. She knows that such awareness can help foster the client's multidimensional development. The worker also helps the client make meaning out of his body's strengths, limitations, and illnesses so that the client can use such meaning to help him interpret his developmental goals and progress.

CASE STUDY 12.6
USING BIOCONSCIOUSNESS TO FOSTER MATURITY

A 23-year-old woman is referred to the social worker by her basketball coach. The young woman, who was a good basketball player in college, had her heart set on becoming a professional basketball player. However, she was not chosen by any team in the draft, and had become despondent as she realized that she was probably not talented enough to play professionally. Over several sessions, the social worker listened to her tell her story about her dream and disappointment. Then he asks her to makes sense out of her physical limitations. The young woman at first is resistant to doing this, so the social worker shared a true story about when he was not hired when he got out of college and decided to move out of the state. The disappointment became a blessing because he moved out of his home state and into a new city where many wonderful things happened. The woman begins to appreciate the idea that a limitation might be a body–mind–spirit blessing. They begin to talk about her future in a more positive way. "Of course, it is a disappointment, but I wonder what greater things you will be doing instead," says the worker.

Collective Consciousness and
Eco-Consciousness

The social worker often encourages the client to engage in service, because she appreciates how meaningful service can help foster adult development. The worker knows, however, that a person will not become more responsible to other people or other living and life-supporting things until he becomes aware of that he has a meaningful *response* to in his world. In other words, the worker first has to help the client understand what kind of service to which he is most drawn.

The worker also helps the client understand what Communities of Spiritual and Universal Diversity are, and how they can help foster the evolution of individual and collective consciousness. As the client understands the value of such communities, he is more likely to strive to help co-create them and to personally benefit from his participation in them.

STUDY QUESTIONS

1. From a spiritual perspective, what could be said is the goal of adulthood? What is your reaction to this definition?

2. What are some common limitations men and women might experience related to their spiritual development?

3. What is an ecstatic state? Have you ever experienced such a state?

4. Describe the definitions of maturity in each of the dimensions. Describe where you judge yourself to be in relation to these definitions. What would you say is your most developed dimension? Which one is the least developed?
   a. Physical development
   b. Emotional development
   c. Cognitive development
   d. Social development
   e. Spiritual development

5. Select a client and describe where she is along the five developmental dimensions. Then describe an example of a method from each of the seven paradigms of spiritual practice that could be used to help this client continue to develop multidimensionally.

RESOURCES

Cortright, B. *Psychotherapy and spirit: Theory and practice in transpersonal psychotherapy.* Albany: State University of New York Press.
   This text reviews transpersonal theories of human development.
Maslow, A. H. (1971). *The further reaches of human nature.* New York: Viking.
   Still an impressive book after 30 years, Maslow lays the foundation for a new psychology of transcendence, later to become transpersonal psychology.

CHAPTER 13

SPIRITUALLY ORIENTED PRACTICE IN MENTAL-HEALTH SETTINGS

From a spiritual perspective, the purpose of social work practice in mental-health settings is to foster the biopsychosocial–spiritual–environmental (BPSSE) well-being of people. Mental health (or cognitive health) is thus seen as inseparable from physical, emotional, social, spiritual, and environmental health. Although most voluntary or court-referred clients in the mental-health environment may initially see themselves as a "mental-health patients," the spiritually oriented social worker also views the client as a body–mind–spirit–environmental being.

Spiritually oriented work in mental health is a comprehensive approach to practice that does not necessarily replace methods popular in current practice but rather *adds* additional perspectives and methods to the work. In fact, the spiritually oriented social worker prefers to work with multiple methods and with multidisciplinary teams because he or she knows that the client is likely to benefit from such an approach.

The spiritually oriented social worker believes that individual symptoms can be viewed as a sign of health in the individual in that situation. The healthy person is connected to his or her body–mind–spirit–environment and therefore responds to changing conditions. For example, anxiety might be a healthy reaction to a culture that oppresses gay, lesbian, and transgendered people, because such a culture creates fear in most people, regardless of their sexual orientation. Or in a state where the forests are dying because of acid rain, moderate depression might be a natural healthy reaction in healthy children and adolescents.

BASIC SPIRITUAL APPROACHES TO PRACTICE IN MENTAL HEALTH

A Radical, Inclusive View

In general, the spiritually oriented social worker takes a *radical* approach to mental health in that he looks for and works with all the many *roots* of people's life challenges. The social worker takes an *inclusive* view of the etiology of mental-health

■ ■ ■ ■ ■

BOX 13.1

INTEGRATIVE VIEWS OF THE SPIRITUAL, ENVIRONMENTAL, AND GENETIC ROOTS OF SYMPTOMS

Spiritual	The soul is creating "pathology" so that the client can re-discover and re-embrace her spiritual "path."
Environmental	The person has been traumatized by some life experience that still needs healing, so the soul "echos" the original trauma until it is "heard."
Genetic-Evolutionary	The person inherited a predisposition to develop limitations so the soul can challenge the person through the symptom to develop off-setting strengths.

symptoms in that he anticipates that every symptom probably has spiritual, environmental, *and* genetic-evolutionary roots (see Box 13.1). Genetic-evolutionary roots of symptoms are viewed not only as the "weak" genes of the client's parents but also the distant genetic history of the species.

Symptoms Are Signs of Both Dis-Ease and Health

The social worker is aware that mental-health symptoms usually bring suffering to the client, and that the client is not "at ease" with himself. However, the social worker also views mental-health symptoms as signs of health, in that they let the person know more about the needs of his soul, the status of his unhealed trauma, and the nature of his biological limitations and strengths. The worker takes an integrative view of symptoms (see Box 13.1) and sees symptoms as having interconnected spiritual, environmental, and genetic roots.

A Radical View of Suffering

The worker often views symptoms as painful communications from the soul, the environment, and genetics. The social worker knows that suffering can often lead to spiritual transformation, because people usually seek spiritual and religious comfort and meaning when in pain. Thus, instead of only seeking to help the client reduce or eliminate suffering, the spiritually oriented social worker also tries to help the client do the work that his suffering may seem to be inviting him to do.

The social worker has compassion for the suffering of the client, of course, and does not want the client to experience excessive or unnecessary pain. The worker, however, also recognizes that many clients suffer excessive pain precisely because they have tried to avoid their suffering, through such addictive behaviors, for example, as substance abuse, worry, busy work schedules, overeating, or destructive sexual adventures. The social worker does not want the client merely to substitute one method of avoidance or addiction for another.

A Radical View of Healing

The social worker thus does not want to measure success merely by the absence of symptoms, for symptoms may actually be "gifts" from the soul that can lead to further transformation. In addition, the worker realizes that life on Earth can never be free of pain, regardless of what the client wants or does.

The social worker also does not want to help the client merely become "functional" or "stabilized." The worker knows that functional and stable people can still live miserable lives. If a client is potentially self-destructive or violent toward other people or living things, then the worker of course acts to protect the client and others who are threatened. However, "dysfunction" and "instability" can also be viewed as messages from the soul and opportunities for transformation.

Instead, healing is wholing; the process of owning all of the "parts" that make up the body–mind–spirit–environment human organism. The social worker realizes that when people heal, they seldom become symptom free and suffering free. They also do not necessarily become more functional and stable, in the sense that they make more money, go to work on time, or get their grades up. They may, however, become free to be fully alive, with access to all of their emotions, thoughts, sensations, spiritual experiences, and behaviors.

Transformation of Identification

Another goal of spiritual work in mental-health settings is transformation. Deep healing is transformational as the client dis-identifies from one stage of consciousness so that she can identify with the next stage of consciousness. As such development occurs, the client may gradually move through her own unique levels of identification (see Box 13.2). The spiritually oriented social worker at a mental health setting strives to support this process because he believes that people who are moving through these developmental stages tend to co-create individual well-being and Communities of Spiritual and Universal Diversity.

Multiple Challenges and Multidisciplinary Teams in Spiritually Oriented Practice

The social worker also views most clients as having multiple life challenges that may require assistance on many levels. For example, a client who presents with anxiety may also have issues with housing, substance abuse, employment, and physical health. Such a client might benefit from a multidisciplinary team approach that incorporates interventions from the social worker who coordinates with the local Housing Authority, a substance abuse treatment agency, the Work Force Services office, and a free health clinic. Such teams work together to conduct multidisciplinary case staffings, reduce the need for separate intake and assessment procedures, and support the multiple needs of each client.

■ ■ ■ ■ ■

BOX 13.2
DEVELOPMENTAL LEVELS AND DESCRIPTIONS OF IDENTIFICATION

Ego-centric	Identification with my self
Ethno-centric	Identification with my family, tribe, culture, religion
National-centric	Identification with my tribe, community, culture, country
Human-centric	Identification with my species
Life-centric	Identification with all living things
Eco-centric	Identification with my environment
Nothing-centric	Identification with nothing (connection Creative Spirit)

Source: Wilber (1997).

A SPIRITUAL PERSPECTIVE TO COMMON MENTAL HEALTH DIAGNOSES

The spiritually oriented social worker is open to seeing mental-health diagnoses from many perspectives. She is willing and able to use diagnostic language when she believes that such language can support her clients (such as when preparing or disseminating a case report or insurance form). However, she refuses to "shrink" her client down to only a diagnosis, preferring instead to "expand" her client, seeing him from multiple lenses. The client is seen as a spiritual being who is in a human body with many strengths and symptoms, rather than as just a diagnosis.

In general, the social worker considers the possibility that symptoms of "mental illness" are more likely to be indicators of individual and societal imbalance than chemical imbalance. Box 13.3 illustrates examples of spiritual perspectives that might be taken with some diagnoses. In each of these examples, the traditional view of the "disorder" is expanded to include a broader perspective of how the individual or community may be imbalanced.

Anxiety and Depression

Anxiety and depression are among the most common diagnoses given to clients by helping professionals. They also have many related elements. Although there are a growing number of types of depression and anxiety described in the literature, the most common symptoms, usually seen in what is called *dysthymia* and *generalized anxiety,* will be considered here.

On the *physical* level, anxiety and depression can both be seen as "diseases of the head," associated with the common tendency to live too much "above the

BOX 13.3

SOME SPIRITUAL PERSPECTIVES AND EXAMPLES THAT MIGHT BE USED WITH SOME MENTAL-HEALTH DIAGNOSES

Depression	Soul is asking client to notice that he has forgotten who he is
Anxiety	Client is anticipating danger rather than trusting in her own spiritual path
ADHD	Client's soul needs more creative expression and less focus and function
Substance abuse	Inability to move consciousness out of consensus reality without drugs
Antisocial	Client has forgotten that on a spiritual level everyone is the same
Narcissistic	Client has no loving connection with self so has become egocentric instead
Sexual identity	Client was born twin spirited into a culture that fears such spiritual balance

neck." Although the brain is an important and vital organ of the body, most of the body resides, of course, outside of the brain. Many people today live primarily in their heads, anticipating future negative events and reliving negative memories of the past. Such a focus on the negative may, at first, give a child or teen a sense of mastery and control in a scary world. However, negative thinking usually becomes excessive and creates unnecessary suffering. A lack of physical exercise and poor diet may also often associated with living in the head, and this lack may intensify the symptoms of anxiety and depression.

Physical therapy for depression might help the client move more often down below her neck into the rest of his body. This might be accomplished through the use of such transformations drawn from the body consciousness paradigm, such as breath work, walking, meditation, yoga, or aerobic exercise. The social worker also strives to help the client listen with and to his body for communications about his soul, environment, and genetics. For example, the client may decide that his lack of physical energy is related to a need to experience deep relaxation in his life.

On the *emotional* level, both anxiety and depression are associated with the suppression of the full range of emotions. This suppression is not the same thing as the responsible self-control of feelings that the adult hopefully creates, but is a more childlike, unconscious, self-protective reflex. As a child, the person may have learned not to feel or express her anger, for example, or his sadness, perhaps because it was not safe to feel or express such feelings. Eventually, the result of such suppression of emotion might be a general flatness of affect, since it is difficult to extinguish negative emotions without doing the same thing to the more positive emotions. Other clients may express all of their emotions through one emotional channel, such as anger or sadness. Transformations drawn from the Spirit with Heart paradigm may assist in the recovery of emotions and the development of love, compassion, and forgiveness. The client learns to feel all of her feelings again and then to let them put her in "e-motion" toward her dreams. The client may also learn to listen to her heart for clues about her soul, environment, or evolution. For example, the inability to feel sadness may be a clue that the client has had significant losses in her life that she needs to grieve before she can move on developmentally.

On the *cognitive* level, anxiety and depression are generally associated with a belief in an unfriendly universe and a sense of shame (personal inferiority and inadequacy). To use a computer analogy, the depressed and anxious mind does not have a hardware problem; the difficulty is with the software, which could be labeled "negative thinking." Such negative thinking can reduce joy, spontaneity, and spiritual growth.

Methods drawn from the Mindful Daily Living paradigm may help the client go beyond believing that he *is* his thoughts and learn instead to watch his thoughts from his Overseer Self. The client also learns to assert more positive thoughts in his mind through affirmations. The client may choose to view his thoughts as communications from his soul, environment, or biological inheritance. For example, his tendency to worry about something terrible happening may be seen as a communication from the soul that he still has little faith in his God (soul), that he has been traumatized in his family of origin (environment), or that his family has a tendency to worry when under stress (biology).

On the *social* level, anxiety and depression are usually associated with a difficulty in vertical and horizontal intimacy. As discussed in an earlier chapter, *vertical intimacy* is the connection a person has with all her "parts," including the physical, emotional, cognitive, social, and spiritual. *Horizontal intimacy* is the connection a person has with other people, living and nonliving things. The anxious and depressed person has difficulty in vertical intimacy in as much as he is unable to relate to some part(s) of himself, which may show up in a discomfort in being alone and quiet with himself. The anxious and depressed person has difficulty with horizontal intimacy when he cannot relate with other beings or things, and he may practice social withdrawal or excessive control of others instead.

The social worker can use methods of community consciousness to help foster social development. For example, she can have the client work on expressing the social behaviors that are still underdeveloped, which may be contemplative time or more social-interactive time. Social interactions may also be viewed as communications from the soul, environment, and evolution. The client, for example, may decide that her tendency to withdraw socially may be a communication from her soul that she needs more contemplative time in her life right now.

On the *spiritual* level, anxiety and depression may be viewed as signs that the soul is asking for more attention. The client may have become dis-spirited, perhaps because she has forgotten to continue her conversations with her soul. The soul may be "concerned" that the person has become separated from her spiritual path.

Methods drawn from the Religious Self paradigm may help the client explore and respond to her soul messages. For example, the client may practice meditation, prayer, or other forms of supplication to increase mindfulness. In other words, the client can purposively engage in some kind of discipline in which she practices "listening" to her own soul messages.

Attention-Deficit and Hyperactivity Disorder

From a spiritual perspective, the large numbers of people, mostly young men, who are now diagnosed and medicated for ADHD may generally be more a symptom of collective "societal imbalance" than of individual "chemical imbalance." The social worker understands that pressures to be functional, stay productive, and operate in consensus reality are stronger than the invitations to be creative, foster multidimensional development, and access meditative states of consciousness. If many children and adolescents are unable or unwilling to stay "on task" in their public schools, perhaps the schools are expecting young people to do too many of the wrong tasks.

Working from such an expanded perspective, the spiritually oriented social worker may still work with traditional approaches to ADHD clients. However, she also helps the child and his caretakers change their view of the child from a "problem child" with learning and behavior problems to a spiritual being with considerable potential who (like everyone on the planet) has to sometimes learn to live in unfriendly environments. The worker may teach the child methods that can help him do well in such environments, such as meditation, compassion toward self and others, and connection with his God. The worker may also help the child find success in the "more friendly" environments he may find himself in, such as sports, computers, or art classes.

Bipolar Disorders

From a spiritual perspective, the social worker can view bipolarity as a human condition that most people experience to varying degrees. The worker realizes that there are clients who suffer from severe bipolar disorders that seem to at least occasionally cripple them. However, the worker also knows that polarities can be found throughout life, usually dualities between what the culture or individuals believe to be good and to be bad. Such polarities may be experienced between religions, political parties, sexual orientations, philosophies, and practically any other mental constructs. Polarities can also be found in a person's judgments about what thoughts, moods, and behaviors are acceptable and which are not. For example, a client might have a hard time accepting joy in his life and even become "allergic" to feeling good. Clients can also have a hard time accepting such emotions as sadness or anger.

From a spiritual perspective, polarities or dualities are associated with mental identifications that ultimately create unnecessary suffering for the client and other people and living things. For example, a client who identifies herself as a "liberal democrat" might create a duality in her life in which all people who she perceives as "neo-conservatives" are foolish and all people she perceives as liberal democrats will save the world. By letting her mind split people into such categories, she cheats herself out of opportunities to experience herself and other people as whole people and to have deeper interpersonal intimacy with them. Or, for example, a young man may experience himself as "not good enough" because he is only five feet tall (tall is good and short is bad). He becomes disconnected with himself by seeing himself as less worthy than taller men.

The spiritually oriented social worker may use the traditional approaches to bipolar disorder currently in use. However, he also adds a spiritual approach to the work. He helps the client understand, accept, and use her own bipolarity for her own spiritual development. When and if the client is in a manic state of being, for example, the social worker helps her use her high energy in highly active ways—for example, doing service work, art projects, aerobic exercise, and construction ventures. During a more depressed state of being, the client might do less active meditative work, such as creating peace of mind, higher consciousness, and compassion. The worker also helps the client view herself as a spiritual being who has certain symptoms rather than as a just a person with a severe mental illness.

Narcissistic Personality Disorder

The client who presents with narcissistic traits is usually a "nonvoluntary" client who has been "persuaded" to see the social worker by a judge, spouse, or parent. This is because the very narcissistic client, by definition, usually does not think that she needs to work on anything; she believes that other people have the problem. The social worker thus has the initial challenge of co-developing a helping relationship and therapeutic goals with the client before they can do deeper work together. The worker is not fooled by the client's attempt to present herself as somehow superior to other people, since the worker knows that the client needs her narcissism when she does not feel deeply that she is "enough." The worker knows that the mainstream culture supports widespread narcissism by encouraging the worship of such goals as wealth, power, beauty, and fame over peace of mind, equanimity, compassion, and forgiveness.

Successful practice with narcissism must therefore focus on the core beliefs that the client has about herself and the world. On the psychological level, the social worker wants the client to learn to love herself more. On the spiritual level, the client is assisted in dis-identifying from egocentric, ethnocentric, nationalcentric, and humancentric levels of development so that her need for self-importance can be reduced. Then the worker helps the client replace her feelings of shame with a deep sense of connection with God or Creative Spirit and replace her indentifications with specialness and self-importance with a sense of the importance of service to other people, living things, and ecosystems.

Work with Externalizing and Internalizing Behaviors

Some psychological systems divide mental-health diagnoses into externalizing and internalizing disorders. *Externalizing disorders* are described as those that manifest in the client acting out in socially unacceptable ways, and thus are usually identified first by other people in the client's life. *Internalizing disorders*, in contrast, are seen as those that the client experiences inside himself, and thus are usually identified first by the client himself. Although this classification system is certainly simplistic and although there are many clients with both kinds of disorders, the spiritually oriented social worker can link these classifications to transpersonal theory.

In transpersonal theory, the client who presents primarily with an *externalizing disorder* (which are generally also called *Axis II disorders*) can be viewed as someone who is operating primarily at the prepersonal level (see Chapter 1) consciousness. Such a client may have an overdeveloped child ego state, which means that he has a childlike primary interest in his own immediate gratification. The spiritually oriented social worker can draw methods from each of the paradigms of practice (see Table 13.1, column 2) that may encourage such a client to become more sensitive to responsible toward other people, living things, and ecosystems.

TABLE 13.1   Examples of Methods that May Help Heal Externalizing and Internalizing Disorders

PARADIGM OF SPIRITUAL TRANSFORMATION	HEALING EXTERNALIZING DISORDER (PREPERSONAL CONSCIOUSNESS)	HEALING INTERNALIZING DISORDER (PERSONAL CONSCIOUSNESS)
Spiritual Momentum	Teaching respect and responsibility for the continuity of life	Healing trauma in past and current lifetimes that contribute to symptoms
Mindful Daily Living	Teaching mindfulness and right actions to others	Using symptoms to teach the need for a pattern of more mindful living
Spirit with Heart	Teaching love, forgiveness, and compassion in service to other beings	Experiencing and sharing the emotions that are speaking through the symptoms
Religious Self	Teaching the responsible practice of a ritual from a wisdom tradition	Using rituals from world's wisdom traditions to address symptoms
Body Consciousness	Using body work or body expression in service	Using body work and embodiment to express and heal symptoms
Community Consciousness	Co-creating and practicing in Communities of Spiritual Diversity	Addressing symptoms of imbalance by creating more balanced Communities of Spiritual Diversity
Eco-Consciousness	Co-creating and practicing in Communities of Universal Diversity	Addressing symptoms of imbalance by creating more balanced Communities of Universal Diversity

In contrast, the client who presents primarily with an *internalizing disorder* (which are usually seen as also belonging to the *Axis I disorders*) can be viewed as someone who is operating primarily at the personal level (see Chapter 1) consciousness. Such a client may have an overdeveloped parent ego state, which means that he is more or less driven to be grown up and successful in traditional ways. The social worker can draw methods from each of the paradigms of practice (see Table 13.1, column 3) that may encourage such a client to become more sensitive to and responsible toward his own deeper feelings and needs.

The methods described briefly in Table 13.1 may help the client heal his symptoms. As described earlier, from a spiritual perspective, healing does not necessarily reduce suffering but rather helps change the relationship that the client has with his suffering. In general, the client begins to understand the root cause of his suffering and begins to reintegrate his body–mind–spirit–environment connection.

STUDY QUESTIONS

1. How is spiritually oriented social work practice *radical* in nature? How is it *inclusive?*

2. From a spiritual perspective, what are mental-health symptoms for? Think about one of your own mental-health symptoms that has persisted over time. Describe how you might relate to that symptom from a Western medical model perspective. Now describe how you might view that symptom from a spiritual perspective. Which perspective do you like better? Why?

3. From a spiritual perspective, what is healing? From this perspective, how healthy are you today?

4. What are dis-identification and identification for? What do you hope to dis-identify from next in your life? What is the next level of identification you anticipate you are moving toward?

5. Why does the spiritually oriented social worker believe that mental-health symptoms have multiple causes? Describe the multiple causes that you believe are associated with one of your symptoms. Do you think you understand all of the causes of your symptom? Why or why not?

6. Describe a spiritual perspective to mental-health diagnoses. How might such a perspective be helpful to the client? What dangers might there be in taking a spiritual perspective, and how would you minimize them?

RESOURCES

Canda, E. R., & Smith, E. D. (2001). *Transpersonal prespectives in spirituality in social work.* New York: Haworth Press.
    This edited text contains articles that describe transpersonal approaches to social work clients.
Muller, W. (1992). *Legacy of the heart: The spiritual advantages of a painful childhood.* New York: Simon and Schuster.
    This book reframes the childhood trauma that many adults with mental-health disorders suffered as gifts to the soul.
Wilber, K. (1997). *The eye of the spirit: An integral vision for a world gone slightly mad.* Boston: Shambhala Publications.
    Wilber introduces many concepts that may be helpful to the social worker in the mental-health setting.

CHAPTER 14

SPIRITUALLY ORIENTED PRACTICE IN PHYSICAL-HEALTH SETTINGS

Since the spiritually oriented social worker views her client as a biopsychoso-cial–spiritual–environmental (BPSSE) being, she sees physical health as inseparable from mental, emotional, social, spiritual, and environmental health. The social worker's practice in physical-health settings is thus inclusive and integrative, because she strives to help the client reconnect his body with the rest of his BPSSE self.

BASIC SPIRITUAL APPROACHES TO PRACTICE IN PHYSICAL HEALTH

The Social Worker as Spiritual Advocate

The spiritually oriented social worker is a spiritual advocate who is committed to supporting the biopsychosocial–spiritual–environmental development and Highest Good of the client. As a spiritual advocate, the social worker strives to help all health-care settings become Communities of Spiritual and Universal Diversity that prioritize equal access to quality affordable health care to all people, regardless of their wealth, power, or social status.

The social worker in a health setting often finds herself in a professional team in which decision-making power is concentrated in the hands of physicians and other health administrators. Although the spiritually oriented social worker does not seek power for its own sake, she becomes concerned when decisions are made that are not in the Highest Good of her clients. The spiritually oriented social worker may be the only professional in a health setting who is concerned about the total health of the client as BPSSE well-being. Therefore, part of the role of the social worker in the physical-health setting is to advocate for the Highest Good of the client. Such spiritual advocacy might include not only speaking out in staff meetings but also working to reform administrative structures so that all health-care professionals have equal decision-making power.

The social worker also recognizes the educational, institutional, and legal restrictions that limit her ability to work with her clients in health settings. Again, the worker does not wish to engage in conflicts with other professionals simply to win battles about "turf," control, or more formal legal boundaries and rights of practice. She respects the unique educational training and licenses that each professional brings to patient care. However, she does want to advocate for the co-creation of democratic power sharing in health settings because she wants to give her clients a spiritually oriented voice in their own health care. The client's voice needs to be heard not only in staff meetings but also in the public policy forum. The social worker helps to co-create health-care policies and guidelines that support the BPSSE well-being of all people.

Healing Is Connecting

The spiritually oriented social worker approaches physical health and healing in much the same way that she approaches mental health and healing. From this perspective, the physically healthy person is seldom presenting symptom free, but he is becoming whole as he becomes increasingly *connected* with his body, mind, spirit, and environment. Thus, healing is not necessarily the elimination of suffering, but rather an ongoing process in which the person connects in an increasingly profound and deep way with his BPSSE "parts."

What is connection and connecting? A person can connect with all of his parts in many different ways, through various physical, emotional, cognitive, social, spiritual, and environmental processes. The client can use any combination of processes in his own healing work. The social worker can invite the client to use these processes to express and experience body presenting symptoms, healing practices, and healthy states.

Three levels of connecting work that the client can engage in include work with the presenting symptom, the healing practice, and the ideal health. These are described in Box 14.1. As will be seen, each of these levels can be worked with physically, emotionally, cognitively, socially, spiritually, and environmentally.

On the *physical* level, the person can use his own body images to connect with his ecological, physical, emotional, cognitive, social, or environmental "parts." For example, the person could make three drawings, one of which represents his presenting symptom (that currently ails him), one his healing practice (that he currently uses to heal), and one his ideal health (that he ultimately hopes for). The

---

BOX 14.1

LEVELS AND DESCRIPTIONS OF CONNECTING WORK

Presenting symptom	The physical illness for which the client initially asked for help
Healing practice	The method the client imagines would heal the presenting symptom
Ideal health	The state of well-being that the client hopes she ultimately will have

client could also express his presenting symptom, healing practice, and ideal health through physical movements or dances. A third physical method might utilize music; the client can express his presenting symptom, healing practice, and ideal health by singing songs or playing instruments. All of these body images act as bridges that help the client reconnect with his BPSSE self. The following case study provides an example of healing through the physical dimension.

CASE STUDY 14.1
HEALING THROUGH THE PHYSICAL DIMENSION

An elderly woman is under medical care for a chronic cough. The social worker discovers that she loves music but is uncomfortable singing or playing an instrument. The social worker asks her to pick out three songs—one that would best represent her physical problem, one her healing practice, and one her ideal health. She selects three old songs recorded by a favorite male vocalist of hers. One of them is about rainy weather and a romance gone bad, and this one she selects as representing her chronic cough. One of them is a popular Christmas song, and this one she picks as her healing practice. The third song, representing her ideal health, is a religious song about God.

The woman and the social worker set out to find recordings of the songs. As they listen to the three songs in the office, the client is able to make some connections among her symptom, healing practice, and health as well as her other parts. She decides, with her social worker's help, that her symptom is about her complicated grief following her husband's death, that her best healing practice would be to open up her heart to her family again, and that her ideal health would be a new spirituality that accepts the realities of life and death.

On the *emotional* level, the client seeks emotions that seem linked to his presenting symptom, healing practice, or ideal health. Like the body images mentioned above, the emotions are bridges that reconnect the client to his BPSSE self. One method of doing this work is to ask the client to choose feelings from a list of feeling words, such as *sad, mad, glad, scared, excited,* and so on. Another method would be to have the client sit in an empty chair and then experience and express the emotions that seem associated with the symptom, healing practice, and health. An example of healing work through emotional dimension is given below.

CASE STUDY 14.2
HEALING THROUGH THE EMOTIONAL DIMENSION

A 14-year-old girl is referred by her nurse to a social worker. The girl has been extremely concerned about her facial acne. The social worker asks her to sit across an empty chair and pretend that her acne can talk and then to imagine what her acne would say. The girl is at first reluctant, but then starts to yell, "I am going to ruin your life!" "Why do you want to ruin my life, acne?" asks the social worker. The girl says, "Because you are such a bad person!" and then starts to cry. This psychodrama leads to a discussion between the worker and client in which the girl talks about why she thinks she is so unlovable. It turns out that she is still blaming herself for her parents' divorce. The emotions that the girl experienced have now acted as a bridge to some of her core issues.

On the *cognitive* level, the client uses his mind as a way to bridge the BPSSE disconnections that may be associated with his body symptoms. The social worker can help the client explore the beliefs that he has about his presenting symptom, healing practice, and ideal health. She can help the client explore such beliefs by simply asking him to explore his own self-talk that is associated with the presenting symptom.

CASE STUDY 14.3
HEALING THROUGH THE COGNITIVE DIMENSION

An 80-year-old man diagnosed with Alzheimer's disease is visited in the board and care home by a spiritually oriented social worker who works with the local Adult Protective Services. The aging client has also been given a diagnosis of dysthymia. The client and social worker are able to quickly develop a good helping relationship, and both look forward to their visits together. During one visit, the worker asks the client about his depression. The client talks about his frustration and anger related to having Alzheimer's disease. The worker asks the client, "How has your view of yourself and the world changed since you started to get sick?" The client replies that he now feels that he is worthless and just a burden to his family and the world. Together, the client and social worker explore the roots of these unhelpful beliefs, and they discover that the man probably has never believed in his own worth, at least since his early childhood. They explore how he started to believe that his brilliant mind could make him valuable, because then he could make contributions at work and home. The man started to look for new ways to look at himself. "If I had never had this disease," the man told the social worker before he died, "I would have never truly learned to love myself."

On a *social* level, the social worker helps the client explore what social patterns seem to be associated with his presenting symptom, symbolic medicine, and ideal healthy state. The client might, for example, become more introverted or extroverted when he is experiencing a particular symptom. Since religious activity often involves interaction with a community, the client might also want to study how he may use his religious community as one of his sacred medicines. The social worker might also ask the client to act as if he was in his ideal healthy state.

CASE STUDY 14.4
HEALING THROUGH THE SOCIAL DIMENSION

A 20-year-old ski racer went to the sports medicine facility with a knee ligament injury. She was referred to the sports medicine facility for rehabilitation. When the social worker and young woman meet, the client presents as angry and bitter. "I was on the verge of getting an invitation to the international competition in Italy when I had this stupid injury!" she says. The social worker asks what she has been doing since then and the client shrugs and says, "Nothing." The worker asks, "When was the last time you did nothing?" "I can't remember," replies the client. "What is it like to be by yourself?" asks the worker. "I hate it," the client says, and she starts to cry. The client agrees to explore her social life and soon discovers that the reason that she fears being alone is that she has been trying to avoid her self. Pressured to be a successful athlete by her parents, she had never wanted to reflect on what she really wanted to do or on who she really is. She agrees to begin a meditation practice, with the social worker's help, to rediscover her true vocation and self.

The social worker can also help the client explore the *spiritual* significance of his presenting symptom, symbolic medicine, and ideal healthy state. The worker can ask the client, for example, why he thinks his God or Creative Spirit gave him this particular symptom at this particular time in his life. The worker can ask the client to meditate on what sacred medicine he might need in his life now to become more whole and on what ideal health really is.

CASE STUDY 14.5
HEALING THROUGH THE SPIRITUAL DIMENSION

A 30-year-old woman is recovering from a brain injury in the local hospital. The social worker makes a visit to her room and asks if he can talk with her. The woman shares that she was just recently engaged to marry an older man she had met through an Internet dating service. The social worker asks the client about her spiritual and religious history and finds out that she considers herself a mainstream Christian. The worker asks her if she believes that everything happens for a reason and she says, "So you want me to speculate on why I got hurt right now? Well, I have been thinking about that a lot. You see, Frank fell in love with me very quickly and started talking about marriage within a month. I was not really ready but I felt that he was a good man and I agreed. Now I can see that I was not really ready yet to marry. I wish I hadn't had to have had this accident to get some time to reflect on all of this, but I suppose I have to trust that it is all for the best."

Finally, on the *environmental* level, the client can explore how his presenting symptoms, symbolic medicines, and ideal healthy state are related to the larger environment he lives in. The spiritually oriented social worker realizes that in an unhealthy environment, healthy people will have symptoms. For example, a child diagnosed with serious food allergies to dairy and wheat products might be seen on a spiritual level as also having a painful reaction to factors in his family, community, and/or local ecosystem. Such factors might include his parents' unhappy marriage, the pressures in his neighborhood for children to be successful, and the loss of natural habitat around the edges of his community.

CASE STUDY 14.6
HEALING THROUGH THE ENVIRONMENTAL DIMENSION
(FAMILY ENVIRONMENT)

A father brings his 11-year-old daughter to the health clinic. The girl has been having chronic headaches and stomach aches. The physician cannot find any physical cause for these symptoms, so she asks the social worker to visit with the child and her father. The worker discovers that the father has been a single parent for almost 11 years and that the child's mother abandoned the family and has not contacted the girl since she left. The worker also determines that the girl is a straight-A student in school but has few friends and very low self-esteem. In another family session, the social worker invites the father to imagine that the symptoms that his daughter is experiencing are actually messages from not only her soul but also from the family's soul. The father breaks down and starts to cry. "I am sorry," he says, "it is not like me to cry like this." The worker responds, "Perhaps it actually really *is* like you to cry like this. I wonder if your tears might help both you and your daughter heal." Although her symptoms do not immediately go away, the daughter begins reporting that she feels better.

CASE STUDY 14.7
HEALING THROUGH THE ENVIRONMENTAL DIMENSION
(ECOSYSTEM ENVIRONMENT)

A 44-year-old woman has been diagnosed for years with Chronic Fatigue Syndrome (CFS). Although she lives in a rural upper mountain valley, she travels into the city once a month to see a physician who is a CFS specialist. Her physician recommends that she see a social worker in the city and she makes the appointment so that she can see both health care providers on the same trip next month. During that visit, the social worker realizes that the client is very connected to her natural environment and they decide together to use natural metaphors for the healing work. The client imagines her CFS is like an extended drought in the upper desert. Then she imagines that her healing practice might be like a series of winter storms that build up the snow pack in the mountains. She imagines that her ideal healthy state would be like a gently warming spring, during which the snow pack slowly melts and nourishes a rich return of plant and animal life to the mountain slopes and valley floor. The client makes drawings of these images and hangs them in her study at home. She also has occasional dreams about these images that she journals. She reports in later sessions that as she works with these images, she has had insights into the value and meaning of her own body symptoms. "I am just beginning to value the different cycles of energy of my body, just like I value the cycles of the seasons and weather in the mountains I live in," she said.

Use of Body Symbolism and Rituals from Religious Traditions

The spiritually oriented social worker is always respectful of any religious beliefs, doctrines, and rituals that the client may have. She or he also recognizes that the religious client's beliefs, doctrines, and rituals can be very helpful in the healing process, and so remains open to working with the client's religious language and metaphors. Spiritual and religious work is often some of the most personal work

BOX 14.2

SOME PRACTICE STRATEGIES FOR SOME DIFFERENT INTENTIONS AND TYPES OF PRAYER

Client prays for her self	Social worker supports client's intentions prior to prayer
	At her request, social worker listens to and supports client's prayer
	Client shares with worker her experiences of process
Client prays with others for her self	Social worker supports client's intentions prior to prayer
	At her request, social worker may pray with client
	Client shares with worker her experiences of process
Client asks others to pray for her	Social worker supports client's intentions prior to prayer
	At her request, social worker may pray for client
	Client shares with worker her experiences of process
Client prays for self and others	Social worker supports client's intentions prior to prayer
	At her request, social worker may listen to or pray with client
	Client shares with worker her experiences of process

that a client can engage in, and because of this, clients will often feel especially vulnerable when engaged in such work.

Prayer and other practices of supplication can be helpful to the client. Prayers can be offered by the client as well as by other people who may wish to support the client's healing process. The social worker determines during the assessment whether the client would like to use any supplication practices and then supports the client's intentions. The social worker recognizes that each client may have unique intentions and prefer unique types of prayer (see Box 14.2).

There are many different types of prayer. Some clients may prefer praying alone, and in such cases, the social worker respects the client's wishes and may process the client's intentions before the prayer as well as the experiences and outcomes of the process afterwards. Some clients may want to pray in the company of another person or with many other people. In such cases, the client may or may not want the social worker to pray with him. In other instances, the social worker may agree to pray with the client. The client may also want to pray for other people's healing as well as his own. Again, the social worker may participate in the client's prayers and process if both client and worker agree to this.

> **CASE STUDY 14.8**
> **LISTENING TO GOD THROUGH THE LANGUAGE OF ILLNESS**
>
> As part of the health-care team at the city clinic, the social worker visits with a 40-year-old woman who has been having chronic stomach pain. The woman has already been seen by the physician who has recommended a new diet. During the assessment interview, the woman reported that, in her religious tradition, she was taught that the human

body was created by God in God's image. The worker then asks her if she would be comfortable doing some exploration of the meaning of her illness from that perspective, which they agree suggests that all of her body experiences are God-given. When the woman consents, the social worker has her do a drawing of her body, including her strengths and diseases. Then the woman decides to ask for insight into her illness through prayer. The worker sits with the client as she prays to her God and contemplates God's answer. The woman eventually reports that she now thinks she has not trusted God enough to give her the challenges she needs to have as well as the solutions. She decides that she will look at her stomach pain as a message from her God. Eventually, in further sessions in which she uses more prayer and contemplation, she has the insight that God wants her to stop "stomaching" so much abuse from other people. Building on that insight, the worker helps her do some assertiveness-building work. She learns to establish healthier boundaries with her children, husband, and co-workers.

Social Worker's Participation in Religious Rituals

Similar practice strategies can also be used by the social worker when the client wants to engage in rituals that are familiar and sacred to him (such as blessings, prayers, and baptisms). In general, the social worker continues to be respectful of the client's beliefs and rituals and continues to dialogue with the client about what roles the worker should take in supporting the client's process. The worker assesses the openness and readiness of both her client and her self to do religious work. At times, the worker will participate and process in little, if any, of the client's religious experience. At other times, the worker will be very much involved. The worker may also involve clergy to assist in religious work. For example, in many hospices a pastoral counselor or clergy member is on the staff who conducts religious rituals with the client at the client's request.

Ethical Issues in Spiritually Oriented Practice in Health-Care Settings

The spiritually oriented social worker is aware of a number of ethical or value issues that are related to everyday practice in health-care settings. The way the social worker handles these ethical challenges is critical to the outcomes of her or his practice. This is true for a number of reasons.

First, one reason why many clients struggle with their physical symptoms is because their very personal spiritual (and sometimes religious) experiences have not been valued or supported by other people. Because of such experiences, they may not feel safe doing their spiritual work and may even neglect their spirituality (and sometimes religiosity) as a tool in the healing process. They may have great difficulty trusting the social worker enough to do spiritual work with them.

The spiritually oriented social worker is always sensitive to the feelings and beliefs of such clients. The social worker never demands that the client engage in any spiritual practice without the client's permission, and respects where the client is at developmentally. The social worker does "open the door" for the client in as much as he is ready to talk about any of the client's issues with her. He respects when and how the client may be ready to "go through" that door and talk about or engage in spiritual practices. The social worker realizes that he has to take the client "where she is at" and therefore may have to process how and why it is hard for the client to do spiritual work *before* the two of them ever engage in such work.

Second, the spiritually oriented social worker may find himself working with other professionals who also have not had their own spiritual or religious experiences valued and supported. These others may value only scientific ways of knowing and devalue spiritual and religious processes. In such situations, the other professionals may be uncomfortable or even threatened by the social worker's methods, and may even object to the use of spiritual or religious methods in any health-care setting. He is flexible enough to use the language of the client, whether it be religious, scientific, or spiritual, to foster effective communication.

In such situations, the social worker realizes that his effectiveness in working with other professionals in the conference and lunch rooms is as important as his effectiveness in working with his clients in the office room. He makes a point of forming and developing relationships with those professionals who will let him relate with them. He respects the right of other professionals to disagree with him, but is also willing to educate other professionals about the role of spirituality in healing and life in general. The worker is flexible enough to use the scientific language that other professionals may prefer if he thinks that such language will help him foster positive change.

Third, there may be many people in the mainstream culture who do not yet understand how spirituality and religiosity are often related but still different processes. They may also strongly identify with a particular religion but devalue spiritual processes. With such a value system, such people may not believe that it is appropriate for a social worker to work in any of the religious or spiritual realms. They may instead prefer that clients (or their loved ones, or other members of their religious community) only go to their own clergy to do spiritual work.

The spiritually oriented social worker respects the beliefs and rituals and need for privacy and exclusivity that such people may have. The worker understands and accepts that such people may never be willing to accept his work. He does not try to force his work on any client. He does, however, also respect the right of adults in any community who freely choose to come see him for services. In such cases, he will support the client's process as well as the client's own autonomy and freedom. He will try to help the client deal effectively with the reactions she may experience from others in her community who oppose her work with the social worker, so that the client can hopefully both stay in integrity with her self and stay in relationship with her community.

Fourth, there may also be people in the community who feel strongly that certain religious beliefs, doctrines, or rituals essentially "belong" to their own religion or culture. Because of these feelings, they may oppose the use of certain beliefs, doctrines, or rituals by a social worker, particularly if the worker does not belong to their religion or culture.

The social worker respects such concerns and understands that many people who feel that way are still understandably angry about the way their family, or community, or ancestors were treated by other peoples. The social worker would never try to represent himself as someone he is not, or pretend to be an expert in some sacred ritual in which he has insufficient training. However, the social worker also hopes that the people of the world will eventually find ways to share their resources, traditions, and wisdom with each other freely and equally. With that goal in mind, the social worker tries to help people heal the wounds that make them fearful, suspicious, and withholding of others. He also strives to help educate all people to be respectful of all religious traditions and to help co-create the globe into an international Community of Spiritual and Universal Diversity.

Other Methods for Healing

The spiritually oriented social worker can also try to help clients find methods of healing that come from traditions with which the clients are still unfamiliar. Across time, most religions have found diverse symbolic meanings in the human body. Because of this history, and because of the religious freedom that people in the United States and many other countries enjoy, spiritually oriented social workers can draw from a large number of traditions in developing practice methods in physical-health settings. The social worker can help clients discover more about various traditional meanings and then help them identify which symbols they are most drawn to and with which they want to work.

For example, in many traditions, the human body is viewed as a microcosm of the entire Multiuniverse. Some religions teach that the human body is created in the "image of God." Such a tradition might teach that, just as the spiritual nature of God is understood to be less apparent but more important than the material manifestation of the God through the Universe, the spiritual nature of the person is viewed as less apparent but more important than the material nature of the body. The client who is drawn to this perspective can use these symbolic meanings in his or her own healing.

In general, the method is first to help the client discover the religious symbols and rituals that are most meaningful to the client. The most effective social worker is flexible enough to work with diverse symbols and rituals because he honors the belief system of each client and realizes that, from a spiritual perspective, they are all potentially useful in fostering healing. Then the social worker helps the client use the symbols and rituals to foster her healing.

CASE STUDY 14.9
RECOVERING SPIRITUALITY IN THE RECOVERY ROOM

A 22-year-old woman is recovering from a bicycle accident, in which she was hit by a careless motorist. She had a concussion, broken ribs, bruised internal organs, and a separated shoulder. She asks to see a hospital social worker in her room. She tells the social worker that she has been thinking as she has laid in her bed recovering, that this is a good time for her to do some personal work. The social worker explains that she is spiritually oriented and that she could offer the client many different kinds of methods of self-exploration. The client asks about these, and after hearing about some of the traditions that the worker is familiar with, decides that she is especially interested in Buddhism. The worker explains that, although she is not a Buddhist, she would be able to work with her with some of the Buddhist techniques she has studied. The woman is especially interested in the Dalai Lama's work, and they begin a study group where the worker reads from a book and they discuss the ideas and try some exercises.

The worker can offer the client simple ideas about healing that are drawn from different traditions, without going into all the beliefs, doctrines, and rituals of each tradition. For example, the right side of the body was seen in some traditions as masculine, the left side as feminine. Ancient warriors, for example, often held their swords in their right hand and their shields in their left. A client who is attracted to this perspective might use this simple rule as a way to make meaning out of his or her body presenting symptoms. For example, if a series of physical injuries have occurred on the left side, the person might consider the possibility that there is an imbalance of masculine energy being expressed in his or her life. Similarly, in some traditions, the right side of the body is understood to reflect current psychosocialspiritual issues and the left side more long-term psychosocialspiritual issues. Such ideas might be fascinating to some clients and might offer ways to begin working with body symptoms.

Box 14.3 below summarizes some ways to work with the body in each of the seven paradigms of transformation. The social worker draws from all the paradigms in her practice.

BOX 14.3

EXAMPLES OF METHODS THAT MAY HELP FOSTER TRANSFORMATION IN HEALTH SETTINGS

Spiritual Momentum	The client explores the body–mind–spirit relationship that people had across the history of her culture, family, and own life.
Mindful Daily Living	The client develops mindfulness of how he listens to and cares for his body.
Spirit with Heart	The client uses her feelings to communicate with her body.
Religious Self	The client uses rituals from his own and/or other religions to heal his body.
Body Consciousness	The client develops her body–mind–spirit connection through intentional exercises.
Community Consciousness	The client engages in physical service to his community.
Eco-Consciousness	The client engages in physical service to her ecosystem.

STUDY QUESTIONS

1. What is a spiritual advocate? How do you feel and what do you think about the concept? Could you do such work?

2. How is healing the body also a "wholing" process?

3. How is healing also connecting?

4. What are the three levels of connecting work?

5. With a partner, identify a body symptom, healing practice, and ideal healthy state for yourself. Then work with those levels in the physical, cognitive, emotional, social, spiritual, and environmental dimensions. What did you learn about yourself?

6. How can a social worker help a client who wants to use prayer to heal? Would you be comfortable doing this?

7. Name the four kinds of ethical issues described in the chapter. Which have you encountered yourself? Explain.

RESOURCES

Mindell, Arnold. (2004). *The quantum mind and healing*. New York: Hampton Roads.
   Arnie Mindell's pioneering work describes approaches to working with symptoms of the body and mind. His other books are equally helpful to the spiritually oriented social worker.
Murphy, M. (1992). *The future of the body: Explorations into the further evolution of human nature*. New York: Jeremy P. Tarcher/Putman.
   This well-documented book describes the literature on body–mind–spirit research.

CHAPTER 15

SPIRITUALLY ORIENTED PRACTICE IN CRIMINAL JUSTICE SETTINGS

Clients referred to social workers in the criminal justice system are often challenging. Social workers are faced with not only the apparent low motivation often seen in such clients but also by the often hostile attitudes directed at their clients by other professionals and the public.

BASIC SPIRITUAL APPROACHES TO PRACTICE IN CRIMINAL JUSTICE

Busted Open to Spiritual Transformation

Spiritually oriented practice in the criminal justice system begins with the recognition that the suffering the client is experiencing is also an opportunity for transformation. The client in the criminal justice system has usually been "busted" in more than one way. First, he is busted because his behavior has been identified as inappropriate by someone else who has the power to force "corrective action" on him. Second, the client's heart and mind and soul may also have been, at least temporarily, "busted" open. It is in this window of opportunity, opened by suffering, that there is also an opportunity for transformation.

On the emotional (heart) level, when a person is "busted," he may feel guilt and shame, as well as fear and anger and sadness. He may be suddenly flooded with intense feelings, as he is suddenly thrown into a new situation, with little sense of control over events.

Since the person's integrity, or wholeness, has been publically challenged, the person may also experience a conflict between his view of himself and the view that others have of him. Thus, on the cognitive (mind) level, the client may suddenly have to deal with all kinds of new "input" that is flooding in from his environment. He will be called a criminal and he might be treated abusively. He may start to question the views he has held about himself and the world.

On the spiritual (soul) level, the client may feel especially challenged to make sense out of his suffering. He might ask how he got to this point in his life. He might feel like he is also a victim in life, and feel like he is being unfairly treated. He could also start to wonder what the root causes of his behaviors really are, and think about what he might want to change in the way he thinks, and feels, and acts in the world.

Remaining Busted Open to Spirit

The client who has been busted by other people often wants to return to the much more comfortable guarded position that she has been used to. The spiritually oriented worker strives to help the nonvoluntary client stay busted—that is, stay open to and accepting of spiritual experience and transformation. The work can involve all the biopsychosocial–spiritual–environmental aspects of being. The purpose of helping the client stay open is not to punish her, but to help her heal.

On the *physical* level, the social worker can work with any body symptoms that the client may have, in order to help her stay "busted open." The experience of being busted is often associated with some kind of body reaction. The client has been in a state of high, ongoing stress, and may have changed her patterns of eating, sleeping, rest, and exercise. Her body may react in any number of ways (for example, the client may catch a cold, have headaches, or experience persistent stomach problems). The worker helps the client listen to her symptoms, take better care of herself physically, and make meaning or significance from the symptoms. This process of listening to and caring for the body is often an important first step in the transformative process. The following four case study examples all describe work with the same young woman.

CASE STUDY 15.1
WORK ON THE PHYSICAL LEVEL

A social worker working in the juvenile justice system is given a case of a 15-year-old girl who was caught shoplifting drugs at a local grocery store. Although she claimed that it was her friends' idea to steal (who were not caught), she was given a fine, community service time, and ordered into counseling by the judge. The girl is crying when she comes in for her first session with her mother and the worker.

The social worker asks the mother to stay outside and then first asks the girl to tell her story. The girl explains to him that she was stealing cough medication to get high. She used to be an A student and a cheerleader. "Now I am a druggie," she says. During that first session, they talk about her crime. The worker also asks her about her physical symptoms. The girl says that she has been worried and unable to sleep. She has also been depressed and has had some suicidal thoughts. The worker finds out that the girl has had insomnia earlier in her life during periods of stress. The worker asks the girl what she thinks about at night when she cannot sleep. The girl cries again and she says she worries about "everything." The social worker asks the girl to start exercising. He explains that exercise may be the simplest way for her to help herself feel better again. She is reluctant but agrees to design an aerobic program for her to begin. Although she struggles at first with her commitment, she eventually exercises regularly three times a week. Later in the sessions, she starts to feel better. She admits to him that "exercising does make me feel better; I know that now." They then begin to explore the root causes of her addictive behaviors.

On the *emotional* level, the worker can help the client process, understand, and accept her emotional reactions to what has happened, so that she can stay busted open. The social worker asks the client what emotional reactions she has had and then together they can explore the roots and meanings of these feelings. Often a client's feelings can act as a compass, guiding the client in transformative work. The social worker can sometimes help the client stay open to feelings by asking the client to do nonverbal expressions of those feelings.

CASE STUDY 15.2
WORK ON THE EMOTIONAL LEVEL (CONTINUED FROM CASE STUDY 15.1)

The worker asks the girl to talk about how she feels about her life. This is difficult for the girl at first, because she is not used to talking about her feelings. So the worker has the girl bring her favorite music (which is rap music) to the office. When they play it, the worker encourages the girl to try movements to the music. Eventually, the girl identifies emotions in the music through her body. Gradually, through more movement and discussion, she is able to also identify feelings that she has. She talks at first about how she "really does not like anything" about her boyfriend but that she sleeps with him anyway. She also talks about how she does not like her friends, mostly because they usually act like they do not like her. When the social worker asks her about her family, the girl says her mom is too controlling and her dad is distant. The social worker then asks her what does matter to her, and she says, "I don't know." They agree to make her discovery of what matters to her a goal for the next months.

Eventually the girl decides that she wants to go to a trade school and learn to do hair styling work. The next fall she is admitted into a night program at the local community college so she can finish her high school degree during the day. "How do you feel about your plans for next year?" asks the worker. "How do you want my answer, in dance or in words?" the girl replies. The social worker leans back in his chair and replies, "Maybe both."

On the *cognitive* level, the social worker helps the client become more aware of her thought patterns and how they are related to her emotions and behaviors. The client also may want to learn how to use her mind in new and more constructive ways, to practice such methods as yoga, meditation, or contemplation. Sometimes storytelling can be one of the most effective ways to lead a client to an idea.

CASE STUDY 15.3
WORK ON THE COGNITIVE LEVEL (CONTINUED FROM CASE STUDY 15.2)

"What do you think about when you worry?" asks the social worker. The girl replies, "I think about everything, whether my mom is ok, if I am going to flunk out of school, if Billy and I will break up . . ." The social worker asks her why she worries about her mom, and the girl says that she has been concerned since her mother and father got a divorce five years ago. "Well, I can see why you started to worry, but I am not sure it serves you very well any more. Do you really want to be worried about everything like this your whole life?" "Well, no," replies the girl, "but how can I stop worrying? I have tried but I just worry more." "Did you ever hear the story about the Zen master and the wind?" "No." "Well, one day one of the master's students asked her the same question you asked me just now. It was a breezy day and the master took her outside and asked her to stop the wind. The student said that it was impossible to stop the wind and the master smiled and said that the student was correct, and as long as the wind was not of typhoon strength, that she need not be concerned." The girl looks at her social worker, half puzzled and half amused. Then she says, "Did the master mean that you shouldn't worry about worry, unless there is a real danger?" "You're starting to get it," says the social worker.

On the *social* level, the worker helps the client stay open to new social behaviors. The most common method is to co-design, support, and evaluate a "homework" assignment. The homework is a way for the client to act her way into new ways of thinking and feeling, which is often easier for her than to feel or think her way into new ways of acting. The new behaviors can also lead the client to her soul.

CASE STUDY 15.4
WORK ON THE SOCIAL LEVEL (CONTINUED FROM CASE STUDY 15.3)

The social worker asks the girl to talk about what kinds of relationships she would want to have. The girls replies, "I don't know . . ." "Yet," adds the social worker. They begin to explore that question. The worker teaches the girl that it is usually easier to figure out what you do not want first and then figure out what you do want after that. With that in mind, the girl is able to identify that she wants to have friends that do not want to "just get high and steal." Later she realizes that she wants friends who "are nice to me." She decides that her homework assignment will be for her to be true to her own self, regardless of what her friends think. When the girl discovers how hard this is to do, the social worker supports her progress and process, regardless of the pace at which she is progressing.

The worker also asks the client about her relationships with her parents. The girl says that no matter what she does, she never feels like she is "good enough" for her dad. She adds that her mother is "even more uptight than her dad" because she is "always finding something wrong" with what she does. "How do you want to respond to them?" asks the social worker. "Maybe I would like to just not get angry with them, just stay cool." She starts working on this change. Over time, the girl discovers that she is not "as charged" by her parents as she was. The social worker tells her, "You are beginning to learn to do something that few adults are good at, which is not to go into emotional reaction to your family of origin."

On the *spiritual* level, the social worker employs Conscious Use of Higher Self to assist the client to stay open. The social worker always sees his clients in the criminal justice system as spiritual beings who are living in human bodies. He refuses to give up hope that they can eventually use their suffering as an opportunity to further their own spiritual development. He takes seriously the suffering that his clients have inflicted on others, and accepts the laws that regulate the criminal justice system, yet he also refuses to join in trying to inflict unnecessary suffering on his clients. Instead, he works to help the client shift her spiritual perspective, from viewing herself as a victim who has the right to take anything she wants to viewing herself as a blessed being who has the responsibility to serve other people, living things, and ecosystems. The social worker knows that his clients live in a real world in which there are consequences for every action. He also knows that his clients need to experience compassion, forgiveness, and love at least as much as they need the enforcement of consequences.

One way to help a client continue opening up to his or her own experience of Creative Spirit is through the use of creative expressions. Some clients in prison may use creative writing, for example, as a means of self-expression and exploration. Some clients may write daily entries in a journal or work on poetry. Such writing may be a private and therefore a relatively safe way for clients to begin exploring their spiritual lives.

CASE STUDY 15.5
WORK ON THE SPIRITUAL LEVEL IN A PRISON SETTING

The new social worker begins her first day at the juvenile men's lock-up facility at the state prison. Some of the other prison staff are impressed with how she seems unafraid of the clients and becomes involved in getting to know them. The young men in the prison respond to her friendliness and openness. She soon discovers that several of them are writing in their rooms every day, although they prefer to hide their creative writing from other people in the prison. She asks her clients to let her read their writing and soon these sessions evolve into opportunities for the social worker also to do talk therapy with her clients, in individual and group sessions. She learns that many of the men write about their emotional and spiritual experiences and that they share vocational and relationship dreams similar to most people in mainstream culture. Eventually, she starts to run another support group for the men as they leave the prison and transition into mainstream life again. When her first client finishes high school, the support group attends his graduation ceremony.

Moving from Crucifixion to Transformation

The spiritually oriented social worker knows that the client needs not only to receive compassion and forgiveness, but also to offer compassion and forgiveness to others. The ultimate goal of work in the criminal justice system is transformation, and the client must eventually take responsibility for his own behaviors if he is to further develop spiritually. As the client takes increased responsibility, he stops looking at himself as a victim of life and looks instead at the world with gratitude and for opportunities to be of service to other people, living things, and the ecosystems that support all life.

The social worker knows that suffering is often the greatest therapist. Some clients struggle with their belief that they do not deserve their suffering. Most people experience unwanted and what seems unjust suffering in their lives. This experience of *crucifixion*, or unfair and cruel treatment "from life," challenges the client to reach deeper inside of himself to find new ways to still have love, compassion, and forgiveness for himself and the world. From a spiritual perspective, the experience of crucifixion can lead to deep transformation in a person's life. The social worker realizes that many, if not most, of her clients in the criminal justice system have experienced crucifixion in their lives, and that such clients may need assistance in moving beyond their reactions of bitterness and resentment. Although the social worker may have to wait until the client is ready and the timing is right, sooner or later, she must try to help the client use his suffering as an opportunity for spiritual growth.

CASE STUDY 15.6
NO TRANSFORMATION WITHOUT CRUCIFIXION

The client walks into the social worker's office for the first time. "I don't know why I am here," he says angrily. "They say that I was drinking and driving." The social worker replies, "Tell me what happened." The client explains how he was not only falsely blamed for driving when intoxicated (DUI), but that this has happened to him several other times in the past two years. Instead of challenging this obvious falsehood immediately, the social worker replies, "It sounds like you have had a lot of things happen that have been really hard for you." "You got that right," says the client, "I never get a break! Other people—those rich people—are getting breaks all the time and look how much they get away with, but not me, never me!" The social worker lets the man tell the story of his life, from his perspective.

Later, as the work progresses, the social worker asks, "Well, I can see that you have had tremendous suffering your whole life, but I keep wondering, what are you going to do with this suffering you have now?" "What do you mean?" asks the client. "Well, what do you think suffering is for?" "Got me, you tell me, you are the educated one," he replies. "The word *educate* originally just meant to 'draw out' wisdom that is inside of us. So if the wisdom traditions of the world, discovered by our ancestors who were basically like us, do indeed contain the collective wisdom of humanity, then it seems that maybe each of us, including you and I, are sometimes nudged by the universe, so to speak, to finally decide to learn to love our selves," says the worker. "I already do love myself—and how is suffering supposed to make you love yourself anyway?" asks the client. The social worker answers, "Well, maybe when no one on the outside is supporting me, and things are going badly, it almost forces me to go inside and get 'educated,' and find out who I really am meant to be, and then try to be that person I am meant to be, and even learn to love that person. Maybe there really can be no transformation without a crucifixion."

Still later in the work, the client says, "You know, I did not realize how my anger had become like a fog that gave me a false sense of security but also kept me from seeing reality. I always knew down deep that I was 'bull shitting' everyone, including myself. I am beginning to see that I have never loved myself very much at all, and that I have always been at war with everyone, including myself. I am tired of fighting. I want to learn to love myself, once I figure out who he is. I want to try to give up my anger, even if it takes the rest of my life." "What else is life for?" smiles the worker.

The Prisons in Our Lives, External and Internal

The spiritually oriented social worker is curious about the spiritual purpose of the prisons in each client's life. He can see that most people have both kinds of "prisons"—those imposed externally by others and those imposed internally by themselves.

In his work in the justice system, the social worker knows, of course, that the client has been imprisoned or "seized" against her will and has probably experienced a profound loss of control, accompanied with intense feelings of anger, fear, and sadness. The social worker addresses these concerns at the beginning of her work with the client, knowing that they must be addressed before deeper work can be done. The helping relationship often develops slowly, and the client's difficulties need to be heard.

Self-work is hard enough to do when it is entered into voluntarily; the client must often face very painful realities about herself and the world in order to grow. However, when the self-work is court-ordered, the client must also face the personal demons that often arise from having her integrity publically questioned. In such situations, the client may feel and think that she is the victim. When the client is also imprisoned, then she must also face the public humiliation of being treated like a child—a child who must be watched and confined and punished. The spiritually oriented social worker understands, however, that the client's suffering can help liberate her from the prisons in her life into true freedom.

The client has been "convicted" but the "convictions," or strong beliefs, that supported her imprisonment are usually held by other people, rather than by the client herself. The worker's task in part is to help the client find her own convictions, and live with integrity in relationship to them.

CASE STUDY 15.7
FIRST DAY IN PRISON

The social worker reaches his hand out to his new client, who just arrived at the prison. She refuses his invitation and instead sits down with her head in her hands. They sit there quietly for a minute, and then she starts to sob. The worker listens to her cry, and when she is still again, he says, "I am glad you can cry. I don't blame you for being bummed." "What do you know? What kind of a world puts a mother in jail? I know it is illegal to do drugs, but why must I be separated from my children?" The worker is quiet again for a few moments and replies, "You are right. I do not know what it is like for you. But I am willing to listen." The client looks up at him and wipes her eyes. "Nobody ever listens to me, especially any man." "I don't blame you for not trusting me. Is there anyone in your life you trust?" "Not really," she says. "Well, if it takes you a long time before you decide you can maybe trust me a little, then that's OK. Take as long as you need," the social worker says.

The practice of *penitence,* which is the experience of sorrow for one's actions, may or may not be facilitated by imprisonment. Imprisonment can lead to feelings of sorrow that one has been busted. However, deep (or real) penitence may begin when the client's heart and mind and soul are open to see that suffering that he has caused to himself, to other people, and/or to other living things and ecosystems. When facilitating penitence, the social worker's task is to help the client enhance his own conscious awareness of the consequences of his actions, perhaps through such methods as meditation, contemplation, and prayer. Some clients will feel penitence in relation to both other people as well as to their God or sense of Creative Spirit. The worker also facilitates the client's awareness and appropriateness of his own emotions. Such work can be done with individuals or in a group context.

CASE STUDY 15.8
WORK ON PENITENCE

The social worker sees clients at the Family Trauma Center, which treats perpetrators and victims of child maltreatment. She has found that many of her male sexual abuse perpetrators respond to a film that she found in which three women who were molested as children talk about the short- and long-term consequences of their victimization.

In the group she is running now, she has five men who are participating in a 12-week group that uses multiple methods of treatment. In the first week, the men meet each other and tell the stories of their abusive behavior. In the second week, they are asked to consider the physical, emotional, cognitive, social, spiritual, and environmental etiologies (causes) of their abusive behavior. It turns out that most of them have histories of sexual trauma themselves, as well as poor impulse control, low self-esteem, anger at their God (like most people, each of these men stated that he believes in a God), and alcohol abuse. In the third week, the men are introduced to the concept of penitence, watch the film, and then discuss their reactions. One of the men is visibly shaken and he tearfully talks about his sorrow, guilt, and shame about molesting his daughter. Most of the other men also own their own feelings of sorrow and remorse. The one man that states that he "did not feel anything" and does not see "what the big deal is" actually turns out to be the one who makes a suicide attempt a month later.

The practice of *repentance* is a practice of will, in which the client resolves to have a transformation of heart, mind, and behavior. Repentance is thus an active process in which the person puts penitence into action. The social worker supports the client as he takes increasing responsibility for the well-being of other people, living things, and ecosystems.

CASE STUDY 15.9
REPENTANCE (CONTINUED FROM CASE STUDY 15.8)

The sexual abuse perpetrator group starts to talk about repentance during their sixth meeting. The social worker recognizes that all of her clients have felt "dis-eased," and she asks the men to consider what they need to do to feel "at ease" again with themselves, with their families, communities, and their Gods.

One of the men, for example, states that he wants a reunification with his wife and family, and that he is "willing to do anything" to get his family back. The group helps him identify his next step, which is to ask for permission to start counseling sessions, both with his children and with his wife.

Another man says that he would like to find inner peace again, and he wants to find a way to feel forgiveness from his God. The group asks him to find a way to have a conversation with his God, and he selects prayer as his method of supplication. He role-plays his first prayer in group, selecting an empty chair to talk to, and he tells his God (in the empty chair) that he wants to feel a sense of peace again. Then the social worker suggests he sit in the empty chair and say what he thinks his God would say back to him. The man sits down (in the chair representing God) and tells the other empty chair (now representing himself) that "I have been quite unhappy with your behavior. However, I still love you and therefore give you another chance to turn your life around. But I expect that you do a better job this time."

Paradigms of Practice in Criminal Justice Settings

The most effective spiritually oriented social worker utilizes combinations of methods drawn from any or all of the paradigms of practice available to her. As illustrated by the examples given in Box 15.1, these methods may all be used to foster transformations of consciousness.

■ ■ ■ ■ ■

BOX 15.1

EXAMPLES OF METHODS THAT MAY FOSTER TRANSFORMATION IN CRIMINAL JUSTICE SETTINGS

Spiritual Momentum	Help the client explore the causes of his own behavior and the consequences of his behavior in the lives of others.
Mindful Daily Living	Help the client change her sense of herself as a victim to new attitudes and behaviors consistent with gratitude and service.
Spirit with Heart	Help the client increase his love, compassion, and forgiveness of self and others.
Religious Self	Use religious rituals, beliefs, and doctrines to foster transformation of the client's relationships with others.
Body Consciousness	Transform the client's consciousness through body awareness and body work.
Community Consciousness	Transform the client by supporting his awareness of, responsibility to, and service to the community.
Eco-Consciousness	Transform the client by supporting his awareness of, responsibility to, and service to ecosystems.

STUDY QUESTIONS

1. What are the two ways people have been "busted" when they enter the criminal justice system? Describe how you have been busted in your own life, perhaps by a parent, or teacher, or some authority figure. How did you feel and what did you think?

2. Why does the social worker want to help the client stay "busted"? Why is staying busted often hard for people to do?

3. Describe the multidimensional developmental approach to helping clients stay busted open.

4. What are the two kinds of prisons that people may have in their lives? Describe the prison(s) in your own life, and what you feel and think about them today.

5. Why does crucifixion often precede transformation? Define both terms. Describe an example of how you have felt "crucified" in your own life, and how it may have challenged your own spiritual development.

6. What is penitence? How can the social worker help foster penitence? What is repentance, and how might it be related to penitence? How can the social worker help foster repentance?

7. Review Box 15.1. What methods appeal to you the most? Which ones are least appealing? Why?

RESOURCE

Tricycle: The Buddhist Review
   This well-edited publication has dealt with issues of imprisonment from a Buddhist perspective.

CHAPTER 16

SPIRITUALLY ORIENTED PRACTICE IN PUBLIC SOCIAL SERVICE SETTINGS

Public social service settings present unique challenges and opportunities for the spiritually oriented social worker. The clients the social workers serve in such settings often suffer from serious and multiple life challenges in interrelated areas such as poverty, employment, education, housing, mental health, physical health, legal issues, transportation, and relationships. Work with clients in social service settings is usually also influenced by multiple and sometimes conflicting administrative and public factors, such as high workloads, constricting practice protocols, lack of interagency coordination, and a shortage of agency and community resources.

The spiritually oriented social worker in such settings knows that many of her or his clients are hungry for some kind of spiritual approach to life that would help them deal with their suffering. The worker develops and implements spiritual methods that are both effective for the clients and also acceptable in the public agencies in which he or she works.

WORK IN CHILD AND FAMILY SERVICES

The spiritually oriented social worker is aware of and has compassion for the suffering of her clients. She is sensitive to the pain that families have when they deal with such issues as poverty, family maltreatment, foster care, and adoptions. She knows that most of her clients are "involuntary" clients who find themselves now involved in a public system that often seems confusing and unfriendly.

Supplication

One method that the spiritually oriented social worker can safely and effectively use in child and family service settings is supplication. The social worker develops his own method of supplication and uses it before, during, and/or after his sessions with the client. For many social workers, for example, such supplication may take the form of a prayer. Some workers may develop other rituals that may better fit with their own personal, cultural, or religious background.

Before a session, the social worker can offer a supplication for the client. There is no one correct way to do such a ritual, but some common elements of supplication can be identified. The social worker can hold an intention for the client's Highest Good. The worker can also hold an intention that the client learn from her suffering and have her suffering relieved. The worker can ask for the wisdom and compassion and skill that he needs to help the client. The worker can also ask that other people in the client's life, professionals or lay people, be blessed in some way.

Many workers wonder whether it is appropriate for them to pray privately for a client without the client's permission. Some workers need to deal with this ethical challenge by discussing the issue with the client and actually asking for permission. Other workers decide that praying for a client is always appropriate when done with pure intention for the client's Highest Good.

CASE STUDY 16.1
SUPPLICATION BEFORE A SESSION

The child protective service social worker is sitting in her office. She is preparing to go to a home to talk to a parent about a child abuse report that is to be investigated. This worker has a strong belief in her God and has used prayer in her life since she was a small child. She closes the door to her small office and then closes her eyes and starts to pray. She says, "Dear God, as you know I am going out to work with another family. Please give me the wisdom to sense what the Highest Good is for this child and his mother. Please help me make the right decisions, and act with compassion and sensitivity in all my work with them. Please also bless my supervisor, the judge, the police officers, and all the other professionals that may have to work with this family, so that they also do what is best for them. Finally, please bring hope to this family that the Highest Good will come from all their suffering, and if their suffering can be reduced as they progress in their own spiritual development, then please let it be so."

During a session, the social worker might also pray for or with a client. In such situations, as is the case with all interventions done with the client, the worker is sensitive to the needs and desires of the client. The worker asks the client how she feels and thinks about prayer, and will engage in such a method only with the client's permission. Such dialogue not only gives the client an opportunity to co-create the methods that are used in a session, but it also models methods of spiritual and religious dialogue for the client so that she can dialogue more effectively with other people in the future.

CASE STUDY 16.2
SUPPLICATION DURING A SESSION

The adoptions case worker meets with a pregnant 20-year-old woman and her 20-year-old boyfriend. They have been discussing the possibility of putting their baby up for adoption. The young couple are both tearful and the worker lets them talk about their feelings and cries with them. The theme that seems to keep emerging the most is their concern that they do the right thing for their child. Knowing that both parents belong to a local church and that they both believe in prayer, the worker asks them if they would like to pray together for guidance and support. After they both agree, the worker asks them how they want to pray, and they decide together that they will go around in a circle and will each say something in turn until they are finished. The mother starts the prayer exercise by saying, "We pray today to you God for the future of our beautiful baby boy and ask for Your guidance that we make the best decision for him." The boyfriend speaks next and says, "We ask that we know what is Your will so we can make the right decision soon." The social worker then says, "And we ask that both of these wonderful parents be blessed not only with wisdom and strength but also with peace of mind." The mother then says a few more words.

Supplication *following a session* is similar to supplication before the session. The social worker again is no longer with his clients physically, but wants to be connected with them spiritually. The worker might conduct the supplication alone in such circumstances, or he might do a ritual with another professional or person as appropriate.

CASE STUDY 16.3
SUPPLICATION AFTER A SESSION

The worker visits with her supervisor following a home visit. In that visit, the social worker had met with two men who had applied to be state foster parents. The worker was upset and told her supervisor that she really liked the two men but was afraid that their application would be turned down simply because they were gay. The worker, who had herself grown up in a tribal community, added that in her tribe, a gay couple would be completely accepted by the rest of the community. The worker decides to conduct a simple ritual in the men's behalf by burning some dried herbs and retelling an old story she had learned from her grandmother.

    The supervisor is respectful of the social worker's traditions and she sits quietly with the worker as she tells the story of how a boy was once born to a great warrior and his bride. The warrior was killed during a hunt, leaving the mother and child alone. There were no other men available to marry, but there was another woman who lived alone in the village, and so the mother decided to move in with her. The two women were not only wonderful parents to the boy, who grew up to be a greater warrior than his father, but they also became warriors themselves. No one ever knew for certain whether the two women were ever actually lovers, and no one seemed to think it mattered enough to ask them. The worker ended the story by asking Great Spirit that the community would accept these two men and welcome them as wonderful parents.

An Inclusive Family Values Hierarchy

All social work practice is value based in the sense that a social worker's beliefs fundamentally influence the way he or she conducts assessments, interventions, and evaluations. Those who are spiritually oriented realize that values are by nature in a hierarchy of importance and they are always mindful of their personal hierarchy of values as well as those held by others.

A value hierarchy can be held by an individual as well as by a community of people. Social workers, like any community of people, continue to develop a hierarchy of shared values, based on the evolving collective wisdom of all the social workers in the professional community.

A possible family values hierarchy that might inform spiritually oriented social work is provided in Box 16.1, which can be used as a model for continued discussion and dialogue. In this model, the term *family* is used to include not only the individual's nuclear or even extended human family but also the ecosystems that support the lives of the individual and his or her human family.

The spiritually oriented social worker is aware that many of the decisions made by professionals in the child welfare system (e.g., social workers, judges, lawyers, physicians, psychologists, etc.) are heavily influenced by the professionals' own personally held values. The social worker respects the right of every professional (and every person) to have personal values, but also questions whether value-based decisions are necessarily in the Highest Good of the client child and family.

Just like any other person, the spiritually oriented social worker has her own strongly held family values, and she is always mindful of the nature of her own value hierarchy. She constantly is careful not to confuse her own psychology (values, biases, prejudices, fears) with the nature of the universe. She strives to help other professionals, organizations, and communities to do the same. Her role is not to provide new morals for her clients, practice setting, or community, but rather to

---

BOX 16.1

A POSSIBLE FAMILY VALUES HIERARCHY THAT MIGHT INFORM SPIRITUALLY ORIENTED SOCIAL WORK

1 (Higher)	The long-term well-being of the ecosystems that sustain and contain all life Ecosystems include all human and nonhuman life and the air, water, and earth
2	The long-term well-being of the entire global and local communities Communities include people and their human-made environments
3	The well-being of vulnerable people who cannot care for or protect themselves Such people include children and youth, frail or disabled adults, and oppressed and minority populations
4	The individual's right to live her life according to her own values
5 (Lower)	The individual's right to force her own values on the life of another person

help co-create Communities of Spiritual and Universal Diversity in which all voices can be heard. When there are voices that are not being heard, she acts as an advocate.

CASE STUDY 16.4
FAMILY VALUES IN A CHILD WELFARE CASE

The social worker is asked to present a report to the court regarding a possible reuni-fication plan of a single father with his 8-year-old son. The man's son was having dif-ficulties in school and was referred for a medication evaluation. The boy had been temporarily removed from his custody when reports were filed that the father had re-fused to agree to give the boy psychotropic medication, after a physician determined that the boy has severe ADHD. The social worker makes a visit to the father and de-termines that he loves his son very much but that he also has strongly held religious views that prohibit or limit the use of what he calls "Western Medicine." There are no other family members to help the father raise his son. The boy tells the worker that he misses his father and wants to return home with him. The worker suggests to the court that the father begin visits with his son immediately and that a plan be implemented that gradually returns the son to the father, while a counselor–nurse team works out a compromise plan for medical care with the father. The father agrees to the plan but the judge refuses to consider it, stating that the family values of the community need to be considered and that the father "is another religious extremist" and that the boy "needs a home with two parents."

The social worker decides both to continue to work toward helping this family move toward reunification and also to work toward long-term court reform. After con-sulting with his supervisor, who is supportive, the social worker prepares a complaint about the judge's behavior and eventually the case is transferred to another judge. The worker also helps co-create a community coalition of people who will work toward better training of all professionals who work in child welfare cases. They develop a community-values dialogue group in which professionals and lay people meet once a month and work toward creating an evolving community value hierarchy through their collective wisdom.

Including the Spiritual and Religious Dimensions in Child Welfare Assessments

The spiritually oriented social worker understands the importance of including spiritual and religious factors when making evaluations for child welfare cases. He does not replace standard assessment questions with religious and spiritual ques-tions, but rather *adds* spiritual and religious content to the assessment. Box 16.2 provides some examples of spiritual and religious questions that can be added to assessments.

When assessing any child welfare case, the social worker looks at how both religious and spiritual factors uniquely present in the family being assessed. The worker knows that the religiosity of a parent can be a protective factor, strengthening

■ ■ ■ ■ ■

BOX 16.2

QUESTIONS TO EXPLORE ABOUT SPIRITUAL AND RELIGIOUS FACTORS IN ASSESSING CHILD WELFARE CASES

Religious factors	What religion, if any, does the parent belong to?
	What does the parent believe that religion teaches about parenting practices?
	In what ways, if any, is the parent's religiosity a protective factor in this family?
	In what ways, if any, does the parent's religiosity increase risks in this family?
	What supports does the parent's religious community provide the family?
	In what ways, if any, does their religious community put the family more at risk?
	How, if at all, does the parent teach the child about religiosity?
	Is the family's church a Community of Spiritual and Universal Diversity?
	Is the family's community a Community of Spiritual and Universal Diversity?
	Is the family itself a Community of Spiritual and Universal Diversity?
Spiritual factors	How important is spirituality in the parent's life?
	What has the parent learned about parenting from her or his spiritual experiences?
	In what ways, if any, is the parent's spirituality a protective factor in this family?
	In what ways, if any, does the parent's spirituality increase risks in this family?
	How, if at all, does the parent teach the child about spirituality?
	Is the family's church a Community of Spiritual and Universal Diversity?
	Is the family's community a Community of Spiritual and Universal Diversity?
	Is the family itself a Community of Spiritual and Universal Diversity?

the parent's ability to handle stress and parenting effectively, and/or that the re-ligiosity can be a risk factor, weakening the parent's ability to handle stress and parenting effectively. Similarly, the parent's spirituality can also be a risk and/or strength factor. Thus, the assessment of spirituality and religiosity must be done on a case-by-case basis, since each family will have unique spiritual and religious characteristics.

WORK IN THE PUBLIC SCHOOLS

The spiritually oriented social worker who works in a school setting is often chal-lenged to deal with a large population of children and families with a wide range of issues. Children identified with learning and behavior problems often live in families that also may have financial, housing, mental health, physical health, or legal challenges.

The school social worker includes spirituality in his or her assessments, in-terventions, and evaluations, often using different language to communicate about spirituality with different clients and professionals. The social worker listens care-fully to the language that each client uses, and asks questions to clarify what spir-itual and religious symbols will be comfortable for the client. For example, if a social worker is meeting with a family that has a strong fundamentalist religiosity,

■ ■ ■ ■ ■ ■

BOX 16.3

USING CONVENTIONAL SOCIAL WORK TERMS TO DESCRIBE SPIRITUAL CONCEPTS

Self-esteem	Children learn to love themselves as they feel loved by the universe.
Resiliency	Children are less vulnerable when they feel the world is friendly.
Protective factor	Children are stronger when they believe in something larger than themselves.
Person-in-environment	Children's well-being is related to their sense of connectedness with everything else in their world.
Strength-based	Children's faith in themselves and their world gives them security.
Evidence-based	There is growing evidence of the efficacy of such interventions as prayer and of the linkage between the body and the mind.

the worker may ask them what they believe the Bible teaches them about parenting. If the family has what they call "New Age" beliefs, the worker might ask them what their books on meditation and yoga teach them about parenting.

Similarly, the worker is also sensitive to the language and metaphors that other professionals use. Some professionals are uncomfortable with any discussion of spirituality or religiosity. The worker can still approach spirituality by using more conventional helping language, as described in Box 16.3.

The spiritually oriented social worker knows that most school systems are out of balance, tending to teach mostly to the child's brain. She might be the only professional on the staff who is responsible for the whole person, the biopsychosocial–spiritual–environmental well-being of children and their families. As a result, in an educational setting, she may spend as much of her time educating and supporting parents and other professionals about BPSSE well-being as she does working directly with her client children and families. The social worker may first initiate trainings with her own staff, to prepare them for programs that she will initiate with the parents and children in the year ahead. In these trainings, the worker models the behavior of a leader in a Community of Spiritual Diversity.

CASE STUDY 16.5
INTRODUCING SPIRITUALITY INTO A TRAINING FOR OTHER SCHOOL PROFESSIONALS

The school social worker is asked to offer an in-service training on her work at the two schools she serves. She decides to offer some training that might introduce spirituality, and she titles her presentation, "Supporting Strong Families through Strong Communities." She suggests to the teachers and administrators that children will benefit from a new program that involves parents in helping themselves and each other. One of the principles of the program will be the teaching and practice of dialogue across the cultures and religions that currently divide families and the community. Another principle will be to teach parents a strength-based perspective of parenting that helps children develop self-esteem and resiliency. In a later follow-up training, the social worker uses some of the approaches illustrated in Box 16.2 to further introduce spirituality into her work.

The social worker can also provide workshops for parents, in which spiritual content can be introduced using other, often less-threatening methods. As the social worker develops a trusting relationship with the parents, she may begin to use other strategies of transformation. At all times, however, she models respect for spiritual and religious diversity.

CASE STUDY 16.6
INTRODUCING SPIRITUALITY INTO A TRAINING FOR PARENTS

The school social worker initiates her "Supporting Strong Families through Strong Communities" program by providing a light dinner, donated by a local grocery store, for the parents of her grade schoolers early in the fall semester. She welcomes the parents and then gives each of them two blank sheets of paper and some crayons. She asks them to draw two pictures. The first is a drawing of how friendly the world seemed to them when they were in grade school. When they are finished, she asks them to draw a picture of how they think the world seems to their own children today. Then the worker has the parents sit with someone whom they do not know and share the pictures with each other. Before they talk, the paired parents are to guess which of the pictures represents the other parent and which represents the child. This exercise works very well, and the worker begins the school year with a successful beginning to her new program.

The social worker will also plan and implement educational experiences for the children in her school. She may at times do these trainings herself. Her ultimate goal, however, is to have the teachers and parents learn to lead these trainings, because she wants always to be creating new leaders who will be significant in the children's lives on a consistent and ongoing basis. Therefore, the educational experiences are best integrated in learning settings that are already established.

CASE STUDY 16.7
INTRODUCING SPIRITUALITY INTO LEARNING EXPERIENCES FOR CHILDREN

The social worker develops a curriculum for spirituality trainings for children. The key concepts are designed to be sensitive to all backgrounds, including cultural and religious differences in the community. She meets with a group of parents and teachers who have volunteered to help lead and teach the "Supporting Strong Families through Strong Communities" program. They decide that the topics should include loving yourself, caring for other people, caring for the natural environment, dealing with differences through dialogue, and making a positive difference in the world. The voluntary classes (parental and child permissions required) begin during the lunch hour, during which time participating children are fed healthy and tasty lunches low in sugar, fat, and white flour (as opposed to the school lunchroom that still feeds the children lunches high in sugar, fat, and white flour). The food is donated by the local health food market. The class is all experiential, so the children learn the concepts through play and creative work. The classes are soon full and have waiting lists.

WORK IN ADULT AND AGING SERVICES

The spiritually oriented social worker looks at his work with vulnerable adults, the aging, and their families as an opportunity to foster their spiritual development and, in doing so, help them co-create Communities of Spiritual and Universal Diversity in their families, institutions, and communities. The worker realizes that such clients often have a variety of life challenges and often experience feelings of humiliation when public social services become involved in their lives. Thus, the initial work with many clients is to help them make sense out of their suffering. Few if any clients may have expected that they would some day be nonvoluntary clients of a public social worker.

The worker accepts the client where she is. Recognizing that most people do the best they can under the circumstances as they view them, the worker is compassionate toward his clients. He also knows that the most powerful method of effecting change is not through shame but through radical acceptance of the client. *Radical acceptance* means that the social worker sees the client as a spiritual being who is in a human body and therefore worthy of love.

The worker also knows that most adults feel good about themselves when they experience success in work and relationships. Most of the clients the worker sees are more alone than they want to be in their lives. The worker helps clients find ways to reconnect, not just with other people but also with their selves and with Creative Spirit. The worker also tries to help clients find ways to give back to the world, because he knows that most people find meaning in the work and service they perform.

CASE STUDY 16.8
WORK WITH AN ADULT PROTECTIVE SERVICE (APS) CLIENT

The APS social worker goes out to visit a 70-year-old man who is living alone in his house. A referral was made to APS by the driver of the Meals on Wheels program, who was concerned when he entered the house and saw a great deal of what appeared to be garbage in the house. When the worker arrives at the house, the elderly man is at first reluctant to let the woman in. She explains to him that the driver of the food van wanted her to check on him and then asked the man about the flowers in his driveway. They struck up a conversation about gardening and the man visibly relaxed. He tells her that he has no family left, except for a son he never sees who lives on the East Coast. The social worker could see enough inside the door to determine that the man has been hoarding all kinds of materials in the hallway. From where she stood in the doorway, she could see piles of old newspapers, used milk and juice cartons, letters, and boxes of every size and shape. Instead of trying to force her way in, she says, "Well, I understand that you do not want me to visit with you now, and since you told me things seem to be going well right now, I will just leave you with my card that has a number where you can call me. Would it be OK if I checked back later to see how you are?" The man seemed relieved and said yes.

The next week the social worker returns to the man's home and suggested that they sit outside on the porch and talk for a minute. She asks him whether he has any relationships with anyone, and he tells her that he does not. She also asks about what he does with his time, what kind of work or service he likes to do. He tells her that he loves to garden when he feels well, and that he likes to talk about what he knows about gardening with people. The worker asks the man to talk about why gardening is so important to him. His eyes tear up as he tells her that it was never important until his wife died five years ago, and that she had been an avid gardener. "Will you show me some of your favorite plants?" she asks. As he walks her through the garden, she asks him more questions about his wife. She determines that he has a complicated grief, full of guilt that he was not a better man and resentment that she died before him.

During the two months that the social worker helps the client, she supports him in finding more peace of mind about his wife. She asks him why he thinks God had her die and had him live, since so often the woman lives longer than her husband. He said, "Perhaps I have more to do and learn; she was a better person than me." At her suggestion, the man decides to write a letter about his feelings, which is addressed to his wife. He also goes down to the neighborhood garden with the worker and she sets him up as a volunteer at the neighborhood center there, where he can tutor others with his gardening knowledge. When she closes the case, as required after ninety days, he still has a cluttered house. However, he is starting to heal and to develop service and relationships.

The spiritually oriented social worker may often ask adult clients direct questions about their spiritual views. Such questions, when asked to the right clients at the right time, can facilitate the healing and transformative processes (see Box 16.4).

BOX 16.4

EXAMPLES OF SPIRITUAL QUESTIONS FOR SOME ADULT CLIENTS

1. What is the purpose of adulthood in your view?
2. What is the difference between a child and an adult, from a spiritual perspective?
3. How do you view life and death differently now, compared to when you were younger?
4. Why do people die?
5. Why do people grieve? What does a person do when he or she is grieving?
6. From a spiritual perspective, why do you have your disability or illness?
7. What is suffering for?

BOX 16.5

EXAMPLES OF METHODS THAT MAY HELP FOSTER TRANSFORMATION IN PUBLIC SOCIAL SERVICE SETTINGS

Mindful Past and Future	The client examines how her ancestors dealt with old age.
Mindful Daily Living	The client decides to view the primary goal of parenting as the fostering of the spiritual development of his children.
Spirit with Heart	The client develops forgiveness and compassion for the people in her life who have hurt her.
Religious Self	The client rediscovers the beliefs and rituals of the religion he grew up in by adopting those beliefs and rituals to deal with his life challenges.
Spirit Embodied	The client engages in a physical discipline, such as yoga or a martial art, for the purpose of increasing her own impulse control.
Community Consciousness	The client works toward helping make his own family, church, or community into a Community of Spiritual Diversity.
Eco-Consciousness	The client works toward helping make her own family, church, or community into a Community of Universal Diversity.

USING THE PARADIGMS OF PRACTICE IN PUBLIC SOCIAL SERVICES

The spiritually oriented social worker draws methods of transformation from all the paradigms of spiritual practice, seeking to find the best fit between the method and the unique client situation. Some examples of methods drawn from the paradigms are given in Box 16.5.

STUDY QUESTIONS

1. What is a supplication? Why do most cultures and religions use them? Do you have your own personal rituals of supplication? Have they changed in your life? Why or why not?

2. How might supplication be used in public social service settings? Would you use them in such settings? Why or why not?

3. How might a spiritually oriented social worker view the concept of family values from a more inclusive perspective? What do you think and feel about this idea?

4. What is your reaction to the hierarchy of family values given in Box 16.1? How might you re-order the values in your own personal hierarchy?

5. Review the suggestions for inclusion of religious and spiritual factors in assessment in Box 16.2. Describe your own personal responses to the questions in the box.

6. Give some examples of how a social worker can use conventional terms to describe spiritual concepts. In what kind of situations would a social worker want to do this? In what situations have you done this?

7. What kinds of trainings might a school social worker want to plan and implement? What kinds of trainings do you wish a social worker had implemented in the public schools you went to as a child and adolescent?

8. Ask yourself the spiritual questions in Box 16.4.

RESOURCE

American Psychiatric Association. (2000). *Diagnostic and Statistical Manual of Mental Disorders-IV-TR*. Washington, DC: American Psychiatric Association.
Religious or spiritual problems have been added to the text.

CHAPTER 17

SPIRITUALLY ORIENTED PRACTICE WITH COUPLES

From a spiritual perspective, the purpose of couple work is to help both people co-create a Relationship of Spiritual and Universal Diversity in which the spiritual development of both partners is supported. Such a relationship is a healthy model for other couples in the larger community. This spiritually healthy couple also is interconnected with the larger community and local ecosystem in a variety of ways, and may interact through such activities as service, religious ceremony, and leadership.

Spiritual practice with couples does not replace traditional methods of couple therapy; rather, it *adds* the spiritual dimension to traditional couple work. The symptoms that the couple initially present with are viewed by the social worker as signals from the souls of the partners. These souls are sending messages to the couple about the spiritual nature of their lives and relationship. The task of the social worker is, in part, to help the partners discover their own individual spiritual paths and how their paths interact in the relationship.

From a spiritual perspective, the sexual dimension of the relationship intensifies the possibility of spiritual intimacy and spiritual development for the partners. Thus, sexuality can be seen as a potential powerful catalyst for spiritual growth in each individual's life. Since spirituality and sexuality are both connecting forces, sexuality can also be viewed as a form of spiritual expression that can help people connect with their own bodies, with other people, and with Creative Spirit. From a spiritual perspective, sexual attraction is a gift from God or Creative Spirit that can, like any transforming spiritual gift, bring both suffering and ecstasy.

DEEP SEXUAL RELATIONSHIP

Sexual attraction can lead to a deep sexual relationship. A *deep sexual relationship* is a special connection between two people, characterized by *com-passion* for each other's well-being, ongoing intent to develop *multidimensional intimacy*, the gift of *vertical and horizontal compatibility,* and mutual *commitment to each other's Highest Good.*

Com-Passion

Com-passion is a surrender to love in which each person can experience both the suffering and the ecstacy of his or her partner. In com-passion, the lover "suffers with" her partner when the other is in pain as well as "enjoys with" her partner when the other is in ecstacy. Such intimacy is as intensely connecting as the individual's heart and mind and soul are open to such intensity. This surrender to love can be seen as a surrender to Creative Spirit or God, similar to the transpersonal process of disidentification (see Chapter 7).

Many people experience the beginning of erotic love as a gift from their God or Creative Spirit. Our ancestors often likened the experience to a powerful and sudden loss of individual control or power. The power was now in the hands of the god or goddess of love. Perhaps that is why people still say they "fall" in love. In this sense, sexuality is also akin to spirituality, because people who have intense spiritual experiences also often say that they give up their power to a greater force or power or God.

The spiritually oriented social worker knows that when a person falls in love, the experience always means *something* for that person. Perhaps the experience will lead to a wonderful, life-long marriage. Perhaps the person the individual is falling in love with is someone who is not so good or compatible for him or her. Either way, there are important spiritual life lessons to be learned.

The gift of com-passion can occur on any or all of the levels of consciousness. On the *prepersonal* level, the client may want to fully enjoy the excitement (and the pain) of the falling of the ego into love. On the *personal* level of consciousness, the client may want to examine not only the sexual feelings but also the spiritual, emotional, cognitive, and social experiences she is having. The client does this examination so that she can better understand who the person really is that she is falling in love with, and so that she can begin to understand what the experience means to her. This process could take hours or years. Finally, on the *transpersonal* level, the client may use the sexual experience as an opportunity to have a transformation of consciousness. Such a transformation of consciousness is possible because the heart, mind, and soul are often all opened up, creating a special window of opportunity for spiritual growth. The social worker's task is not to try to create or re-create passion for the client, but rather to help the client uncover and express that passion in ways that support her spiritual process.

Multidimensional Intimacy

Sexuality is the catalyst for some of the deepest intimacy that humans can experience. As described in Chapter 6 (see Table 6.3), deep intimacy is multidimensional, vertical, and horizontal. Deep sexuality is a form of intimacy that is also multidimensional, vertical, and horizontal. *Vertical* sexuality is about how the person's sexuality can help him deepen his own body–mind–spirit–environment connection. *Horizontal* sexuality is about how the person's sexuality can deepen his connection with another person. Sexuality is multidimensional because it can help foster sharing in all the dimensions of development (see Box 17.1).

The social worker's task is to help clients develop the intimacy they need in any or all of these categories. Each client may need intimacy more in some dimensions than in others. The social worker can help the clients become aware of the kinds of intimacy that are most important to them.

Vertical and Horizontal Compatibility

From a spiritual perspective, compatibility with another person is a gift from Creative Spirit or God. The traditional view of compatibility is that there are human characteristics that tend to stay stable over the lifetime and that if two people are not compatible today they will not be compatible tomorrow, regardless of what they try to do about it. This *horizontal compatibility* is thus about the ability of the person to like, live comfortably with, and accept her or his partner. Horizontal compatibility can include compatibility across any of the dimensions of intimacy described in Box 17.1.

The social worker's role is not to enhance horizontal compatibility, but to help the client become more aware of what kind of compatibility she needs, who she is compatible and incompatible with, and what the spiritual meaning of her experiences are. The social worker knows that the client will be attracted to a variety of people, and that some people of these people will be much more compatible with her than others. The worker strives to help the client understand why she is sometimes attracted to people who are not good for her and to let go of such unhealthy patterns so she can have what she does want in her love life.

Another kind of compatibility has to do with the relationship a person has with himself. This *vertical compatibility* is about the ability of the person to like, to live with, and accept himself. A person cannot have more vertical compatibility

---

BOX 17.1

MULTIDIMENSIONAL (DEEP) INTIMACY AND SEXUAL EXPRESSIONS IN HEALTHY SEXUALITY

Spiritual intimacy	Sharing souls
Physical intimacy	Sharing bodies
Emotional intimacy	Sharing hearts
Cognitive intimacy	Sharing minds
Social intimacy	Sharing friends
Environmental intimacy	Sharing nature

than he has horizontal compatibility. Vertical intimacy does not mean that a person must always "bloom where he is planted" and stay with a partner regardless of the level of horizontal compatibility that they share. However, from a spiritual perspective, the individual is a body–mind–spirit–environmental being who is most likely to stay happily in a long-term relationship when he is compatible both with himself as well as with his lover. The social worker can help a client recognize the extent to which he feels compatible with himself, and to recognize the extent to which the lack of horizontal intimacy in his relationship is due to his own discomfort with "parts" of himself.

CASE STUDY 17.1
WORK ON VERTICAL AND HORIZONTAL INTIMACY

A 35-year-old woman goes to see a social worker at the local family counseling center. She says, "My father was an alcoholic and my first husband was an alcoholic. I thought I was done with them. But now I have discovered that the man I am engaged to is an alcoholic. Do I have a sign on my back that advertises me as a woman who likes alcoholics?" The worker helps the woman recognize how the trauma in her early life is part of her unhealthy pattern with men, but the work does not stop there. The worker then asks the woman to look at her life pattern from a spiritual perspective. "Why do you think you have this pattern in your life?" she asks. The woman says, "Well, it seems sometimes that the only way for me to have what my soul most wants is to first have to deal with the exact opposite of that." "Yes," says the worker, "now tell me what it is you most want." The woman states that she wants to love herself and be in a loving relationship. They decide to work first on the woman's vertical intimacy and compatibility, by identifying what she dislikes about herself. She starts to realize how much shame she has, and how she actually does not feel that she deserves a man who loves her. Later in their work, when she starts to date a new man who is healthier, she talks about how scared she is of being close to him because "my heart could get really hurt with someone like him whom I am more compatible with." "Yes," the social worker agrees, "and as you already know, there is no way to avoid that risk if you want to be close."

Mutual Commitment to Each Other's Highest Good

Finally, in a deep sexual relationship, two people share a mutual commitment to think and act in support of each other's Highest Good. Thus, a deep sexual relationship is also a continuing choice to love the other person. The social worker knows that "love" is not the same thing as "like." Whereas a person can choose who she wants to love, she cannot choose what she likes or dislikes most in a person. Just like a person may like chocolate more than vanilla, a person will like some traits in her lover more than other traits. When a person chooses to make a commitment to love her partner, she may be able to transcend the things she dislikes about her partner and herself, and in the process learn to love herself and Creative Spirit or God even more. The social worker's task is not to foster or discourage commitment, but to help the clients continue to become aware of and communicate their level of commitment to each other.

SEXUAL EDUCATION

The spiritually oriented social worker interested in practice in human sexuality may choose to design and offer sexual education classes. The worker thinks of spiritual education as a process of "drawing out" the spiritual wisdom already in the person, rather than just a process of "filling up" the person with her own knowledge and perspectives. The worker respects the client's religious and political views on sexuality. The social worker's primary goal in sexual education is not to change her client's religious or political views, but rather to help the client use her sexuality as a tool in her spiritual development.

Today, most education in human sexuality could be called "unhealthy sexuality education." Students receive only half of what they need to develop the kind of deep sexual relationships that their parents and teachers may want them to have. The half they usually receive is how to avoid unwanted pregnancy and sexually transmitted disease (STD). Often the curriculum teaches a strategy of abstinence until when and if the person is married. The benefit of this education is that, if successful, the individual may be able to escape pregnancy and STD. The risk is that the individual may also learn to avoid her or his sexuality.

The often-missing half of sexuality education might be called *healthy sexuality.* Healthy sexuality education helps people learn to develop their own capacity for consciousness, connection, and intimacy so that they can co-create the kinds of deep sexual relationships they want in their lives. The spiritually oriented social worker believes that people in deep sexual relationships tend to be more effective, loving parents, neighbors, and citizens.

What is healthy sexuality? First of all, it is multidimensional, which means that sexuality is interconnected with the physical, emotional, cognitive, social, spiritual, and environmental dimensions. Second, healthy sexuality is both horizontal and vertical, in that sexuality fosters the body–mind–spirit connection within the individual and also can connect the individual with other people and environments. Third, healthy sexuality is never abusive and is always responsible about avoiding unnecessary risk of pregnancy or STD transmission.

Finally, the spiritually oriented social worker believes that education really is a process of "drawing out" the wisdom that already is in the person, rather than "filling up" the person with knowledge that he or she needs. From this perspective, the best sexual education class is designed to be largely discussion oriented and experientially based. Students are asked to discover for themselves their truths about what healthy sexuality really is.

HEALING SEXUAL TRAUMA

The spiritually oriented social worker is aware of how the majority of people on the planet have experienced some kind of sexual trauma. Such trauma can be the result of intentional and direct maltreatment, such as childhood sexual abuse, date rape, or marital rape. Sexual trauma can also be associated with often less intentional and less direct experiences, such as negative messages about the person's body, mind, and spirit that the person might receive from mass media, institutions, families, friends, and lovers.

With so much trauma in a culture, sexual trauma is more the norm than sexual health, and individuals may not be conscious of their own woundedness. The social worker's initial task may often be to "show the client where he is bleeding until the client notices his own wounds." After the client is aware of what happened to him, and of the short- and long-term damage the trauma has caused him, he can also explore the spiritual dimension of his traumatic experiences. The client can ask the question, Why did my soul need to have this trauma during my lifetime?

The spiritually oriented social worker helps the client see where his sexual trauma has impacted him the most by exploring systematically his current capacity for physical, emotional, cognitive, social, spiritual, and environmental intimacy. The worker then can help the client practice opening up himself again in these dimensions, beginning in those areas that are the easiest for him.

GENDER IDENTIFICATIONS

From a spiritual perspective, there are as many genders as there are human beings on the planet. Each person can be viewed as a spiritual being in a human body, blessed with a unique combination of what could be called "feminine" and "masculine" characteristics, all of which are neither right nor wrong, good nor bad. Gender is not just about the genitals, but is about all of what makes people body–mind–spirit–environmental beings. Most of our ancestors lived in cultures that saw masculine and feminine traits not only in people but also in other living and nonliving things. Many cultures had terms for multiple gender identities, going beyond the duality of masculine and feminine genders. People who had both feminine and masculine traits were viewed in such cultures as being healthy or whole, and sometimes became healers or leaders in their communities.

The social worker can use a gender worksheet, such as the one illustrated in Table 17.1, to help the client develop an understanding of how masculine or feminine she thinks she is in various categories and subcategories. In this worksheet, the client is asked to rate her masculinity and femininity in various dimensions along a five-point gender scale. The social worker can provide the client with a safe and accepting therapeutic atmosphere in which she can see herself as accurately as possible.

TABLE 17.1 Gender Worksheet

	MOSTLY MASCULINE	MORE MASCULINE	EQUALLY MASCULINE AND FEMININE	MORE FEMININE	MOSTLY FEMININE
Physical					
Emotional					
Cognitive					
Social					
Spiritual					
Environmental					

For example, on the physical level, a particular male client might identify himself as being "mostly masculine," based on his appearance, physical activities, and sexual behaviors. On the emotional level, however, he may rate himself as "equally masculine and feminine," because he has access to the full range of emotions and can express them all freely when he wants to. On the cognitive level, the man may say he is also "equally masculine and feminine," not only because he has bisexual fantasies but also because he can be both intellectually authoritative and open minded. The same man might rate himself "more feminine" in the social realm because he is very nurturing and giving in his relationships with other people. He might also rate himself "mostly feminine" in the spiritual realm because he is so receptive to Creative Spirit in his life. Finally, on the environmental level, he sees himself as "more feminine" because he is very nurturing to other living things and ecosystems and because he is so open to the energy of sacred outdoor environments.

The spiritually oriented social worker is willing to look at her own gender identities in an honest way, and works on accepting those identities as spiritual gifts in her life. She values all identities equally, and recognizes that there is a place in the world for every person to play a useful role, regardless of his or her unique characteristics.

SEXUALITY IN CHILDHOOD AND ADOLESCENCE

The spiritually oriented social worker works to help young people discover and affirm their sexuality in safe and responsible ways, even before they begin dating. Many young people are far more alone than they need or want to be, disconnected from themselves and other people often in large part because they are ashamed of their sexuality. Young people who are not ready to date or who are unsuccessful at dating often feel bad about themselves and may withdraw or act out inappropriately in response. Young people who do not fit into the dominant heterosexual community are especially vulnerable to depression and suicide. Therefore an important part of spiritual practice in sexuality is advocacy for young people who are at risk because of they belong to sexual minorities.

The social worker also works to help young people stay in relationship with their families, friends, schools, and communities so that they can receive the support, resources, information, and love they need to navigate through their sexuality. The social worker may offer many kinds of assistance to achieve these goals. She could do individual or groups sessions with young people, perhaps using educational models to "draw their wisdom out" about appropriate sexual behavior. She could do parenting classes, aimed at helping mothers and fathers to stay in relationship with their children during the difficult adolescent and early adult years. Family therapy may be very helpful in many situations, when a family needs assistance in making their family into a Community of Spiritual Diversity (see Chapter 18).

CASE STUDY 17.2
PRACTICE WITH A YOUNG PERSON AT RISK

A mother and father bring their 13-year-old boy to the social worker at the child guidance clinic. The presenting problem is that the boy was caught cross-dressing and masturbating in his room. The social worker determines first that the boy is very embarrassed and also quite depressed and anxious with some suicidal ideation. The boy is willing to agree to a suicide contract. The parents are also anxious. The mother is dysthymic and the father is a successful administrator who works over 50 hours a week.

The social worker tries family therapy first. He invites the other siblings (a younger brother and sister) to the meeting. The therapist has each family member talk about his or her life. The social worker discovers that everyone in the family feels more alone and stressed than they want to be. The middle child, a 12-year-old girl, is a straight-A student who has poor social skills and very low self-esteem. The youngest boy has been diagnosed with ADHD and acts out frequently at home and school.

Next, the social worker sees the 13-year-old boy for individual sessions. The worker finds out that the boy is very creative and energetic. The young teen does not understand himself why he wants to wear women's clothes, and he feels tremendous shame and guilt about his sexual behavior. He denies having homosexual attractions, but does say he is attracted to girls. He has not dated and seems to have poor social skills. The worker tells the boy about how ancient shamans were often cross-dressers who were understood to "betwix and between" the masculine and feminine worlds. The boy is interested to learn that there is a history of other people who are like him, and that they were not always seen as pathological at all, but rather as healers.

The social worker sees the father and mother for a few sessions. He has the parents talk about their greatest fears about their son and their lives. Then he explains how most cross-dressers live fairly normal lives, although they have to hide their desires from the mainstream culture. He asks them to consider why their God may have given their son and family this gift of suffering and potential joy. Eventually, they agree to work on staying in relationship with their son, rather than to work on changing him.

SEXUAL FANTASIES

The spiritually oriented social worker views sexual fantasies as soul expressions and gifts from God. Many clients struggle with some of their sexual fantasies, often feeling guilt and shame about them. The worker strives to help the client understand and accept his fantasies and then make meaning out of them. This process may be difficult for the client, since many people keep their fantasies private, even to the people they are closest to in their lives.

CASE STUDY 17.3
SEXUAL FANTASY WORK

A 25-year-old man visits with a social worker at the university counseling center. The presenting problem is that the man is more lonely than he wants to be. The social worker determines that the client is moderately depressed but not suicidal. In the course of the treatment, the man hints that he has sexual fantasies that are "really sick." The worker lets him know that when and if he is ready, he can talk about any of these fantasies. Eventually the man says that he "is obsessed with the idea of two women making love to each other." The social worker normalizes the fantasy, and tells the man that this fantasy is not uncommon among men. Then the worker asks the client to be curious about why his soul has given him this fantasy. Together, they explore this question, Eventually, the client decides that he would like not only to make love "more like a woman" but also express his feminine side more in his life. He realizes that he has felt that he has to act "more masculine than I really feel" in practically every area in his life. Instead, he would like to be less focused on achieving success, wealth, and power and be more open to "simply being alive." The man discovers that as he makes meaning out of his sexual fantasy, the fantasy no longer seems to trouble him as much.

Dating

Today, there are many single adults in every age category across the life span. Many of these people wish to find a lover and get married. The social worker may have clients who struggle with the dating process. Some of them have given up. They may feel discouraged, and doubt that they will ever have a lover or marital partner. Others are dissatisfied with their dating experiences and are trying to find the right partner.

The spiritually oriented social worker not only strives to support the client in finding people through a dating process but he also helps the client make sense out of her life situation, discover meaning in her suffering, and use the experience of being single as a catalyst for spiritual transformation.

CASE STUDY 17.4
TRANSFORMING OLD LOVE PATTERNS

The social worker, working at a mental health agency, is visited by a 45-year-old woman. The client is despondent, and between tears she talks about how she has been single for five years since she divorced her husband. "It was a terrible marriage. He was a drinker and I did not love him any more," she says, "but I am beginning to wonder if I should have stayed with him, because *this* is worse." The client talks about how disappointed she has been with the men she has met on the Internet. "The young ones are fun but immature and the older ones seem *so* old," she says. "I don't think that there will ever be anyone out there for me." The worker determines that the client has had a long history of deep disappointment in relationships, going back to when she was a child. They start to explore spiritual perspectives that she might want to take toward her past and current suffering. At first she struggles to let go of her anger. She talks about how angry she is at God for letting her be sexually abused as a child and repeatedly hurt in her life. In the sessions she also starts to realize how her anger at men and God, perhaps once necessary to help her fight for her survival, no longer serves her. She resolves to let go of her anger gradually, and begins finding moments of gratitude about something in her life.

PREMARITAL COUNSELING AND EDUCATION

The spiritually oriented social worker might also want to offer premarital counseling to couples who are considering marriage. In some cases, the worker might provide such services for individual couples or groups of couples through an existing church. This kind of service would of course be especially supportive of members of that church. Other social workers might offer premarital counseling that is spiritually based but that is not religious based. Such a service might provide an alternative for clients who are not church members. Premarital counseling offers couples an opportunity to explore their own unique issues in a private setting.

The social worker may offer premarital education classes as well, in order to help young people anticipate the kinds of spiritual challenges and opportunities they may face during the stages of marriage (romance, power struggle, and mutual acceptance). Premarital education would introduce the central role of spirituality in long-term marital happiness and would educate participants about their own spiritual development. The various dimensions of intimacy would be explored along with the quality of the couple's current vertical and horizontal intimacy.

The worker also can help clients resist the messages from the popular media that tend to glorify the falling-in-love process and ignore the rewarding but challenging aspects of long-term relationships.

MARRIAGE AND REMARRIAGE

Spiritually Based Relationship

The spiritually oriented social worker views any marriage-type relationship as an opportunity for two people to develop a deep sexual relationship in which both people commit to support each other's spiritual development. The thought of creating such a spiritually based relationship is often scary for people because one person's spiritual development may well lead her in a direction that is threatening to her partner. In a spiritually based marriage, the most important relationship is the connection each person has with Creative Spirit (or his or her God), and the marriage becomes an expression of that connection. In such a marriage, each person is free to stay or leave, and the couple chooses to stay together because they can, through their love for each other, best support the Highest Good of everyone in their family and community.

Shame- and Fear-Based Relationship

In contrast, in marriage-type relationships that are fear and shame based, both partners prioritize their relationship with each other over their connection with Creative Spirit. In such a relationship, the partners often stay together because they are afraid of the consequences of breaking apart. They also do not feel good about themselves and do not feel that they deserve a healthy relationship. In his fear and shame, the individual tends to try to control his partner's spiritual development and/or give up his own spiritual power. In such a relationship, the ability of each person to support the Highest Good of others in their family or community is limited.

The spiritually oriented social worker uses all the traditional methods of couple counseling in her practice, but she also adds spiritual methods to her work. She encourages the couples she works with to develop spiritually based relationships.

CASE STUDY 17.5
MARRIAGE COUNSELING

A heterosexual couple, with two adult children living outside of the home, comes to see the social worker at his private practice. The first thing the woman says is, "Our marriage is not going well, but divorce is not an option." When asked by the social worker, the husband agrees with his wife's statement. The worker learns that they belong to the ABC Church and that their pastor had referred them to the worker for help with their marriage. The husband had already separated from his wife and was living in a small apartment downtown. It turned out that they had experienced frequent difficulties in their relationship and had other separations. He complained that she was "frigid" sexually and she complained that he was cold and aloof. The worker told them that she could see that neither of them felt free to discover what (in their language) was "God's will" about their marriage. The wife was not willing to consider divorce as an option until her husband stayed away from the home during the holidays. However, at that point she decided to consider a divorce and her husband responded by asking for a reconciliation of the marriage. At that point, the couple came in to see if the social worker could help them create a healthy marriage.

"It looks like you both now are tired of the power struggle and want to see if you can learn to really love each other," says the social worker. They begin exploring that question. Both the wife and husband discover how their fear of divorce and shame about sex has kept them married but distant. They decide to investigate together what a spiritually based marriage would be like. He decides that he needs to support his wife's need to have her own career and that he needs also to tell her what he really feels about things more often. She decides that she needs to stop guarding her heart from him so much, and to pay more attention to her own needs instead of worrying so much about the well-being of her children.

The spiritually oriented social worker sees that all couples have the potential of co-creating spiritually oriented relationships, regardless of their sexual orientation or gender identities. She is also aware that each couple has their own unique strengths, limitations, and environmental conditions to with which to deal. Couple work with gay, lesbian, and transgendered clients often must include consideration of the prejudice such clients experience in mainstream culture.

CASE STUDY 17.6
MARRIAGE COUNSELING

The social worker at the counseling center sees a gay couple who have lived together for 17 years. One man (Mark) is 53 years old and his lover (Bill) is 51. Their presenting problem is a lack of desire that they seem to feel toward one another. The social worker does a history of each man's intimate relationships. She finds that Mark was married for 10 years and had two children by his wife before he "came out" and started dating. Bill, however, had known he was gay since adolescence and had been sexually active with other men since then. Bill had one other long-term relationship before he met Mark. Both men report that they have experienced considerable prejudice from family, community, and religion in their lives. She suggests that their loss of sexual desire may be associated with these kinds of factors.

The social worker first normalizes the experiences of the two men. She explains that most couples do experience a loss of intensity in their initial years of relationship. She also helps them see that they have been both been traumatized by the prejudices that most gay, lesbian, and transgendered people experience in their lifetimes. She asks them to try to spend some time together again—in effect, date each other again. She also has them discuss their resentments toward each other.

Then the worker asks the couple if they have ever looked at their relationship from a spiritual perspective. They are interested in her question and want to know about what she means. She explains to them that from a spiritual perspective, one could examine everything that happens in one's life as an opportunity for transformation. Bill and Mark want to try doing this work, so the social worker asks them to consider first why they may have decided to be gay men in this lifetime. After wrestling with that question, they each come up with different answers. Bill feels that his sexual identity has led to him becoming a better person. Mark thinks he decided to become gay because he was meant to be a healer in his community. Then the social worker asks them to consider why they might have decided to have this lack of desire now in their lives. Mark smiles and says, "Maybe to bring us closer together again." Bill nods in agreement, "Yes, and it is working."

DIVORCE

Today, the majority of couples experience divorce at least once in their lifetimes. The spiritually oriented social worker looks at divorce as another opportunity for spiritual transformation. Divorce from a marriage involves not just the loss of a partner but also often the loss of financial security, family connections, and even institutional and community acceptance. Such profound loss can strip away the identifications that the person has made with her home, her wealth, her social roles, her sense of stability, and her beliefs. This process of rapid dis-identification can give the divorced person access to spiritual insights that she may never have had if her life had remained more stable. The social worker strives to help the person continue to develop spiritually.

CASE STUDY 17.7
WORK WITH A DIVORCED COUPLE

A divorcing couple is referred to the social worker by their lawyer. The two women come in together. They are both crying as they talk about how their 12-year relationship is ending. They have been raising two children (each woman had a child from a previous marriage) but now they find that they need to move on. "I am impressed with how strong you both are to be able to come in together to discuss these issues," the social worker says. The women tell him that they are most concerned about their children and that they need to find a way to minimize the impact their divorce will have on the children. The worker asks them why they believe that their divorce has to have a more negative effect on the spiritual life of their children than an unhappy marriage type relationship would. They uncover in therapy that the women still feel guilt and shame about divorcing their husbands and living together as lovers. The social worker normalizes their feelings and supports them, noting how much they both love their children and want to continue being effective parents for both of them. The worker tells them that their children do not need perfect parents, but rather parents who are aware of their imperfections. They talk about how the two women can continue to support their children's spiritual growth during the divorce by showing them how an adult can have a spiritual transformation from intense suffering. They then discuss what kinds of transformations of consciousness the divorce has opened up for both of them.

CASE STUDY 17.8
DIVORCE COUNSELING WITH AN ANGRY INDIVIDUAL

A 34-year-old man comes in to see a counselor at the clinic. The man presents as very angry and tells the counselor how furious he is at his wife who has told him she wants a divorce. "She has been a bitch since the day I married her," he says. The counselor lets the man complain for half of the session and then she asks him, "Why do you think you married such a woman and stayed with her as long as you did?" He stops and then replies, "Well, she pretended to be someone she was not when we were dating." "You don't think she ever loved you?" asks the worker. The man says, "I doubt it." "It sounds like you loved her, and still do," she responds. He fights back a tear and says, "I hate her now." The worker says, "It must be hard to have so many disappointments in your love life." "You have no idea." "You are right; tell me about it," she says. Realizing that he is not ready yet to let go of his anger, she lets him talk more about how not only his wife but also many other people have let him down.

When the timing is right, the social worker again tries to help the man feel his other emotions. She has him draw a picture of his heart and then describe it to her. It is torn apart by bullets and is bleeding terribly. Then she asks him to draw a picture of what would cure his heart. He draws a picture of a blood transfusion. "What poured out of your heart when it was shot, and what is going back into you in the second picture?" she asks. "I am losing my hope in the first picture, and . . . I am getting it back in the second picture," he replies. Fascinated, the worker asks him to talk about hope. He said that he used to believe that there was a place for him in the world and that things would work out. "It sounds to me like your anger is actually more at God than at your wife or your mom or your boss." "You could say that," he said. "I know it is not right." "It is OK to be angry at God," replies the worker. "Perhaps everyone is at some point in their life, but now you must decide if you want to stay inside of the prison you have constructed." "What do you mean?" The worker replies, "Well, if you want, we can look at the price you have paid for staying angry all of these years." The client starts to look at how his anger, which once helped him fight life's battles, now keeps him "stuck" in one place in his spiritual path.

In her work with sexual relationships, the spiritually oriented social worker utilizes methods drawn from all the paradigms of transformation. Examples of methods are given in Box 17.2. For example, in the Community Consciousness paradigm, the worker might work to help transform such institutions as churches, schools, and court systems into Communities of Spiritual Diversity that allow all people equal rights and power, regardless of their sexualities.

BOX 17.2

EXAMPLES OF METHODS THAT MAY HELP FOSTER TRANSFORMATION IN WORK WITH SEXUAL RELATIONSHIPS

Spiritual Momentum	The client explores the kinds of sexual relationships that her ancestors and descendants had.
Mindful Daily Living	The client develops mindfulness of how his sexuality is connected to his body–mind–spirit–environment.
Spirit with Heart	The client notices and expresses how she feels about her own sexuality.
Religious Self	The client uses rituals from his own and/or other religions to heal his body.
Body Consciousness	The client develops her sexuality through body–mind–spirit expressions, such as practicing masturbation.
Community Consciousness	The client helps foster Communities of Spiritual Diversity that especially honor sexual diversity.
Eco-Consciousness	The client helps foster Communities of Universal Diversity that especially honor sexual diversity.

STUDY QUESTIONS

1. What is the goal of spiritual couple work? How is the work related to traditional couple counseling?

2. What is a deep sexual relationship? What do you think and feel about the concept?

3. Why is com-passion important in a deep sexual relationship?

4. What are the elements in multidimensional intimacy? Do you think that it is possible to have a relationship that has intimacy on all of these levels? Why or why not?

5. What is a commitment to someone else's Highest Good? How does one know what the Highest Good is?

6. What is missing from most sex education today?

7. Give your own definition of healthy sexuality. How did you learn your own concept about healthy sexuality?

8. Why is sexual trauma so common? How does sexual trauma heal?

9. How can one person have many gender identifications? How can there be more than two genders?

10. What kind of sexual behavior makes some children and adolescents particularly at risk?

11. Why do most people hide at least some of their sexual fantasies? What can people learn from their sexual fantasies, particularly those fantasies of which they are most ashamed?

12. What do you personally think is the spiritual purpose of dating? Of marriage? Of divorce?

13. Could you work with someone who has a different spiritual or religious belief structure than you do about dating, marriage, and divorce? Why or why not?

RESOURCES

Deida, D. (2002). *Finding God through sex: A spiritual guide to ecstatic loving and deep passion for men and women.* Austin, TX: Plexus.
   This book offers a perspective on how sexuality and religion can be seen as related.
Raphael, D. (1999). *Sacred relationships: A guide to authentic loving.* Novato, CA: Origin Press.
   This text is one of a number of books that describe spiritual aspects of romantic relationships.

CHAPTER 18

SPIRITUALLY ORIENTED PRACTICE WITH FAMILIES AND GROUPS

FAMILY THERAPY

From a spiritual perspective, the purpose of family therapy is to help members co-create a Family of Spiritual and Universal Diversity in which the spiritual development of every member is supported. Such a family is a healthy model for other families in the larger community. This spiritually healthy family also is interconnected with the larger community and local ecosystem in a variety of ways, and may interact through such activities as service, religious ceremony, and leadership.

Methods of Transformation in Work with Families

Spiritually oriented family therapy does not replace existing traditional methods but rather *adds* spirituality to assessment, intervention, and evaluation strategies. When an individual in a family goes through a spiritual transformation, every other person in the family is also challenged to take the next step in his or her own spiritual path. As illustrated in Box 18.1, spiritually oriented family therapy can use methods drawn from the paradigms of spiritual transformation. The social worker may use any combination of these methods with the family as she or he tries to find the best fit of methods with the needs of the family system.

Basic Methods of Spiritually Oriented Family Practice

The spiritually oriented social worker sees each *presenting problem* as a symptom of the deeper spiritual issues in the family. Often, the presenting problem in family therapy is the behavior of one of the children, the *identified client*. This child may indeed be involved in behaviors that are destructive to self and/or other people.

■ ■ ■ ■ ■ ■

BOX 18.1

EXAMPLES OF FAMILY THERAPY METHODS DRAWN FROM THE PARADIGMS OF SPIRITUAL TRANSFORMATION

Spiritual Momentum	The family co-explores the spirituality and religiosity of their ancestors and descendants.
Mindful Daily Living	The family co-develops mindfulness of the spiritual development and current spiritual issues of each member. Family members practice supporting each other's spiritual development.
Spirit with Heart	Family members share their feelings about themselves, each other, and their spiritual lives.
Religious Self	The family uses rituals from their own and/or other religions to foster each other's spirituality.
Body Consciousness	Family members develop their spirituality through shared body–mind–spirit practice, such as hiking, yoga, dance, and so on.
Community Consciousness	The family fosters Communities of Spiritual Diversity through modeling, service, religious activities, and leadership activities.
Eco-Consciousness	The family fosters Communities of Universal Diversity through modeling, service, religious activities, and leadership activities.

However, the identified client is often, from a spiritual perspective, the healthiest child in the family simply because the child is connected enough to his or her soul to express what is going on in the family.

The social worker sets out to help members discover what indeed is going on in the family on the deepest spiritual level. She may do this by having them take the broadest perspective on their issues, across time and space, exploring the experiences of people in other families across time and space. She may also ask family members to increase their mindfulness of the spiritual process of each other. They sometimes may also perceive that the entire family shares a spiritual direction (although not all families have this experience, and such experience is often temporary). With these new insights and perspectives, the family then may decide to make some changes in the way they think about and act toward each other.

CASE STUDY 18.1
FAMILY THERAPY: A RITE OF PASSAGE FOR A TEEN IN A SINGLE-PARENT FAMILY

A single parent brings in his son, Frankie, who is now age 17. The boy has been depressed and the father is concerned because he found a note in the boy's room in which he writes about how he wishes that he was dead. The social worker first addresses the suicidal threat and the boy agrees to a suicide contract. In the assessment, the worker determines that Frankie has all the symptoms of dysthymia, but that he has many strengths, such as high intelligence, creativity in writing, and the ability to play several instruments. The boy says that he is tired of being depressed but sees no end in sight. The social worker assesses that the father, like many single parents, is probably overinvolved with his son.

One of the interventions that the social worker uses has a spiritual component. The worker says, "I am curious about how your ancestors did the transition an adolescent boy makes as he becomes a man." "What do you mean?" asked the father. "Well, Frankie, you are between a boy and a man right now, as every 17-year-old boy is. In past times, the whole community would have been involved in assisting you in the process. There may have been rituals enacted that had roots going back thousands of years. Today, it is just you and your father having to figure it out by yourselves. So let's imagine what other 17-year-old boys went through in other times." The social worker then tells the father and son a story of a young man who lived in a tribe in what is now the Great Basin.

The boy is turning 17 years old and he prepares to go out into the desert on a vision quest by himself for six days and nights. All he is given is a knife and a bowl and some pine nuts to eat. Each day, the boy sits by a cliff over a stream and watches the clouds and animals go by. He prays for a vision. On the third day he is bitten by a snake on his left hand. He lays down by the water and washes his wound, wondering if he will die. Instead, a trout comes up to him in the water and swims around his hand, splashing the cool water with its fin as it turns. The boy takes the fish and, thanking it, he cooks it for dinner that night. He survives and comes back to the village, believing that the trout saved his life.

The three men discuss what the story means to each of them. Frankie decides that he needs to have a vision quest too. To his dad, he seems more excited about that idea than he has been about anything in a while. Frankie decides to go on a camping trip. He plans the trip himself and has his dad take him to the trail head, where Frankie will leave with a cell phone in case he needs any help. The trip turns out to be helpful to Frankie, and he does have some spiritually meaningful experiences. He tells his dad in a later session that he wants to move out of the home when he finishes high school. The worker supports the boy's plans to differentiate from his dad and helps the dad start to "let go" of his son.

Sometimes spiritual family therapy focuses on the here-and-now thoughts and behaviors that seem to be somehow rewarding the child's misbehavior. The social worker might use creative expressions to facilitate awareness of the spiritual dimensions of the presenting problems, as well as teach methods of meditation that might help families co-create healthier attitudes and behaviors.

CASE STUDY 18.2
FAMILY THERAPY: CREATIVE EXPRESSION WITH YOUNG CHILDREN

The social worker sits down with a new family that has come to the clinic. There are two children and two mothers in this family. Susan and Marcy have raised their two adopted children, Freddy (age 7) and Mark (age 10), for five years. The presenting problem is that Mark has not been doing well in school. He is getting poor grades and lately has been off task most of the time in the classroom. At home Mark seems to do well, especially when he is sitting in front of the television or computer games. The parents had Mark tested by the school psychologist and he diagnosed him with ADHD and recommended that Mark take stimulants and go to counseling. The mothers decided to wait on the medication and took their sons to the counselor first. The social worker gives everyone in the family two sheets of white paper and a handful of crayons. The instructions are that each person is to draw two pictures. The first is a drawing of how it feels now to live in their family and world. The second drawing is to be about how the person *wants* to feel about his or her life. Everyone makes their drawings. Freddy draws a picture about his soccer team, in which he is trying to score a goal, and in the second drawing he shows himself scoring the winning goal in a game. Mark draws a picture of his family, in which everyone is smiling except for him. In the second picture he is moving away. When asked about his picture, Mark says that he does not want to be a problem for everyone else and that he is willing to move out so everyone else can be happy. The social worker notices that both the mothers have drawn pictures in which they are worried about the children and then they are doing better and no worry is necessary.

The social worker decides to start with the theme of worry. "Everyone in this family is very smart and everyone seems to worry a lot," she says. They all nod. "Why do people worry?" she asks. "Because bad things can happen," offers Freddy. "But it doesn't help, does it?" says Susan. Knowing that this family goes to a local church, the worker says, "Why would someone pray that bad things would happen?" Mark looks up and says, "That would be stupid." "But isn't that what worry is, like a prayer that wishes for negative things?" asks the worker.

Then the social worker invites the family to practice a family meditation every day in which all the televisions and computers and video games are turned off. During the meditation, the family holds hands and everyone shuts their eyes and imagines that they are being held in God's hands and being taken care of.

Family Values in Spiritually Oriented Practice

The spiritually oriented family therapist sometimes works to help parents become more mindful about their view of what parenting actually is and should be. If a parent believes that his fundamental task is to nurture the spiritual development of his child, then all of his parenting interventions will flow from that belief. What does it mean to nurture the spiritual development of a child? When spiritual development is the priority, then the parent is willing to let go of (or disidentify from) his own fantasies of what he wants his child to be, and surrenders to Creative Spirit (or the will of God). As illustrated in Box 18.2, the spiritually oriented social worker can offer alternative family values.

Letting Go

In this impermanent world, one parenting task that seems to persist across the life span is the task of letting go. When a child is born, for example, the mother has to literally let go of the child so he can have life as a separate being, and she lets go as

■ ■ ■ ■ ■

BOX 18.2

POPULAR VERSUS ALTERNATIVE SPIRITUALLY ORIENTED FAMILY VALUES (NOT IN ORDER) THAT CAN GUIDE PARENTS

Perfection (seek external acceptance)	Good enough (live with internal self-acceptance)
Wealth (seek external material abundance)	High-quality free time (have internal abundance)
Power (control and express through others)	Self-empowerment (self-control and expression)
Success (win over others)	Letting go (help everyone succeed)
Fame (seek publicity and recognition)	Wisdom (develop and apply self-knowledge)
Beauty (seek external appearance)	Love of self (see divine in both shadow and light)
Go to war (destroy whom we project as evil)	Seek peace (give forgiveness, compassion, love)
Consumption (take from nature)	Conservation (in harmony with nature)

he comes out of her body and the umbilical cord is cut. When the child leaves home to go to preschool or grade school, the parent has to let go of the child so he can start to have new experiences in a new learning environment. When a child starts to become more socially and eventually sexually active, the parent has to let go of the child so he can practice new kinds of relationships and perhaps create a family of his own.

The process of letting go has a spiritual dimension. When a parent lets go of a child, she is in part dis-identifying from the fantasies that she has about what she hopes the child will be and do. Instead, she gives the child radical acceptance, which is support for the unique spiritual path that the child is on.

The task of letting go is a balancing act. On the one hand, a parent can let a child go too quickly. For example, a parent can fail to watch a small child and as a result the child can walk out in the street and get injured. On the other hand, a parent can fail to let go fast enough. In such situations, the parent may fail to recognize when a child is ready to do something on her own or make decisions on her own and the parent can unintentionally cripple the child by being too controlling, anxious, or worried. For example, a parent can fail to let an adolescent make her own decision about who her friends should be or what school she wants to go to, perhaps sending messages to the child that the child is incompetent or the world is dangerous.

No parent will ever have the wisdom to consistently both let go and protect in a perfectly balanced way that always fits the changing needs of the child. Indeed, from a spiritual perspective, each child chooses to be born into an imperfect world with imperfect parents, and she does not need her parents to try to be or appear to be perfect.

Thus, the social worker's task is not to help the parent reach perfection in his parenting approach; instead, the worker's task is to help the parent see and accept his own imperfections and strengths, and to gradually improve his own self-awareness, self-acceptance, and parenting wisdom. The social worker can, for example, help the parent learn to meditate on his parenting. The worker and parent can pray that the parent learn more wisdom and strength. The worker can help the parent plan and implement new ways of interacting with his child. The worker always supports the parent, and helps the parent love himself and model a spiritually oriented life for his child.

CASE STUDY 18.3
FINDING A BALANCE BETWEEN LETTING GO OF
AND BEING INVOLVED WITH A CHILD

The social worker is helping two parents who are raising a large family of eight children. The parents have a variety of challenges, but they are most concerned with two of their girls. Katie, the youngest, is 6 years old. She just started school this fall, but she was referred by her school social worker for counseling because she seems to have a delay in social development. She has no friends and acts immaturely with her peers. Millie is 12 years old and has been failing all of her classes in school, but is active after school in sports with her friends. The social worker does a traditional assessment of the family and discovers that neither girl seems to have a history of family trauma or any significant genetic predispositions for learning, social, or emotional problems.

Seeing that the parents are very worried and guilty, the worker explains to the parents that family therapy is not about blaming the parents for the problems of their children, but is about helping the parents change what they can change to help the child. The worker talks with the parents about the concepts of letting go and being involved. The worker asks them to consider how their parenting has been out of balance with Katie and Millie. They meditate and discuss together and decide that the parents have been a little overprotective of Katie and need to let go of her a little more. They will do this in part energetically (change in attitude) and in part by letting her spend more time with other children in safe and supervised situations rather than keeping her at home as much as they do. They also decide that they need to be a bit more protective and involved with Millie right now. Their plan of action with Millie is to get her a tutor for school and to spend more time with her in ways with which she is comfortable (like going mall shopping or out to eat). The social worker congratulates the parents on being strong enough to see their own limitations and to support the spiritual growth of their daughters.

Parenting Adult Children

Today, many parents find that their children may leave home and return multiple times. During this process, parents are challenged to rebalance their attitudes and behaviors with their children. As children get older, they usually need and want far less care. However, sometimes there are life emergencies, such as the loss of a job or marriage, that bring children back home, asking for housing, money, or love. The parent may need to meditate or pray for the wisdom she needs to give her adult child the right amount of help the child needs, without encouraging unhealthy dependency or other unhealthy thinking and behaviors. In blended families, the issues are often intensified because the two parents often have different views; frequently the birth parent is more sympathetic to the child than the step-parent.

CASE STUDY 18.4
SPIRITUAL PERSPECTIVES ON CO-PARENTING

Bob, age 58, and Betty, age 56, are struggling to decide how to deal with Bob's son (and Betty's step-son), Mark. Betty and Bob married five years ago. Both have children from other marriages, although none now live at home. Unfortunately, Mark is a 33-year-old who has been a heroin addict for a decade. Lately his health has deteriorated and he lost his part-time job and his apartment downtown. He started asking his father for money again, and Bob secretly started giving him a weekly "allowance" for several months until Betty found out about it a few days ago. She insisted that they go to a counselor about the issue, because two years ago Bob had promised Betty that he would not give Mark any more money. In addition, Mark has been asking Bob if he could move back home "for a few months" and Bob started cleaning out Mark's old room without talking with Betty.

The social worker meets with Bob and Betty and listens to their stories. Betty is furious at Bob and says, "Although we have a good enough marriage and I love Bob, I told him I will divorce him if he lets Mark move back home again and I mean it." The social worker asks Bob to respond. He shrugs his shoulders and smiles. The social worker asks, "What does that mean, Bob, when you shrug your shoulders and smile like that?" Bob looks down at the floor and says, "Betty has never liked Mark, but you know she bought her daughter a car a year ago." "That's different and you know it," replies Betty. She turns to the social worker and continues, "My daughter is a hard worker and never does drugs—it was just that her husband had left her and she had to get to work."

The social worker tells Bob and Betty that many other couples share the same kinds of issues that they have in their marriage, and that they could continue to fight about their children for the rest of their lives unless they make some changes in the way they think about and act toward each other. The worker suggests that both Bob and Betty probably have some deeper issues that are being activated by this conflict about Mark and she asks them if they would be willing to work on them. Bob and Betty agree to look at the issues from a spiritual perspective. During the time that they do this work, the social worker agrees to meet with Mark and offer him connections to resources in town, including addictions work and harm-reduction services.

First, the social worker works with Bob, with Betty watching and listening. She asks Bob to tell the story of Mark's life and soon understands that Bob still feels guilty about divorcing Mark's mother. The worker challenges Bob to look at the deeper reasons why he still takes so much responsibility for Mark, and Bob eventually agrees that his actions "were all designed to keep me from feeling too guilty, of course, and to prove to him that I was a good daddy, instead of really giving Mark what he most needed." He starts to work on self-forgiveness and agrees to reflect on what he could do that would support Mark's Highest Good.

Now the social worker asks Betty to tell her life story, with Bob watching and listening. It turns out that Betty feels that everyone ultimately lets her down. She has never trusted Bob completely, and feels that he cares more about his children than her. Betty also still feels guilty about leaving her husband 15 years ago, and she has also often put her need to "make up for the pain I caused my children" over the real needs of her children. Betty also agrees to do self-forgiveness work and to "try to find some inner peace finally in my life." She decides that "the person I really don't trust is God herself, and I suppose also myself."

Eventually, Bob and Betty reaffirm their love for each other. They agree to continue to dialogue about how much they will help their children, and how much they will not.

Caring for Aging and Vulnerable Family Members

As a person's parents age, she finds herself between her aging children and her aging parents. She is probably in the prime of her life, and blessed to be in a position to be able to provide for her family. In such cases, she is challenged to make the best decisions about her family's Highest Good. She lives in a culture in which people have become increasingly disconnected from one another, and she knows that she can no longer rely, as her ancestors once did, on her extended family or tribe to help her care for her vulnerable family members.

Just like parenting, caring for vulnerable family members has a spiritual component. Service to others comes from the common spiritual need to help relieve the suffering of others. In addition, the caregiver is challenged to support the Highest Good of another person, which requires spiritual insight and wisdom. The caregiver seeks to find the balance between giving too much and not giving enough. If too much is given, the caregiver herself can become exhausted and dis-eased. If not enough is given, the vulnerable family member suffers unnecessarily. Finally, the presenting problem in these families is often that the adult female in the home (who is usually given the caregiving role) is stuck in either overresponsibility (personal consciousness) or underresponsibility (prepersonal consciousness).

The social worker's task is often to support the caregivers who support the vulnerable family members. The social worker helps the client get in touch with the spiritual dimension of his or her family challenges and find sustenance and wisdom from that dimension. The social worker also assesses the level of consciousness that each adult in the family tends to be most "stuck" in, and tries to help each member become more fluid in his or her consciousness.

CASE STUDY 18.5
CARING FOR FAMILY CARETAKERS

The social worker at the Aging Unit of the Mountain Mental Health Program visits with a family who was referred to him by a physician at the local hospital. Ms. and Mr. White came to the session. The presenting problem is that Mr. White's mother, Bertha, recently had her third stroke, and now needs more care than ever. Bertha had been living in the Whites' home for about four years in an apartment downstairs, but now has moved upstairs so that Ms. White can cook and clean for her.

In his assessment, the social worker determines that Ms. White (who is 63 years old) is functioning primarily on the personal level of consciousness, and Mr.

White (who is age 67) is operating at more of a prepersonal level of consciousness. Although retired himself and in good health, he seems to have avoided his mother as much as possible, and wants his wife to do all of the caregiving.

The social worker is not judgmental of either Ms. or Mr. White, but he wants them to expand their ability to operate at all levels of consciousness. He sees their challenge with Bertha as an opportunity for them to grow spiritually, and he explains these concepts to the couple in the first session: "Ms. and Mr. White, I am impressed with the love you both have for each other and for Bertha. I would like to invite you both to look at Bertha's illness as an opportunity for everyone in the family to grow spiritually. I would like to help support you in making the right decisions about Bertha and the family. I would also like to support you in discovering what this next period of time in your life will be about."

The social worker helps Mr. White see that part of his unhappiness is that his golf game will not be enough to bring him the peace of mind and fulfillment he misses in his life. The worker works with Ms. White to help her understand and transcend her feelings of responsibility for everyone else and her lack of awareness of her own feelings, needs, and boundaries.

GROUP WORK

The spiritually oriented social worker uses group work to foster the spiritual development of her or his clients. Group work (including marital and family work) gives clients a special opportunity to practice developing and running a Community of Spiritual and Universal Diversity. As in couple and family therapy, the social worker can also assess clients in part by observing their interactions with other people. Often people can benefit more from their interaction with their peers than from their interactions with their social worker. The skillful social worker can help clients help each other in their spiritual work.

Bereavement Support Group

The social worker can use spiritual group work to help clients who are grieving the loss of a loved one. Generally, the worker helps clients use their spirituality to help them not only cope with their loss but also to revisualize their entire lives and deaths. The worker sets up the group, but can usually "get out of the way" as the clients learn how to support each other.

CASE STUDY 18.6
GROUP WORK WITH BEREAVED CLIENTS

The hospice social worker begins a new bereavement group. In this group there are six women and two men; all are over 50 years old except for one of the women. All have lost their spouses in the last six months. The worker initially asks each client to tell his or her story, and one by one the group talks about the loss of their loved ones.

The social worker knows that the work of bereavement is feeling sadness, and she explains to the group that in a healthy person, "emotions stay in motion" instead of getting denied and "stuck." The worker asks the group, "What is sadness for?" and the participants talk about how loss seems to be part of life from birth through death. One woman says, "It has been when I am sad that I seem to feel closest to God." Others agree, and another client offers, "Maybe pain is what brings us to God." "Well, when things are going well, I sometimes forget to say my prayers," says another.

When one client says, "Sometimes I feel my husband's presence in the house, especially at night," the worker is at first unsure of what to say. The worker had read in a book that many survivors have such experiences but the book did not explain what the professional should do in response to such comments. In a moment, however, another client says that he has also had a similar experience, and then another client shares her experiences regarding her deceased husband. The social worker starts to realize that the group itself has become the healer and that her task is to act as a safe "container" for the participants to help each other.

Parent Group Work

The social worker can also use the spiritual healing power of a group to support parents. Often the very parents who may most need a parenting class are afraid to attend such a class, perhaps because they worry that they will be seen as incompetent. Thus, in voluntary parenting classes, the social worker's first and most difficult task is to successfully create a safe environment in which parents may work. The disease model used in many professional settings contributes to such reluctance, because people have to have a diagnosis before they can get help. Thus, parents might especially fear that they will be judged as inadequate if they ask for help. A spiritual model is a strength-based perspective that respects both client and helper as seekers of spiritual development. In such a model, there is no shame for asking for help, since we are all on spiritual paths together.

CASE STUDY 18.7
EXERCISE AT PARENT SUPPORT GROUP NIGHT

The social worker helps prepare a light dinner (donated by local corporations) for parents who come to the first parenting class evening. She welcomes everyone after they eat and has them do an introduction exercise. Then she speaks: "I want to invite you all to consider your children from a different perspective than you may ever have done before. I want to ask you to imagine that your soul chose the child or children that were born to you because they were to bring you an important spiritual gift or gifts in your life. I want you to take the piece of paper in front of you and the markers and draw a picture of the spiritual gift that each of your children has, is, or will bring to you in your life. Just do the best you can with your drawings. Everyone is an artist because all an artist is is a person who has her own vision of the world and creates an image of it for herself."

After the parents finish their drawings, the social worker has them choose other parents they do not know and share their drawings in dyads. First, each parent is to look at his partner's picture and share what he sees in the picture. Then, each parent is to explain what the intent of the picture originally was, and what she now sees in her own picture.

Couple Group Work

The spiritually oriented social worker recognizes that many couples are disconnected from other couples and the communities in which they live. People often do not know the extent to which their relational and other life issues are shared by couples not only in their local but also global communities. This isolation creates a number of challenges. In some families, maltreatment, addictions, and other destructive behaviors can occur in secrecy, and the family perpetrators and victims also suffer from their collective denial or minimization. In many other families, couples feel unnecessary guilt and shame about themselves, because they believe that their experiences, thoughts, and behaviors are unique.

The purpose of spiritually oriented couple groups is to decrease that isolation, and in doing so, to help people heal themselves, each other, and their communities. The social worker encourages the couples to explore the spiritual dimension of their relationships.

CASE STUDY 18.8
EXERCISE AT COUPLE GROUP

The social worker meets again with four couples that have contracted to meet weekly for 12 weeks. The worker asks each person to find a partner from another relationship to do a spiritual exercise. Then he asks them to talk with each other about this question: Why do you think your soul wanted you to fall in love with your partner? After about 20 minutes of sharing, the group comes together again and people have a chance to discuss their experience with the whole group.

One woman says, "I was surprised with what I came up with in response to your question. I realized that my soul wanted Ann because she can see my soul, through all my protections." A man then says, "What I realized when I did the exercise was that I do not know yet why my soul made me fall in love with my wife. In fact, I didn't know that I didn't know. But now I want to know." The social worker responds, "I am proud of you that you can admit to the mystery in your relationship. I suspect there is an element of mystery in all of our relationships. Maybe you can use this group to help you learn more about the spiritual dimensions of your relationship."

Men's and Women's Spirituality Groups

The spiritually oriented social worker may run a spirituality group for women or men. Such groups may help adults who especially want to find a connection or explore spirituality with other people who share their biological gender. The motivation for such groups might also be to find or create wisdom traditions that are not patriarchal, hierarchical, or otherwise oppressive to minorities. When the social worker wants to structure a men's or women's group, the worker may ask her or his clients to consider such issues as:

1. Why do you think your soul wanted to come into this world in a woman's (or man's) body?

2. How did the family, school, religion, and community you grew up in treat men and women differently? How do you feel about these biases?

3. If you believe in God, do you believe that God has a gender? Why or why not?

4. Regardless of your gender, to what extent have you developed your feminine and masculine traits? How is such development related to your spiritual growth?

STUDY QUESTIONS

1. What do you think and feel about the spiritual purpose of group work given in the chapter?

2. With what methods of transformation (Box 18.1) are you most comfortable? With which are you least comfortable? Explain why.

3. How can a child's or teen's rite of passage be seen from a spiritual perspective? Give an example from your own life.

4. What do you think and feel about the family values given in Box 18.2? How would you modify the values described?

5. How is the process of letting go a spiritual process? How does it relate to parenting? What is the importance of letting go in your own life?

6. Explain how a caretaker who is "stuck" at the prepersonal level of consciousness might behave with a parent who needs care. Do the same, compare and contrast, for the personal and transpersonal levels of consciousness.

7. How can group work facilitate spiritual development? How comfortable are you running groups? Explain why.

RESOURCES

Dalai Lama. (2000). *Dzogchen: The heart essence of the great perfection*. Ithaca, NY: Snow Lion Publications.
  Another of the books by the Dalai Lama that has advice that may be useful to caretakers.
Vaughan, F., & Walsh, R. (1983). *Gifts from a course of miracles*. New York: Penguin Putman.
  A wonderful summary of key concepts from the "Course of Miracles" that can be inspirational to caretakers.

CHAPTER 19

ADVANCED SPIRITUALLY ORIENTED PRACTICE IN INDIVIDUAL TRANSFORMATION

In this chapter, some methods in advanced spiritual practice with individual transformations are described. Three different populations at risk are considered: people with addictions, straight white males, and the dying.

PEOPLE WITH ADDICTIONS

Momentum

From a spiritual perspective, addiction can be thought of as negative Spiritual Momentum. Momentum is more positive, for example, when the person is moving toward her own multidimensional developmental healing and maturity, is learning to love herself and the world more deeply, and is participating in the creation of Communities of Spiritual and Universal Community. Momentum is more negative, for example, when the person is losing loving connection with parts of herself and her world, is becoming increasingly regressed into and stuck in some stage of her development, and is losing reverence for the diversity of human beings, other living things, and the ecosystems that support all life.

Addiction has roots in the individual's relationship with pain and pleasure, and spiritually oriented work with addictions is directed toward modifying that relationship. Most human beings hunger for pleasure, such as what one can experience when eating a meal, having sex, and participating in music and dance. We also seem to want to avoid suffering, such as in the experience of physical pain, anticipated and real loss, and the sense of disconnection with ourselves and the world.

Our need to have pleasure and avoid pain is understandable and human, and the social worker can normalize such activities for the client. However, as most of the world's wisdom traditions teach, pleasure is always temporary and pain is an unavoidable part of life. From a spiritual perspective, pleasure and pain can be thought of as two of the greatest teachers of the soul; for example, our pursuit of pleasure can teach us about impermanence and our avoidance of suffering can teach us about attachment.

Most addictions begin simply as activities that increase pleasure or decrease pain. On the psychological level, an addiction in moderation could be thought of simply as a coping strategy, a strength, or a resiliency factor. Said another way, when an imbalance occurs, any strength can also become a weakness, any coping strategy can become an unhealthy habit, and any resiliency factor can become a vulnerability. For example, a woman who runs at first to relax and foster her health might begin to run every day for increasing distances until she begins to injure her body seriously. Or a man who is a good listener as a boy might avoid saying much of anything about himself in his intimate relationships as an adult.

On the one hand, this relationship between addiction and coping, strength, and resiliency can be confusing in the helping process. Clients may not understand that their best efforts to deal with the world can also lead to addiction if they become out of balance. On the other hand, understanding this relationship can also support the helping process. The social worker can help the client see that his addictive behavior is rooted in a desire for healing and health and that he could still find another way to achieve the body–mind–spirit–environmental health he seeks. The client may get hope from the realization that every person has the potential to become addicted to something in his life, as well as the potential to develop coping skills, strength, and resiliency.

Creativity

What are the spiritual medicines for addiction? One medicine is creativity. If addiction is thought of as habitual activity, then one opposite of addiction may be creative activity. Although habitual activity is predictable and therefore initially seems to reduce pain and increase pleasure, such behavior, when done in excess, tends to deaden all the individual's experience. Creative activity, although unpredictable and therefore more frightening, also tends to elicit more growth, be more exciting, and foster a general experience of aliveness in the client. The worker may suggest to the client in addiction that she strive to re-balance her life between habitual and creative activity on all the dimensions, physical, emotional, cognitive, social, spiritual, and environmental. As illustrated by the examples in Table 19.1, habitual activities can be replaced by more creative activities in the same dimension.

Balance

Another medicine for addiction is balance. The social worker helps the client look at what might be out of balance in all the areas of her or his life, including not only the developmental dimensions listed in Table 19.1 but also in such interrelated areas as the tension between work and play, income and expenditures, and individual and community focus. Balance is not something a client does once and then it is

TABLE 19.1   Examples of Habitual and Creative Activities across the Developmental Dimensions

DIMENSION	HABITUAL ACTIVITY	ALTERNATIVE CREATIVE ACTIVITY IN SAME DIMENSION
Physical	Substance abuse Overeating Sex addiction	Use medicine to transform and heal self and others. Use food to care for self and others. Use sex to celebrate and heal self and others.
Emotional	Rage-aholic Resentment	Use heart to forgive (let go of anger) and heal self and others. Use heart for love and compassion for self and others.
Cognitive	Worry Perfectionism Narrow thinking	Pray for the Highest Good for self and others. Practice radical acceptance of self and others. Expand mindfulness and tolerance for other ideas.
Social	Social withdrawal Avoid being alone	Take social risks as a way to open up to Creative Spirit. Know self as a way to know Creative Spirit.
Spiritual	Spiritual narcissism	Dis-identify from personal spiritual development. Develop pure motives for behaviors.
Environment	Overconsumption	Give to nature more than take.

done. Since change is constant, the client will find things going in and out of balance constantly. Finding balance requires mindfulness, intent, and creativity. Over time, the client can replace addictive habits with the creative habit of re-balancing.

Temperance

Temperance, another medicine for addiction, is an older term that is seldom used today. Perhaps that is because in our era of consumerism and consumption, we do not want to think about the need for moderation in our lives. Temperance is about finding the "right mix at the right time." The client learns to take care of himself, his family, community, and ecosystem without unnecessary waste and hurry. For example, every family vacation does not have to be thousands of miles away at an expensive resort. Or the client may contract with his family not to buy any presents one December, and instead donate all the money they would have spent to the poor. Or the client can start eating simpler food and start buying less expensive new clothing.

Equanimity

Another related medicine for addiction is equanimity. The social worker teaches the client to approach life with more calmness. Instead of reacting to the pain the client may experience in relationship with her body, other people, or the world, the client chooses to approach her suffering with serenity and calmness. Such a transformation is not easy, and the social worker supports the client in patiently working to understand her reactions to pain and anticipated pain, and then to replace her fearful responses to pain with a more calm, centered, and proactive approach to life.

Surrender

Surrender is part of the process of spiritual development. A person chooses to give up her or his own (in psychological terms, the ego's) will and instead follows Creative Spirit (or in some religions, the Will of God). There is the recognition that one must give up something to get something else, like the story of the monk that tells his student to get rid of all the furniture so that there will be room for new things in his room. Although the student at first wants to cling to his old furniture, he eventually realizes that he will ultimately gain much more than he loses as he goes through each spiritual surrender. The social worker realizes that most clients do not want to let go of their "furniture," whether it is their sense of control, their work addiction, their worry, or their alcohol.

In an addictive process, the person surrenders to the desire for pleasure and/or the need to avoid pain. In the addiction process, something is also lost and something is gained, and as the addiction becomes more intense, the individual ultimately gives up more than he or she gains. Since the relief of pain and the experience of pleasure in addiction is temporary, the person needs to go back and back again into addictive activities to get a short-term fix.

Prepersonal-Level Addictions

People who generally function at the prepersonal level of consciousness often tend to have addictions that provide immediate physical pleasure and relief from emotional pain. The child ego state (see Chapters 1 and 4) is in control on the prepersonal level, and so excesses tend to reflect such youthful tendencies as excessive lack of responsibility, playfulness, drinking, or sexual behavior. A spiritual medicine for prepersonal-level addictions is increased personal and transpersonal consciousness, which would help the client balance out her prepersonal excesses. Often prepersonal-level addiction is not dealt with until other people in the person's life become concerned.

CASE STUDY 19.1
WORK WITH A PREPERSONAL ADDICTION

The social worker sees a court-referred client who has a record of both public intoxication and DUI charges against her. The client is at first very resistant to talking with the social worker, but the worker is willing to listen to the client tell her story, which she eventually does. Based on her formal testing and biopsychosocial–spiritual–environmental assessment, the worker gives the woman an alcohol dependency and dysthymia diagnosis and recommends to the court that the woman receive both weekly individual and group therapy. The judge agrees.

The social worker gives the client feedback about her alcohol addiction and talks to her about what a prepersonal addiction is: "You have been seeking pleasure and avoiding pain like every other human being, but the way you have done this has made your life even worse than it was when you were sober. Part of your work will be to remember what your suffering was before you started using. You are like a woman on fire who jumped into a stream to put the fire out and is now drowning. She has forgotten why she jumped in the water to begin with." The client responds, "Yes, but every time I try to stop drinking I can only stay sober for a month or two." The worker says, "OK, so let's make the short-term goal that you start to love yourself more, just the way that you are, and let yourself feel everything again—joy and pain." "How am I supposed to do that?" "Well," says the worker, "we have to start somewhere. How about telling me the story of your life, from the beginning." As the client tells her story over the weeks of therapy, she begins to identify more with the social worker.

As their therapeutic relationship begins to grow, the worker helps the client begin to take more responsibility (personal consciousness) for other people, beginning by doing visits with her two teenaged children, both of whom have been removed from the home. The client also teaches her yoga (transpersonal consciousness) in the group work class on Tuesday nights, so that she can start to develop an Observing Self.

Personal-Level Addictions

People who generally function at the personal level of consciousness often tend to have addictions that help them avoid pain through excessive responsibility. The parent ego state (see Chapters 1 and 4) is in control on the personal level, and so excesses tend to reflect such parental tendencies as excessive responsibility, work, seriousness, self-control, and obligation. A spiritual medicine for personal-level addictions is increased prepersonal and transpersonal consciousness, which would help the client balance out the personal excesses. Often personal-level addiction is not dealt with until other people in the client's's life become concerned.

CASE STUDY 19.2
WORK WITH A PERSONAL ADDICTION

The social worker is doing couple work with a 40-year-old woman and her 50-year-old husband, Frank. Frank's wife, Mary, has insisted that he go to a marriage counselor because she is feeling increasingly lonely in the marriage. The worker assesses that Frank has an addiction to his work. As a leading physician in town, he works an average of almost 60 hours a week between his own practice and his administrative and academic duties at the university hospital.

The worker realizes that she must help Frank with his work addiction, in addition to doing the couple counseling. Frank is not happy coming to counseling. He says, "I am missing an important meeting tonight during this session. I don't really have the time for much more counseling than this, nor do I need it." Mary responds, "You mean you don't have any time for me or your marriage." "No, that's not what I am saying. Why do you insist on always putting words in my mouth?" The social worker says, "It sounds, Frank, like your work is an issue in your marriage. What if we look at the counseling like that, rather than debate at this point about whether you or Mary is right or wrong." Frank reluctantly agrees and Mary is accepting of a plan to meet for four sessions and then to reevaluate.

During those four sessions, the social worker helps Frank start to feel again—feel his fatigue, his sadness, his anger, his longings. Since Frank is intellectually gifted, she works with his cognitive strength to help him, offering him new ways of thinking about himself and the world: "Frank, your greatest strength is perhaps also your greatest weakness." "What do you mean?" he replies. "I am talking about your endurance, which is remarkable and enables you to do all you do so well. However, your endurance has also enabled you to stay in your addiction longer than most people could." "What do you mean by that?" "Well, your need to work is like your heroin. It gives you a little high but then it wears off and you have to continue increasing the dosage. You are able to do that because you can work harder than most people can." Frank smiles and understands. He eventually decides that he needs to figure out what he wants in his life: "I have become successful, but now I am just a machine. I have forgotten, if I ever knew, who I am." The worker knows that Frank's decision could mark a spiritual turning point in his life.

The worker can see that Mary also operates primarily on the personal level of consciousness. The worker knows that any relationship is created by two people, and that Mary must have her issues, too. The worker determines that Mary was willing to put Frank's needs ahead of her own in the first years of the marriage. However, as she became more mindful of her own thoughts and feelings, she also became more assertive in telling Frank what she wanted and did not want in the marriage. At this point she is very scared that she may not ever be able to have the intimacy she wants with her husband. The social worker reminds her that "the work of a relationship is in large part the process of becoming more mindful about where your husband's responsibility ends and where yours begins." "In other words," replies Mary, "it is good for me to be aware of how much of my aloneness comes from my own life process and how much of it has to do with who Frank is." "Exactly," says the worker, "and when you determine what those realities are, you will know more what you need to do." As Mary does become more mindful of the nature of her aloneness, she eventually realizes that although she has been more alone than she wants to be for her entire life, Frank is unlikely to ever give her what she needs. The worker knows that Mary's growing awareness could also be catalytic to her ongoing development.

Transpersonal Addictions

People who generally function at the transpersonal level of consciousness often tend to have addictions that provide pleasure and relieve pain through excessive withdrawal from the self and the world. The Observing Self ego state (see Chapters 1 and 4) is in control on the transpersonal level, and so excesses tend to reflect such tendencies as excessive social withdrawal, practice of rituals, lack of responsiveness to others, and disconnection from self. A spiritual medicine for transpersonal-level addictions is increased prepersonal and transpersonal consciousness, which would help the client balance out the transpersonal excesses. Often transpersonal-level addiction is not dealt with until other people in the person's life become concerned.

For example, some clients who can operate at the transpersonal level of consciousness may develop a sexual addiction. Such an addiction can be more easily hidden than many other addictions, and can give such clients a convenient pleasure and a quick sense of relief from the pain that they experience in their lives. Some leaders of religious and spiritual groups will seek sexual relationships with their followers, and the spiritually oriented social worker always is concerned for the welfare of communities when sexual boundaries are violated.

CASE STUDY 19.3
WORK WITH A TRANSPERSONAL ADDICTION

Marcie works at the meditation center, where she runs lengthy meditation retreats for adults. She is recognized as a skilled meditator and teacher by her community. She and her former husband divorced 10 years ago and she now lives alone in her apartment and takes care of her two sons four days a week. The children still travel between her home and her former husband's home each week. Marcie's sons have become increasingly hostile toward her in the last year and she brings them into the social worker's office to find out why.

In the session, her oldest son, John, says, "Mom, all you do is meditate all day, or you clean the apartment." John's brother, Billy, adds, "Yes, and you have been getting weirder and weirder, Mom." "What do you mean by that Billy?" asks the worker. The boy responds, "When you talk to her she just looks at you and says nothing." As the boys talk, Marcie says very little.

The worker sits down privately with Marcie and asks her to tell her story. It turns out that she has become increasingly withdrawn over the past decade, and now has no one with whom she is intimate. She has been able to do her professional work, but her private life is a life of isolation. Marcie tells the social worker, "I don't blame the boys for being upset with me. I am upset with me. I feel like I have let everyone down. I sometimes don't even believe in my own work, but that is all I have anymore." The social worker comforts her, and says, "You have gone a long way down your spiritual path, perhaps too far, alone. I think that you have identified with your spiritual work, and you have started to believe that your meditation and teaching is all that you are. But Marcie you are much more than that. Your children are your teachers right now, reminding you of what your soul needs." Marcie agrees to work to try to regain access to her prepersonal and personal levels of consciousness again.

Making Medicines Sacred Again

From a spiritual perspective, substance abuse could be seen as behavior rooted in the natural desire to change consciousness from the painful and limiting aspects of consensus reality to a freer state of mind without anxiety, guilt, and shame. Throughout history, many of our ancestors have used sacred medicines to assist in healing rituals or to enhance their individual and collective well-being and spiritual development. When people used sacred medicines, they usually held the intent that their experiences would facilitate their spiritual process and they were accompanied by loving tribal elders, healers, or shamans who supported their intent for spiritual growth. In contrast, when people today use medicines, they hold the intent that they might escape for a few minutes or hours from their suffering and have a few moments of pleasure, and they are accompanied by other people who facilitate their process of temporary escape by escaping with them.

The spiritually oriented social worker realizes that people today use many "drugs" to escape pain and create temporary pleasure, including such diversions as alcohol, cocaine, television, sports utility vehicles, Internet pornography, electronic games, and shopping. The spiritually oriented social worker is not opposed to such diversions, but is opposed to their use without sacred intent. A person has a sacred intent when she holds her own spiritual transformation and the Highest Good of herself, her communities, and ecosystems as the objective of her thoughts and behaviors.

The social worker does not believe that every client must use a substance or other "drug" or "medicine" to foster spiritual transformation, but recognizes that some clients can benefit from the use of sacred medicines, when used with sacred intent. The social worker helps the client see the difference between the addictive use of substances, which can create negative life momentum, and the sacred use of substances, which can create more positive life momentum.

STRAIGHT WHITE MALES

Privilege and Spirituality

The spiritually oriented social worker recognizes that although, as a group, straight white males (SWM) have been blessed in this era with economic, social, and political privilege, such privilege is often accompanied by spiritual poverty. As most of the world's wisdom traditions teach, excessive wealth and power can become addictive, and those SWMs who "win" the wealth and power competition (and become "Alpha males") may be at risk to lose connection with their souls and the universe. The straight white males who "lose" the wealth and power competition (and end up with relatively less) may still live somewhere between the worlds of material privilege and spiritual poverty, perhaps full of shame about being a loser in the material world and resentment toward the material "winners."

The spiritually oriented social worker is compassionate toward all populations, and refuses to turn away SWM clients simply because of the privileges they may enjoy. She knows that if she can help her SWM clients change their spiritual momentum, then as potential leaders, they may bring more compassion, economic and distributive justice, and peace to this suffering world.

Since straight white males may live primarily "in their heads," spiritual work with them can include methods drawn from the Spirit with Heart and bioconsciousness paradigms. In such work, the client is asked to notice his heart and body

TABLE 19.2   Examples of Current and Alternative Male Archetypes of Success

CURRENT ARCHETYPE	DESCRIPTION OF SUCCESS FOR CURRENT ARCHETYPE	ALTERNATIVE ARCHETYPE	DESCRIPTION OF ALTERNATIVE ARCHETYPE
CEO	Make more money than competitors	Volunteer	Service through giving time to others
Football coach	Win more games than competitors	Father	Support children on their spiritual path
Military general	Win more battles than competitors	Husband–lover	Support spouse–lover's spiritual path
Politician	Win more elections and have more power than competitors	Benefactor	Help others in family and community
Academic	Write more articles than competitors	Street artist	Give away to or share art with others
Suburban homeowner	Have bigger house and car but less dandelions than others	Conservationist	Have more efficient house, car, and xero-scaped (water-efficient) lawn

again. Then the worker can offer the client alternative archetypes of male success, which is more a method of the Mindful Daily Living paradigm (see Table 19.2).

Femiphobia and Spirituality

Another common obstacle to the spiritual development of men is femiphobia, which could be defined as the fear of being feminine. Femiphobia is a deeper and more pervasive fear than homophobia, which in contrast is just the fear of intimacy with other men. The fear of the feminine may have ancient roots in the warrior and leadership traditions of our tribal ancestors, as well as more recent roots in the expectations that modern culture has for men.

Femiphobia can interfere with spiritual development because spiritual development always includes both masculine and feminine processes. As illustrated in Table 19.3, any of these feminine and masculine processes can be part of the spirituality of any man or any woman. All of these processes are, from a spiritual perspective, all equally important. Unfortunately, in our culture, most men do not feel free to express their feminine spiritual processes. The worker does not believe that a man has to give up his masculine processes, or of course become homosexual, in order to be a spiritual being. But the worker does know that if a man (or woman) does not feel free to experience and express the full range of his humanity, then he lives in a box too small for his soul.

The worker first helps the client become more mindful of what processes he feels comfortable with and has developed, and those processes with which he still feels uncomfortable. The next task of the social worker usually is to help the male

TABLE 19.3   **Examples of Feminine and Masculine Spiritual Processes**

FEMININE PROCESS	MASCULINE PROCESS
Surrender to God	Preach about religion
Let go of attachment	Lead a church
Give compassion to others	Organize a ritual
Forgive others	Interpret scripture
Allow openness to mystery	Set down rules
Nurture those less fortunate	Discipline church members

client give himself permission to experience and express the full range of his masculine and feminine spiritual processes, particularly those that have been suppressed. The worker can do this through modeling, teaching, and supporting these processes.

CASE STUDY 19.4
EXPANDING FEMININE PROCESSES WITH A VOLUNTARY MALE CLIENT

The social worker in private practice starts to work with a 45-year-old man who came in for therapy after his relationship with his wife started to deteriorate. The man reports to the therapist, "She told me that she wants me to move out, as if I am some kind of major jerk." "What did she say was the reason for her wanting to leave the relationship?" asks the worker. The man replies, "She keeps saying the same thing, that she felt that I was the one who had left her, that she did not feel close to me anymore. I make a lot of money. I work overtime every week. I gave her a beautiful home. I don't know what she wants." "What do *you* want?" asks the social worker. "I don't know," says the man. Knowing that the end of a relationship is often a painful catalyst for deeper spiritual work, the worker asks, "Do you want to find out?" "OK," replies her client.

The social worker helps the client become more mindful, not just about his relationships with women, but also about his life. They start by doing some exploration of the man's life, how he felt as a boy and young man, and what the turning points were of his first three decades. It turns out that, although the man describes his family as "tight knit," he had repeatedly experienced disappointments in love, beginning with his family of origin, when his father was "always at work" and his mother was "busy with my younger brothers." The client talks about how he decided to "make a lot of money" and worked hard to became a computer engineer, and how he became quite active in the church that he grew up in. The social worker discovers with her client that, although he is very religious, he has not had much of a spiritual life. The man had never thought about his spirituality as being any different than religiosity in his life, but he starts to realize that he feels little connection with his deepest self and the world around him. "The weirdest thing," he says, "is that I thought that I was living the right life. Everyone else seemed happy with me. And it wasn't until my wife became unhappy with me that I realized that I had forgotten about my own soul. I still don't know but I am going to find out."

This leads the worker to ask her client to experiment with meditation, explaining that such a practice might give him the insights he now wants. The client has tremendous difficulty sitting still, and the social worker encourages him to be patient with himself. "I don't think you ever had anyone be patient with you in your life, so you don't know how to be patient with yourself." At the same time, the social worker also asks the client to do a ceremony with her. He is to fill cloth pouches with tobacco, each pouch is to represent something he wants to let go of in his life. The man fills six pouches and they go outside, start a fire, and perform a ceremony. One by one, the man is to say what he wants to let go of in his life as he drops the pouches in the flames. He decides to let go of worry, overtime work, having to keep his lawn green, buying a new car every year, pleasing other people, and never having any recreational time. The worker says, "Now you might expect that you will have more room in your life. Maybe you can give yourself permission to discover gradually how you want to use that time."

CASE STUDY 19.5
EXPANDING FEMININE PROCESSES WITH A NONVOLUNTARY MALE CLIENT

The client walks into the social worker's office saying, "I don't know why I need to be here. If you would just write a letter to the judge saying that I came here, I will pay you the money and we can both go on our way." This man was referred to the agency by the court after the man was arrested on a domestic violence charge. The social worker explains to the man that he is not willing to sign off like that, and that he expects all of his clients to work on their issues. The client is furious, but he is resigned because he knows he has been court-ordered to go to counseling.

The worker just lets his new client complain about how unfair his life is for several sessions. He listens patiently as the man complains about his wife is "always nagging," about how the people who work for him in his roofing business all are "slackers," about how the judge is "self-righteous," about how drivers in the city all "drive like idiots," about how his children are "all self-centered," and how his neighbors are all "lazy." The worker feels compassion for this man, who is obviously in great pain, and he supports the goodness he feels is in his soul without agreeing with him that everyone else in his life is evil.

One session, when he thinks the client is ready to hear something different, the worker says, "Well, it sounds like your 'monkey mind' has stolen spiritual empowerment from you." "What do you mean by that?" asks the client. "Well," says the worker, "when your mind blames all of your suffering on people outside of yourself, then there is absolutely nothing you can do, and you are at the mercy of this obviously imperfect world." "What else can I do?" asks the client. "You could love yourself." "I already do!" complains the client. "No you don't," responds the worker. "If you did, you would allow yourself to accept your own imperfections so that you could move on with your life. Instead, you have to pretend that you are perfect and that everyone else is screwed up." For once the client is speechless for a moment, and the client smiles and adds, "There is only one person in this room who thinks you are a bad person, and it is not me."

In the weeks that follow, the client works on letting go of his personal armor that he has worn all his life. As he lets go of his anger toward others a little, he starts to realize how sad and alone he feels. He is in a potential turning point in his life.

DEATH AND DYING

All clients are, of course, eventually going to die. They are also currently still alive, although many are not living fully. The spiritually oriented social worker keeps coming back to these facts when she works with her clients. She tries to touch on the realities of death and life in some way in every session, reminding clients of the inevitability of death, the miraculous nature of life, and how every moment is a precious opportunity. The worker believes that when the client lives with the awareness that death is always possible, in essence "an eyelash away," he is freed to be more fully alive in every moment.

Some clients seem obviously closer to death. They may have a terminal diagnosis and be involved in a hospice program with which the social worker is associated. In some cases, the social worker has opportunities to actually sit with the client while he or she dies. With such situations, the social worker is focused on the spiritual process of the client and on what he or she needs most in the present moment.

Whether the client is actively dying or is still young and far away from death, the paradigms of transformation (as illustrated in Box 19.1) offer some methods that the worker can draw on in his or her work with dying clients. The social worker's responsibility is to be especially responsive to and respectful of the client's unique religious and spiritual traditions. The worker also recognizes that the dying process can be the most powerful opportunity for transformation in life, and that it occurs in every moment.

BOX 19.1

EXAMPLES OF METHODS THAT MAY FOSTER TRANSFORMATION IN DYING CLIENTS

Spiritual Momentum	Help the client find peace and acceptance of his past and create the momentum of his own living and dying process.
Mindful Daily Living	Help the client live every remaining moment more fully alive, so that her coming death is truly a spiritual teacher in her remaining life.
Spirit with Heart	Help the client increase his love, compassion, and forgiveness of self and others, and let go of his guilt, shame, fear, and anger.
Religious Self	Use the client's own religious rituals, beliefs, and doctrines to help her prepare to leave this life and enter the transformation of death.
Bioconsciousness	Help the client experience how his soul has a body more than his body has a soul, so that he can let go of his attachment to his body.
Community Consciousness	Transform the client by supporting her connection with and participation in the communities that are most meaningful to her.
Eco-Consciousness	Transform the client by supporting his connection with and participation in the ecosystems that are most meaningful to him.

STUDY QUESTIONS

1. Describe a spiritual perspective on addictions. How is such a perspective similar to a psychological or biological perspective? How is it different?

2. How many people have addictions? What addictions do you see in yourself? How do you feel about working with people with addictions?

3. What "medicines" can the spiritually oriented social worker use with clients who have addictions? Which of these seem to work best for you? Why do you think that? Would you be flexible enough to use medicines that do not work for you with your clients?

4. Describe each of these concepts and how it has served you in your own life:
   a. Creativity
   b. Balance
   c. Temperance
   d. Equanimity
   e. Surrender

5. Describe the nature of the addictions that you might expect at the following levels of consciousness, and describe the strategy of change you might use with such cases:
   a. Prepersonal
   b. Personal
   c. Transpersonal

6. How have drugs lost their sacredness in modern culture? How could social workers help clients create their own sacred medicines? How do your own values shape your response to these questions?

7. Why are straight white males at risk? How do you feel working with such clients?

8. How does the privilege of straight white males sometimes contribute to their spiritual poverty? Have you seen this relationship in any of the men you know personally? Explain.

9. What is femiphobia? How is it related to homophobia? How is it related to men's spirituality?

10. What are feminine and masculine spiritual processes? Which, if any, of the processes described in Table 19.3 are part of your own spiritual development? Which are not? Why do you think this is true?

11. What are some advanced methods of transformation that a social worker can use when working with the dying? Describe a method drawn from each of the seven paradigms of transformation.

RESOURCES

Anderson, M. (2001). *Sacred dying: Creating rituals for embracing the end of life.* Roseville, CA: Prima Publishing.
   This book has many useful suggestions about how helpers can help people in the dying process.
Fremantle, F. (2001). *Luminous emptiness: Understanding the Tibetan Book of the Dead.* Boston: Shambhala.
   This text is perhaps the best description of the *Book of the Dead* currently in English. An understanding of death and dying seems essential to understanding adult psychology and spirituality.

CHAPTER 20

ADVANCED SPIRITUALLY ORIENTED PRACTICE IN COLLECTIVE TRANSFORMATION

COLLECTIVE TRANSFORMATION AND COLLECTIVE MOMENTUM

Just as an individual can be said to have a spiritual momentum, so can a family or a local or global community also have a spiritual momentum. Humanity's collective spiritual momentum is the shared direction of its evolution, measured in large part by the way we treat ourselves, each other, other living things, and the planetary ecosystem we currently share. The purpose of macrolevel social work interventions is to help create collective transformations that lead to shifts in collective momentum, characterized by the co-creation of Communities of Spiritual and Universal Diversity in human society. Such transformations may occur on many levels, including in the profession of social work itself, in the local community, on a national level, or in the global community.

SPIRITUAL PRACTICE AT MACROLEVELS AND MICROLEVELS

The spiritually oriented social worker is naturally drawn to working on all levels of social work, which includes the so-called microlevels (individual, couple, family, and group) and macrolevels (local and global community and ecosystem). This is because the spiritual perspective is a broad and unifying perspective that finds connections between all levels of reality. Such a perspective is consistent with the person-in-environment, ecological perspective of social work on both the micro- and macrolevels of practice. In this chapter, advanced methods in macrolevel work are introduced, and implications for both practice and research are described.

The spiritual perspective that unifies the micro and macro perspectives is potentially healing for both the social work profession as well as for its clients. As mentioned in Chapter 1, there has been an unfortunate practical and theoretical split between the micro- and macrolevels of social work. Although the vast majority of social workers in practice today work on the microlevel of the profession of social work, the academic world of social work has been dominated for decades by a more macro perspective, as reflected in the lack of practice content in Ph.D.-level programs (that train future leaders), the emphasis on social policy in many schools, and the relative scarcity of academic or Ph.D.-level direct practitioners in social work today. A more balanced emphasis between all levels of practice would be more helpful to the social work practitioner, educator, and client.

GLOBAL SURVIVAL THREATS

The survival of not just humanity but also of most life on the planet is currently at risk because of global survival threats (GSTs) that people themselves have created. These GSTs are the most pressing of the macro issues that the spiritually oriented social worker can attend to, because they threaten the well-being of all people and living things, and also because as these conditions gradually worsen, it is the poor and disenfranchised who currently suffer from them the most. For example, it is the poor who live in the most polluted regions of the globe, breathing toxic air and drinking disease-ridden water.

On the material level, the most fundamental issue for humanity today is "to be or not to be." On the spiritual level, the issue of our survival and the survival of life on Earth is viewed from the largest perspectives. The social worker can ask such large-perspective questions as those given here, and lead discussions based on such questions.

QUESTIONS FOR DISCUSSION ON GLOBAL SURVIVAL

1. What is our obligation to the generations of people and living things we evolved from?

2. What is our obligation to the generations of people and living things not yet born?

3. What is our obligation to the people and living things who are not helping create the current crises of GSTs but who will perish regardless if conditions worsen?

4. In what way is our collective spiritual evolution or momentum as a species related to the current GST crises?

5. Is the survival of humanity and of life of Earth in the Highest Good (or in God's Will)?

The social worker can help large groups find their own collective wisdom about the issues raised by each question. The spiritually oriented social worker supports efforts to eliminate threats to global survival, when those efforts provide equal protection to all people on the planet.

War, Terror, and Deep Peace

The world is currently at war, as it has been for most of human history. Although the wisdom traditions of the world teach that violence never cures violence, people still seem to be addicted to war, based on its continued popularity as a way to relate to other peoples and cultures. War has increasingly become a global survival threat because the weapons of war have become more deadly and more available. If current trends continue, eventually all nations will have access to various weapons of mass destruction. Unfortunately, if nations had mental health diagnoses, the most warlike people could be classified as bipolar, antisocial, and schizoid, with paranoid features.

What can the spiritually oriented social worker do to reduce the threat of war? One strategy is to model and teach nonviolence. Social workers can lead efforts to educate about nonviolent approaches to conflict resolution, particularly for many children and adolescents who currently receive classroom lectures, books, films, and television documentaries that often almost exclusively teach about and glorify war. Another strategy is to help support and build existing institutions that can impact public policy decisions, such as churches, nonprofit agencies, and social organizations. A third strategy is to organize dialogue meetings between grouping of people who now consider themselves enemies, fostering nonviolent discussion of the issues that divide them.

The spiritually oriented social worker is interested in uncovering and dealing with the roots of all violence, including war and terrorism. The cycle of violence is similar in war and terror; the seed of the next round of violence is always in the "victory" of one side over the other "losing" side. The whole concept of "winning" over the other "losing" side is thus an illusion, because the humiliation and anger of the vanquished is a motivation for the conflicts between future generations.

Is there an alternative to retaliation and blame, then, when the individual or his family and tribe is attacked by others? One alternative is to view an attack as an expression of pain and trauma that needs to be healed. The appropriate social work response to someone in pain is to offer compassionate healing. The spiritually oriented social worker can help local and global communities respond to attacks with compassionate healing. The work begins in the social worker's own heart and mind and soul, because she knows she has to learn how to personally respond to attack with healing and without blame before she can model such behavior effectively for others.

Finally, the social worker can model and teach deep peace. Deep peace is not just the absence of violence but also the response of compassionate healing, directed not only toward others but also toward one's self. The concept of deep peace becomes more than just an intellectual concept when it is also modeled by proponents and teachers.

Overpopulation, Overconsumption, and Stewardship of Ecosystems

The Earth is obviously finite. The spiritually oriented social worker has gratitude for the air and water and food that the Earth produces, and wants to be a good steward of the animals and plants that support human life and the ecosystems that support all life. He also feels the kinship human beings share with the whole family of animal and plant life that share the planet Earth, and perhaps the entire Universe. Because he is mindful, the social worker is aware of how overpopulated the Earth now is, and how most population growth has continued for decades to be in the poorest regions of the Earth. In addition, the worker can see how the wealthiest people on the planet have continued for decades to consume and amass disproportionately larger shares of the Earth's resources. Thus overpopulation and overconsumption are social work issues because they particularly impact those people who already are the poorest and least powerful on the planet. The goal of macrolevel practice in population and consumption work is to help people co-create Communities of Spiritual and Universal Diversity that support a sustainable high quality of life for all people.

Macro practice with overpopulation can focus on the co-creation of policies that return populations to sustainable levels without unfairly impacting any particular subpopulations. As populations decrease and stabilize, social workers need to advocate for the redistribution of resources so that resources that become available go to help those in most need, rather than to increase the wealth of populations already in power and wealth. Such policies should be thought of as being neither liberal nor conservative, Democratic nor Republican; they are based on the sincere desire for compassionate healing of humanity and the planet.

The overpopulation and overconsumption of people, as well as our preparations for and activities of war, all contribute to the gradual and ongoing deterioration of the ecosystems that support all life on Earth. The spiritually oriented social worker feels a strong connection with and responsibility for the natural world, which she expresses through her commitment to a stewardship of all local and global ecosystems. Stewardship is the compassionate healing response people can make to the trauma that the Earth has directly suffered from the excesses of humanity.

Although further scientific study may show more precisely how the activities of humanity have contributed to the destruction of habitat, global warming, air and water and soil pollution, and the extinction of species, any mindful person can see that we are gradually ruining our planetary ecosystem. The goal of the spiritually oriented social worker is to help the local and international communities become Communities of Spiritual and Universal Diversity that value the Highest Good of all living things and ecosystems over such goals as increased productivity, consumption, and material wealth.

The spiritually oriented social worker practices stewardship of the environment on many levels. On a personal level, he practices what he preaches. He does not make unnecessary purchases of products that would lead to further environmental destruction. He recycles all products and waste that he can. He walks or bicycles or uses mass transportation whenever he can, and he eats food produced locally whenever possible. He raises vegetables in his garden and xero-scapes his yard.

On the public level, the social worker helps educate people about their natural biopsychosocial–spiritual connections with other living things and ecosystems. Since education means to "draw out," the effective worker teaches by setting up experiences during which people can explore these connections. She can do this by taking people outdoors and into wild areas, or by asking them to reflect, for example, on how their body, mind, and soul respond to changes in the weather and seasons. The worker can also offer her students new concepts, such as "ecological services" (e.g., the oxygen produced by ocean plants) and "real ecological cost of products" (e.g., the full impact of strip farming on the environment), to help them understand the relationship between economics and ecosystem health. Finally, the social worker can work to have such content included in the curricula of the public or religious schools her children attend. Such education may eventually lead to a civil rights movement for all living things, led by a future generation, that would help protect the well-being of all life on Earth.

The worker knows that when people feel like they are doing something about an issue larger than themselves, and then make a commitment to act, they tend to benefit in body, mind, and spirit. The simple act of restraint, for example, can empower people who are concerned about the health of the ecosystems in which they live. When people live in restraint, they may decide, for example, that they do not need that bigger house after all, or that they can do fine without driving a gigantic new sports utility vehicle.

Social workers can also be activists, working to directly change public policy. For example, social workers can help people elect representatives and judges who refuse to allow wild lands to be further destroyed unnecessarily by such interests as the energy industry, suburban sprawl, or highway construction. Social workers can also work with existing public and private organizations to help mobilize them to make better policy that protects local and global ecosystems.

The Global Marketplace and Economic Democracy

Social workers are often not as interested in economy as they are in psychology, and the globalization of the marketplace seems complex and overwhelming if not irrelevant. But however complex the global economy is, there are several clear issues that emerge that the spiritually oriented worker wants to address. Perhaps first and foremost is the fact that economic inequality between the wealthy and the poor continues to *increase,* both in the United States as well as internationally. Although social workers cannot blame this increasing disparity solely on the global economy, it seems increasingly clear that at the very least, the global economy is not helping to reverse the trend. Another related concern is the growing influence that increasingly powerful international corporations have on local and global culture and policy. This is especially troublesome to social workers because the primary motivation for corporate influence is generally not the Highest Good of vulnerable people, but rather their own economic profit. Corporations can influence policy in many ways, including direct political contributions, the purchase and control of media news, and the pressures put on local businesses by underselling them. Many people are increasingly concerned about the loss of local "cultural capital" as world culture is increasingly "Americanized."

The social worker might be especially concerned about the influence of the pharmaceutical and private insurance industries on the well-being of clients. Since these industries are profitable and profit-driven corporations, the worker must question whether their direct and powerful influence over health care is always in the Highest Good of the people who seek health and mental health services. The increased marketing of medicines on television, magazines, and other mass media also concern the social worker for similar reasons.

Given all these concerns, from a spiritual perspective, the social worker's goal is to reverse the trend of growing economic inequality and to help transform the global economy and its international corporations into Communities of Spiritual and Universal Diversity that value the Highest Good over profit. Such communities could also be thought of as economic democracies. Is this an enormous goal? Yes, but evidence suggests that public opinion is swinging toward support of such changes.

The social worker realizes that the education and organization of consumers can have an impact on the policies of corporations. When people understand that their purchases give them power, many will decide to buy only products and services from corporations that work for equality and to watch only those television channels that support media democracy. The social worker might also explore the use of such emerging practices as time-dollar systems and complementary currencies, which may give local communities increased power to solve their own biopsychosocial–spiritual–environmental problems. The spiritually oriented social worker is not necessarily for or against profit, free trade, and the global economy, but she or he is clearly for the elimination of poverty and the unnecessary suffering of humanity.

SPIRITUAL ACTIVISM WITHIN RELIGIOUS SETTINGS

From a spiritual perspective, the common denominator of all religions should be kindness. The spiritually oriented social worker respects the diversity of doctrines, rituals, and beliefs found in the religions of the world and she or he realizes that all religions can either foster and/or hinder spiritual development. The social worker never tries to change the religion of an individual or community, but may work to help make that religion more of a Community of Spiritual and Universal Diversity. The social worker refuses to practice "religionism"; she or he does not evaluate a person or group based upon religion, but does evaluate the individual or group's unique expression of that religion.

The emergence of publically supported "faith-based" social programs give the spiritually oriented social worker an opportunity to influence programs that can potentially benefit many clients. The social worker wants the faith-based program to be a Community of Spiritual Diversity that will respect the diversity of beliefs held by all clients and social workers in the program.

When thinking through the policy that should direct faith-based social programs, the spiritually oriented social worker distinguishes between religious and spiritual faith systems. A faith system can be either religious and/or spiritual in nature. The social worker knows that when people have "faith" in a particular viewpoint, then they will see the world through that lens, for good or for bad. When doing direct practice within a faith-based program, the spiritually oriented social worker respects the religious faith system that the client has, whether the client is a member of a major religion or has no religion at all. Regardless of the setting, the worker believes that clients should have an informed and free choice in whether they attend any program that has a particular religious bias. The social worker does not try to change or influence the client's religion in any publically supported program.

In contrast, the worker also respects the client's spiritual faith system, and will ask the client (as she does in any practice setting) if he wants to work toward his own spiritual growth and transformation. In order to help clients learn how to create a Community of Spiritual Diversity, the worker will also help them learn how to engage in religious dialogue (see Chapter 7) in which they practice sharing their experiences and faith-based lenses without judging or trying to change each other.

The spiritually oriented social worker strives to educate policymakers and agencies that are implementing faith-based programs about the difference between religious and spiritual work and the nature of religious dialogue. The worker strives to help all faith-based programs become models of Communities of Spiritual Diversity in which clients have opportunities to work on their spiritual development and transformation.

PRIVATE PRACTICE IS PUBLIC PRACTICE

The spiritually oriented social worker makes her private practice a public practice. She feels comfortable giving help to people who can pay for her services, but she also offers help to people who cannot pay her fee. The social worker also feels a responsibility to the local and global communities and ecosystems in which she lives. Thus spiritually oriented private practice, usually thought of as microlevel social work, always has a macrolevel component to it. The social worker is as likely to be seen in an urban planning committee meeting in the mayor's office, for example, as she is with a client in her own private counseling office.

By working at both the micro- and macrolevels of practice, the social worker in public practice is most likely to be successful at making a living as well as successful in helping the people of her community. The public practice social worker refuses to separate her work with individuals, couples, families, and groups from her work with institutions and communities. She does this with pure intention, meaning that her motivation is to foster the Highest Good and that she trusts that such intention also brings her enough prosperity to support herself and her loved ones.

SOCIAL WORK IN ACADEMIC SETTINGS

Some spiritually oriented social workers may choose to develop an academic career in social work. The profession needs such leaders because scholarship and teaching in the spiritual dimension is still relatively scarce in academic settings, and social workers indicate that they want more training, research, and model development to help inform their spiritual practice. Many academics express concerns that spiritual and scientific inquiry are mutually exclusive, but the spiritually oriented social worker appreciates that science and spirituality are actually two human and entirely compatible ways of knowing. The social worker respects the value of scientific inquiry and never seeks to replace it with spiritual inquiry. However, he does seek to *include* the spiritual dimension in his scholarship because he appreciates the central role spirituality plays in all human experience. The task of the spiritually oriented social worker in academia is not only to define and describe the spiritual dimension but also to find ways to *bridge* between the domains of spirituality and science.

Evidence-Based Practice

There has also been an unfortunate split in social work between scientific (sometimes called masculine, empirical, or rational) and artistic (sometimes called feminine, intuitive, or full body) ways of knowing. The spiritually oriented social worker agrees that his practice should be "evidence based" but disagrees with narrow definitions of what constitutes evidence for practice. Instead, he prefers a more inclusive definition of evidence that includes all the ways of knowing. He recognizes that scientific study cannot by itself inform practice, and that the most effective social worker needs to use not only his brain but also his entire body–mind–spirit–environmental being when assessing and intervening in his practice. The task of the spiritually oriented social worker is not only to describe spiritual ways of knowing but also to show how both spiritual and scientific ways of knowing can be used together in practice.

Teaching

Spiritual content in social work can be taught either as the main subject of a course (e.g., an elective on spirituality in social work) or as a dimension of the major subject (e.g., a policy class that considers the spiritual and religious issues related to new social policy being studied). Spiritual content can also be part of either an elective or a required course.

There is a spiritual dimension to every social work problem and its various solutions. The spiritually oriented social worker advocates for inclusion of spiritual content in all required and elective courses, including research, policy, human behavior in the social environment, and practice. Spiritual content should also be included on all levels of social work education, at the B.S.W., M.S.W., and Ph.D. levels (see examples in Table 20.1).

Research

The spiritually oriented social worker utilizes existing quantitative and qualitative methods to study spiritual issues in practice. However, the worker also is committed to developing and utilizing additional methodologies that might be especially useful in choosing study populations and methodologies.

For example, since spirituality is a personal process, social work researchers are especially interested in telling the story of the subjects (or clients), with special attention to the key turning points in their lives. Since spirituality is about transformation and change in momentum, the social worker is especially interested in studying the stories of people who have had spiritual transformations, particularly when they have experienced the kind of suffering most social work populations endure. The findings of such studies might help inform social workers who want to support such transformational growth in their clients.

In addition, since spirituality is also about collective transformation, social work researchers also want to study couples, families, groups, and communities

TABLE 20.1   Examples of Material that Can Include Spiritual Content in Social Work Curriculum across All Three Levels

	PRACTICE	HBSE	POLICY-ACTIVISM	RESEARCH	PRACTICUM
B.S.W.	Spiritual case management and social services	Multi-dimensional development	History of relationship of church and state	Evaluating spiritual case management	Including spirituality in B.S.W.-level placements
M.S.W.	Paradigms of transformation	Assessing in spiritual dimension	Lobbying from a spiritual perspective	Single-subject study of client's spiritual development	Including spirituality in M.S.W.-level placements
Ph.D.	Teaching practice Supervision Model building Research	Strategies of teaching and researching in spirituality	Writing grant proposals for spiritual scholarship	Developing and using research methods for spiritual issues	Using spiritual content as a teaching assistant or a research assistant

that have been successful at co-creating Communities of Spiritual and Universal Diversity. In this era of religious war, such researchers might especially want to study religions and nations that practice nonviolence to determine how and why they function the way they do. Similarly, societies that refuse to take more from nature than they give back might also be examined. Such studies would require multidisciplinary approaches because methodologies from such disciplines as history, anthropology, sociology, religious studies, political science, and peace and conflict studies may all be very useful in understanding the processes involved.

RE-VISIONING THE MISSION OF SOCIAL WORK

Social work has spiritual roots. The roots are historical; the first social workers were generally women in religious organizations who volunteered to help others. The roots are also motivational; the United States continues to be a highly religious nation and many social workers report that they view their work as having a spiritual basis. The profession has been cautious about embracing spirituality as part of its ecological, person-in-environment perspective, but science has increasingly shown a strong connection between spirituality and biopsychosocial functioning. In the next decades, the social workers in practice are likely to continue to lead the way in developing methods of assessment, intervention, and evaluation that incorporate the spiritual dimension.

Every person has a spiritual dimension, although that dimension may be underdeveloped, just a person's emotionality or social functioning could be neglected and underdeveloped. Since spirituality is universal, in a world that appears to be increasingly divided by religion, the spiritual perspective can be a healing force that bridges across religious differences to identify individual similarities. Spirituality has become a very popular subject in our literature, films, and art, prompting some observers to suggest that the culture has a "spiritual hunger." Such a hunger is more likely to increase than to abate over the coming decades, as an increasingly frightening world collides with a culture that has largely lost touch with spirituality. This public hunger for the spiritual may well influence social work in the coming years.

Perhaps much of the fascination people now have with ancient ancestors also reflects our hazy memory of a time when most people lived more spiritual lives, more connected with their bodies and environment than we are today. To those who long for those days, however, we can see that ancient ancestors did not live in a paradise, but rather in a scary, unpredictable world, just like ours. Even if we could go back to that time, which we cannot, we would find that their lives were full of suffering, just like ours. Perhaps our biggest collective delusion is the idea that we can avoid pain. To escape that scary, unpredictable, often painful world, most humans, whether we are social workers or clients, now live primarily in our minds. We remember our bodies mostly when we are diseased or dying. We remember our environment when there is a tsunami or a hurricane. In other words, it is our suffering that brings us back to the body–mind–spirit–environment connection within which we seem designed to operate.

However, our ancestors, or at least some of them, seem to have lived ecstatic, soulful lives. Such lives are not free from pain, but they are also not free from joy. There is hope that people today, or at least growing numbers of us, can again live ecstatic, soulful lives, full of pain and joy. Such a people, fully alive, in transformation, are likely to build tomorrow's Communities of Spiritual and Universal Diversity. Such communities are likely to reduce the dangers that threaten our global existence and increase the Highest Good of all living things and the ecosystems that support all life.

STUDY QUESTIONS

1. What is collective transformation? What is collective momentum? How are they related? Have you experienced or been a part of such transformation? In what way(s)?

2. Why is spiritual practice both micro and macro oriented?

3. What are global survival threats? Which ones seem to impact you the most? How can a social worker help foster collective transformations of consciousness about global survival and well-being?

4. How does stewardship help heal overconsumption? In what ways do you still overconsume?

5. Why is the spiritually oriented social worker concerned about ecosystem health? What macrolevel methods might help protect the natural environment?

6. Describe what spiritual activism might look like within a religious institution.

7. Why and how does the spiritually oriented social worker have a public practice?

8. What kinds of collective transformations does the spiritually oriented social worker want to make within academic social work?

9. How can a spiritually oriented social worker expand the idea of evidence-based practice?

10. From a spiritual perspective, how can the mission of social work be transformed? What are your reactions to the suggestions in this section of the chapter?

RESOURCES

Adbusters
This journal offers the reader alternative views of the global economy, militarism, and politics that can help inform social work practice.
Derezotes, D. S. (2005). *Revaluing social work: Implications of emerging science and technology.* Denver: Love Publishing.
This book describes the global survival threats and possible social work responses to them.

ADDITIONAL RESOURCES FOR SPIRITUALLY ORIENTED SOCIAL WORK PRACTICE

SELECTED INTERNET SITES

http://www.csp.org/
    The Council on Spiritual Practices
http://sehd.binghamton.edu/affprograms/sssw/
    The Society for Spirituality and Social Work
http://www.spirituality-and-social-work.net/
    International Symposium on Spirituality and Social Work
http://www.ecosocialwork.org/
    Global Alliance for a Deep Ecological Social Work
http://www.cswe.org/spirituality
    CSWE's Social Work and Spirituality Resources

SELECTED READINGS

Bart, M. (1998). "Spirituality in Counseling Finding Believers." *Counseling Today,* 41(6), I, 6.

Carroll, M. M. (1997). "Spirituality and Clinical Social Work: Implications of Past and Current Perspectives." *Arete,* 22(1), 25–34.

Doherty, W. J. (1999). "Morality and Spirituality in Therapy." In F. Walsh (Ed.), *Spiritual resources in family therapy.* New York: Guilford Press.

Ellerman, C. P. (1999). "Pragmatic Existential Therapy." *Journal of Contemporary Psychotherapy,* 29(1), 49–64.

Ellison, C. G. (1993). "Religious Involvement and Self Perception among Black Americans." *Social Forces,* 71, 1027–1055.

Ellison, C. G., & George, L. K. (1994). "Religious Involvement, Social Ties, and Social Support in a Southeastern Community." *Journal for the Scientific Study of Religion,* 33(1), 46–61.

Furman, L. D., Perry, D., & Goldale, T. (1996). "Interactions of Evangelical Christians and Social Workers in the Rural Environment." *Human Services in the Rural Environment,* 19(3), 5–8.

Genia, V. (2000). "Religious Issues in Secularly Based Psychotherapy." *Counseling and Values*, 44, 213–221.

Haight, W. L. (1998). " 'Gathering the Spirit' at First Baptist Church: Spirituality as a Protective Factor in the Lives of African American Children." *Social Work*, 43, 213–221.

Hodge, D. R. (2000). "Spiritual Ecomaps: A New Diagrammatic Tool for Assessing Marital and Family Spirituality." *Journal of Marital and Family Therapy*, 26, 229–240.

Hodge, D. R. (2000). "Spirituality: Towards a Theoretical Framework." *Social Thought*, 19(4), 1–20.

Hodge, D. R. (2000). "Spiritual Assessment: A Review of Major Qualitative Methods and a New Framework for Assessing Spirituality." *Social Work*, 46, 203–214.

Hodge, D. R. (2004). "Spirituality and People with Mental Illness: Developing Spiritual Competency in Assessment and Intervention." *Families in Society*, 85, 36–44.

Pargament, K. I. (1997). *The Psychology of Religion and Coping.* New York: Guilford Press.

Perry, B. G. F. (1998). "The Relationship between Faith and Well-Being." *Journal of Religion and Health*, 37(2), 125–136.

Sheridan, M. J., Bullis, R. K., Adcock, C. R., Berlin, S. D., & Miller, P. C. (1992). "Practioners' Personal and Professional Attitudes and Behaviors toward Religion and Spirituality: Issues for Education and Practice." *Journal of Social Work Education*, 28, 190–203.

SELECTED ACADEMIC RESOURCES

Beit-Hallahmi, B. (1996). *Psychoanalytic studies of religion.* Westport, CT: Greenwood Press.

Boorstein, S. (1997). *Clinical studies in transpersonal psychotherapy.* New York: State University of New York Press.

Clarkson, P. (2002). *The transpersonal relationship in psychotherapy.* London: Whurr Publishers.

Corrogan, J., Crump, E., & Kloos, J. (2000). *Emotional and religion: A critical assessment and annotated bibliography.* Westport, CT: Greenwood Press.

Horovitz-Darby, E. G. (1994). *Spiritual art therapy: An alternate path.* Springfield, IL: Charles C. Thomas.

Koenig, H. G. (1994). *Aging and God: Spiritual pathways to mental health in midlife and later years.* New York: Haworth.

Palmer, M., & Finlay, V. (2003). *Faith in conservation: New approaches to religions and the environment.* Washington, DC: World Bank.

Richards, P. S., & Bergin, A. E. (1997). *A sporotia; strategy for counseling and psychotherapy.* Washington, DC: American Psychological Association.

Sperry, L. (2001). *Spirituality in clinical practice: Incorporating the spiritual dimension in psychotherapy and counseling.* Ann Arbor, MI: Brunner-Routledge.

INDEX

Page references followed by *t* indicate tables